PARADISE BURNING

Adventures of a _High_ _Times_ Journalist

PARADISE BURNING

Adventures of a <u>High</u> <u>Times</u> Journalist

Chris Simunek

St. Martin's Griffin ✹ New York

Many of the pieces contained herein have appeared in abbreviated form in *High Times* magazine. They have been altered, edited, and expanded upon for this book.

Design by Bryanna Millis

ISBN 0-312-18753-X

First St. Martin's Griffin Edition: June 1998

10 9 8 7 6 5 4 3 2 1

"Walking on water wasn't built in a day."

—*Jack Kerouac, after first psilocybin trip, 1961*

ACKNOWLEDGMENTS

Most of all, I'd like to thank Steven Hager for giving me the opportunity to do all this crazy shit and also for rescuing me from the Board of Ed. Thanks also to Michael "Wildwood" Reich, Frank Max, and Jim Fitzgerald for making it all happen.

I'd also like to thank my parents, Phil Simunek, *High Times*, Steve Bloom, Harry Crossfield, Jr., Peter Gorman, the *HT* 4:20 crew, Michael Kennedy, Gillian McCain, Richard Luhrs, Brian Jahn, Earl "Chinna" Smith, the Dirt Farmer, Adora McDougal, Mort Todd, George Bethos, Eileen Cope, whoever invented beer, and the Henries.

And special thanks to my sweetie, Catriona Morgan, without whom I'd be a bigger basket case than I already am.

TABLE OF CONTENTS

PARADISE BURNING

Adventures of a _High_ _Times_ Journalist

1

Introduction

I'm here in Kent, Connecticut, a New England town of the *Stepford Wives* variety where American flags fly proudly in front of people's homes, Dole/Kemp stickers still hold prominent positions on the backs of people's minivans, and the self-serve Mobil station runs on the honor system. As I write, the sparrows fuck in the grass and frogs sometimes jump in the pool, causing me to stop and rescue them before they clog the filters. This is America as they like to teach it to you in grade school. This is the country that John Cougar Mellencamp sings about. This is the most boring place on the face of the fucking earth.

My friend Harry gave me the keys to his summer home after I sold him a long semibullshit story on how I couldn't write in New York anymore, how I needed to go someplace where I could take a swim or just breathe real air when the mind bats came to visit and I started pulling the ideas from my head like they were ticks. After four years at *High Times* I can con my friends into anything, and for my sins, I wound up here in Kent.

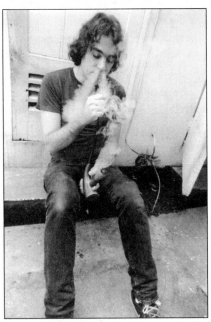

This place is a prison with saccharine bars. There are no pubs down the street where I can "take a break from writing" (such breaks usually last a week). My barracuda-faced landlord can't piss into my ear about New York rent control laws and how someday soon she'll have my ass on the pavement if she has to drag it there herself. There's no Managing Editor here to panic in my face because I haven't chosen a "Bong of the Month" yet.

What, me worry? Chinna Smith's porch, June 1996. (Brian Jahn)

All I've got to do is sit here next to this secluded white house and think about these past few years spent running around the world for a dope magazine.

I dig the scenery in Kent: trees and grass—you can't go wrong with that combination outside of New Jersey. Down the block there's a Revolutionary War cemetery and the Daughters of the American Revolution make sure there are always fresh flowers on the graves of our country's forefathers. Violent death comes not without its privileges, I guess. This would be a great set for one of those poolside porno movies you used to see in the seventies. You could dress a bunch of studs up like Redcoats and have them bang the Daughters of the A.R. two at a time. Call it *When Johnny Cums Marching Home.*

Everyone eats in Kent. The townspeople carry their guts with them the way those dead Freedom Fighters carried their muskets. The birds fly around with writhing crickets clenched in their beaks and the kids swing on monkey bars like Christmas hams on hooks. I've spent enough time in the snow-white suburbs to know a bastard training ground when I see one. When I look at who's inherited this "one nation under God," I wonder if the "shot heard 'round the world" wasn't a dud.

And since this is the last stop for many people on the path known as the American Way, I have to assume that boredom—*exclusive* boredom like this—is Uncle Sam's crowning reward to his constituents. After a life spent climbing your way through the front door of the American Dream, your kids live like milk-fed calves and you get to spend nights and weekends watching a comfortably abridged version of reality on your TV.

If you ask me, it's a lousy payoff, but ultimately I don't give a shit what the good people of Kent do with their downtime. I've learned, these past years visiting various points of interest on the Dope Culture map, that there are still people who risk their lives, freedom, and sanity to write their own versions of the American Dream. They don't worry about doors, they tunnel their way in like the Vietcong. For them, things like security take a back seat to bliss, and usually they die in obscurity, rot in prison, or end up babbling nonsense in your ear while you're trying to buy a subway token.

It's getting harder and harder to party in the Land of the Free and the Home of the Brave. Once you admit you like to alter your consciousness, you become part of a subculture that is systematically hunted. Nancy Reagan might talk about you as if you're her prodigal son, she might act as if there's always a home for you in the Big House once you cast off the shackles of recreational drug use, but you and her both know, if you ever tried to come home again she'd meet you at the door with a RICO warrant and a noise grenade.

Of course exceptions are made for Oprah Winfrey, who has her own TV show and can look into the camera, into the eyes of America, and say "I smoked crack and it was bad." That's how they let Lou Reed back in. I've only smoked crack once and I didn't like it, but I'd do it again with Oprah if she was buying. Later I'd have to talk about how horrible it was on her program, but it would be worth it just to have her show me the working end of a stem.

I wonder what it was like for Oprah, back in the days when she hit the pipe like a lab rat? I hope my drug experiences will have as positive an effect on my career. I grabbed any story that got me out of the city. Rastas, bikers, felons, hippies, rock stars—if it involved a plane ticket, I was there. When someone offers to bankroll a tour through Drug America, you accept first and worry about the consequences later. Working for *High Times* I've learned that words like "free" and "brave" are negotiable.

Sitting here with the horny sparrows and the suicidal frogs I realize I don't like the good people of Kent. I have no sick hatred of them, I just think this place peaked some two-hundred-odd years ago when the musket balls flew through the air like mosquitoes. Sitting around jugs of corn whiskey and talking shit about the enemy? That's entertainment. When there's nothing else there's always the fun of picking the world apart and deciding who gets the first bullet.

In the nineties there are so many enemies you can basically start shooting and never run out of targets. The NYPD, the KKK, the music industry—I've observed them in their natural habitats many times while on assignment for *High Times*. My problem was always finding allies, people like me digging their own crazy foxholes. I looked for those desperate sorts who live where the logic dies off and the id explodes like a seed pod in all directions. The mutants. They're always the cutting edge. Darwin's little nasties.

But after four years of looking for answers, I'm more confused than ever. The front line of this war is invisible. The enemy no longer wear red coats and the mutants don't stand out in a crowd. Even the good kids of Kent are wearing Marilyn Manson T-shirts. But that's progress. When people like that start posing as the same kids whose haircuts their older brothers used to laugh at and whose gym lockers they used to piss in, I say it's time to reach for our revolvers. And as those ghosts down the block will tell you, "Don't fire 'til you see the whites of their eyes," it's more fun to watch them die.

So here's my shot in the dark. I still don't know if I found what I was

looking for. I found what I needed at certain moments, and that's the best
you can hope for from a magazine. Along the way I met a lot of people who
said they had the answer—Manson-eyed iconoclasts who've tripped with
the Great Spirit or Hare Krishna or the Hemp God. Looking at them I always had to conclude that the chase was better than the catch. That's the
soul miner's tragedy in the late twentieth century—most times when you
turn over a rock you find out that the enemy is there, too.

Chris Simunek
July 8, 1997
Connecticut

2

The Dark Days Before the Gravy Train Arrived

I'd been working in Queens as an unlicensed high school teacher for about two years. In New York City all you need is a bachelor's degree to start teaching, as long as you sign something promising you're going to take some education courses over the next few years. I finished the courses pretty fast and then one day the principal called me and two other schmucks into his office. He poured us each out a brandy, him being the fat, well-liked kind of guy he was (that sort of happening personality was a big hit with the PTA, I guess) and then he said, "Congratulations, for you are now teachers," and we all toasted and I remember thinking to myself, you're gonna have to give me that whole bottle if you want me to swallow that one. But swallow I did and that's how I knew I'd entered adulthood—I was able to keep my medicine down.

As I rode that R train home—looking out at the factories, the billboards, the smokestacks, the clapboard houses—I felt like I'd betrayed every dream I ever had, every woman I ever loved. I felt like I'd just left every Christmas gift my poor dead grandmother ever gave me out on the street to be humped by dogs. I always viewed teaching as a temporary thing, a way to pay my rent until my novel got published or my band got signed.

Professor Afghani in his sanctum sanctorum. (Andre Grossmann)

While I was busy banking my paychecks they were luring me into their cult, and I went along with it because it was so easy getting my milk straight from the tit.

A year before I'd so ceremoniously become a "teacher," when I still carried the somewhat classier rank of "substitute teacher," I used to find joy just sitting with my girlfriend and drinking wine where Roosevelt Avenue crosses the BQE and you can watch the cars stretch out in one long line until they disappear into the future. I would tell her stories about the teachers, the kids, the system, and I would laugh as if I were somehow excluded—as if all I had to do was tell the stories and make her laugh and then it was someone else's life.

Two years later, I was neither a published novelist nor a rock star, and my girlfriend, she wasn't dumb. She could smell that stink on me no matter what I did to hide it—the reek of paranoia, depression, boredom, and hatred—the four horsemen of my own personal apocalypse. It's hard to convince somebody why they should keep going out with a teacher. Aside from pimple-faced fifteen-year-olds, the profession doesn't have many groupies.

As my R train rattled methodically over its rusted rails, the realizations penetrated my skull like machine-gun fire. How many times had I told myself that I couldn't take it anymore? Only to find out the next day I was a liar.

The next morning I sat in the teacher's lounge waiting for homeroom to start. The saddest humans on earth rested their feet in that room, and I was now one of them. The room was like a last chance saloon without the booze. I stared out the window at the elevated trains while a three-hundred-pound woman named Darlene peeled the tinfoil back on her Weight Watchers pepper steak and belched forth a torrent of indictments that included everyone from the principal to the Pope. She rambled on and on about the legal battle she'd been having with the Board for the past five years and the lousy traffic on the LIE and how in Africa teachers were given the same respect as priests and how convicted rapists should be castrated and left to bleed to death. There was no love in her life from or for anything, and that was the only thing we had in common.

Wolfkill was about the only one who ever listened to her, even there among the dead she wasn't worth the effort of simple attention. Wolfkill was in his seventies and had been the music teacher at the school since the prohibition days. I don't know what it's like to be old but it seems to me you must forget a lot of things. I can't see any other way it could be remotely bearable. He moaned on about how the educational system could go to hell if it wanted to, but Adolf V. Wolfkill still maintained standards of conduct and behavior in his classroom.

Perhaps the reason for Wolfkill's exaggerated sense of discipline was the fact that five years before a kid threw a desk out of a third-floor window that cracked Wolfkill's head open, leaving a scar that ran from his scalp to his upper lip. The kids called him Frankenstein. Kids are good for that. They may not know the ins and outs of long division, but they can spot your weak point and turn it against you.

There was another woman there. I called her the Manatee. Her hair was permed to a frizz and dyed the color of beets. I think she might actually have been brain damaged. I'd watch her every morning as she stuffed donuts and cheese danishes in her face. "Darlene, you are so right," she said to every word of the litany. She admired Darlene; I don't know why. I guess because Darlene was probably the only one in the world who ever spoke to her. Darlene herself knew this and would in turn talk down to her and treat her like a moron and disagree with everything she said, even when she was just reiterating what Darlene had told her a moment back.

When the bell rang, I trudged off to homeroom. There I was, hungover again, trying to get the kids in their seats. Even at that early hour they had enough energy to overpower me.

"Hey, Mr. S, why you always wear them booty-huggers?"

"Yo, Mr. S, you been drinkin'? Your breath smell like my uncle Tito's."

"Hey, S, you smoke weed, right? You get high, I know you do . . . "

A new kid, a transfer student, walked up and ceremoniously told me, "I'm in your class." I looked at him. He must have been eighteen already, in a tenth-grade homeroom. The upper row of his front teeth was capped in gold, he wore a hat that said BLUNT in huge letters, a gold chain with a dangling pot leaf, and a gold three-finger ring that read his name: "Allah."

"Fill this out," I said, handing him an attendance card.

"I'm gonna fill this out, then I'm gonna knock you out," he said.

"I don't think so, partner. Find a seat—and don't sit in the back."

"I'm sittin' *near* the back," he said but didn't sit down at all.

My hands were already covered with chalk dust, my breath reeked of coffee. I felt like an idiot, standing there while the kids laughed and chased each other around the carved, broken desks. Homeroom was short enough that no incidents had time to occur, so I just let them go beserk. I fumbled over the names—the Greeks, the Indians, the Chinese, the Koreans, the Colombians, the Ecuadorans, the Bengalis, the Peruvians—even the blacks mostly had African names and would sometimes cop serious attitudes when I mispronounced them.

By the end of roll call, Allah was standing in the doorway screaming, "WE WANT BLUNTS! WE WANT BLUNTS!" and banging his fists against the wall like he was at a Mets game. "WE WANT BLUNTS! WE WANT BLUNTS!"

"You and me both," I said. I was ready for a joint the size of a Cadillac. I tried to interest him in a seat, and even suspended my back-row rule, but I couldn't persuade him. He was going to chant this mantra out in the hallway loud enough for all the neighboring classrooms to hear. In his mind he was probably in some movie, he was some great freedom fighter like Sally Field in *Norma Rae*. From where I was standing, he was just another obstacle in my way to an early grave.

"WE WANT BLUNTS! WE WANT BLUNTS!"

I had neither the strength nor the will to help him along on his road. Finally I took an unbreakable comb out of my pocket and promised five dollars to the first student who could break it in half. Allah liked that idea. That inspired him. That kept him busy until the bell rang.

In the hall I walked past the kids screaming, smiling, running, wrestling, flirting, and beating the shit out of each other. Sometimes I got tangled up in all that nearsighted optimism. I'd be working one on one with a kid, teaching him or her something they should already know like the difference between a noun and a verb, and I'd get the desire just to wrap my arms around them and hug them, to be close to what they had and I'd lost.

At this point I even had my personal biology down to a routine. Between homeroom and my first-period class I had four minutes to drain myself of any unwanted nasties. Every day this act presented me with an existential dilemma.

You see, some little miscreant shit in the teacher's bathroom and it stayed there on the floor for three weeks. Every morning I would stare at it, knowing that it had some significance, but I wasn't sure what. Maybe just the fact that it was a part of my life, a part of my day. To me it was a benchmark as to how far I'd come in my twenty-four years. I didn't want to forget it, and in a way it was therapeutic because I figured if I could deal with that, then the rest of the day was easy.

The teacher's bathroom was right by the music room in the basement and, while I again contemplated the turd, Wolfkill was trying to get the kids to sing along to "Joy to the World." That was his idea of being hip. "Joy to the fishes in the deep blue sea, Joy to you and me." I don't think a class ever went by when he didn't have a major freakout. It was his own daily Stalingrad and I guess in a strange way it gave him a reason to go on living.

So there we were—me, the turd, and Three Dog Night.

I zipped up my fly and flushed four years of college and two years of education classes down the toilet. I left the building and never went back.

Now that I'd taken myself off life support, I had to find something to do. I decided to drink more and experiment with drugs. I didn't feel any better after I quit my job, but I could at least sleep late and avoid the hangovers.

It was a good time to be an unemployed drunk in New York City. The Green Door parties had given the Lower East Side rock'n'roll scene a feeling of solidarity, and everybody united behind the two causes common to any New Yorker under forty: punk rock and free booze. After sharing my drugs with a few key people, I found that I'd accidentally achieved something that for me was never an option: popularity. I guess when you're vomiting in a gutter, your best friend is whoever's holding your beer. I hung around mostly with musicians and artists and various other ego cases.

My oldest friend Mikey had just broken up with his girlfriend as well, and together we'd go out to clubs and drink and sulk and talk about how ripped off we felt to have been born into such a regrettable age as the nineties. I'd known Mikey since seventh grade, when we used to scream Sex Pistols songs in our homeroom until our teacher told us to shut up. Mikey gave me the nickname "Gene" after Gene Simmons. Mikey played drums for D Generation, which was the biggest underground band in New York at the time, and I had written a novel about a seven-hundred-foot monster that goes around stepping on things I hate.

I kicked around the city for a few months before forming a band called U.S. Drag with Frank Max, then the Assistant Art Director of *High Times*. Soon after I met Frank, Mikey and I went to the Continental to see our friend Sto's band. Mikey had a copy of *Journey to the End of the Night* with him that he'd borrowed from me. Steve Hager, the Editor-in-Chief of *High Times*, walked in with a motorcycle helmet in his hand and Mikey called him over, figuring he probably had a joint on him. Steve flipped when he saw *Journey*.

"You're reading this?" he asked Mikey, cracking up. My first impression of Steve was of a guy who laughed a lot.

"My friend Gene lent it to me," Mikey said, and we were introduced. I was surprised that the Editor-in-Chief of *High Times* rode a motorcycle and read Céline. I always thought *High Times* was run by a bunch of Deadheads from the back of a Volkswagen bus. Hager and I talked about authors for a while and Mikey told him I wrote this book about a seven-hundred-foot monster.

"Cool!" he said.

"You should read it," Mikey told him.

"Yeah!"

He invited me up to the *High Times* office the following week and told me to bring a copy of my novel. Steve was the first professional person I'd ever met who was willing to look at an unpublished manuscript. He didn't read it until months later, after he'd hired me, but he did come to watch me read a selection of the book at the St. Marks Poetry Project. He liked it, and that's how I began writing for *High Times*.

Four years later, people are a little surprised when I tell them what I do for a living. My parents are still shocked I managed to find work at all. I'm often told I have a strange job, but it never seems that way to me. Teaching was a strange job. Babysitting the welfare state of tomorrow? A day didn't go by when I didn't come face to face with the futility of my efforts. Hanging around with drug people was a much more appropriate way to make a living. It's what I did on my off-time anyway, it made sense that I should some day turn pro.

As Cultivation Editor I'm in charge of the horticultural section of the magazine. Every month I've got to make sure *High Times* is filled with information for readers interested in growing their own dope. Not counting the slime that grows in my toilet, I've never cultivated any sort of vegetation in my life, so my job is to talk experienced growers into writing me articles of the "how to" variety.

It sounds easy, but think about it. What keeps your average writer relatively coherent and time-conscious? What motivates the writer to hit a deadline? Cash! Shekels! Moolah! The stuff that keeps the bill collectors from calling and buys the next beer. There are so many hungry writers out there who would pimp their parents to a leper colony for the chance of writing a one-hundred-word movie review, your average magazine editor is able to make three phone calls in the morning and then spend the rest of his day sitting around his office pretending he's God.

My writers are different. I don't work with scavenging, bowl-scraping wage slaves. The people I depend upon for monthly copy are independently wealthy. Things like production schedules are hazy, indistinct entities for them. There is *now*, which is me begging them on the phone to write something for me, and there is the *future*. You know, where Darth Vader lives. The "deadline" is somewhere in between. Not only do I have to deal with the usual setbacks of production, but with arrests, probation, rehab, sudden changes of address, vacations in the Virgin Islands, you name it. I'm often the only connection to the legit world these people have. I'm the guy telling them, "Hey man, put down the nitrous, these things don't write themselves, you know." I often have to decipher hieroglyphics scratched out on scraps of paper or translate whole articles into some recognizable form of English.

Sometimes my job takes me into the DMZ of the Drug War, into those illicit marijuana gardens that are the cause of so much controversy these days. The first time I was invited to a growroom the proprietor, Kyle Kushman, met me and a photographer in a shopping mall, tied bandannas over our eyes, and made us curl up on the floor of his Ford Taurus before he drove us to his spot. He explained to us that what we didn't know couldn't hurt him.

The car bounced through a labyrinth of country roads, and right before I was going to throw up, we stopped and he removed my blindfold. We were in a wooded area where the houses had plenty of land between each other. He showed me his drying room and the pounds and pounds of pot he was preparing for the market. Then he started showing me around his indoor garden, explaining his own personal experiments, techniques, and mishaps. Enthusiasm exploded from him and I got the impression he'd been waiting a long time for an excuse to say these things to another person—preferably someone from *High Times*. His garden was his art, an expression of himself that he wanted recognized, if only anonymously.

When the shoot was over I was sitting in Kyle's kitchen with him and his girlfriend. Any sound I heard from outside the house—a tree branch falling, a car driving past—made me wonder how I'd look in a prison outfit. The Fear can flash on you mighty quick once you're in the company of those who eat it for breakfast. It was almost dawn and I still had reservations about sleeping above Kyle's garden. Kyle's girlfriend asked me when we were going to do an article about the wives and companions of pot growers. I could see the strain of the lifestyle like a tattoo on her face. It's a lonely life, she insisted, not being able to make friends, give your phone number out, have your family over for an afternoon. As I told the photographer to hurry up—I wanted to get out of there—I could only agree with her.

As Kyle put the bandanna back over my eyes, and I realized I was going to leave this scene with my civil liberties intact, I had a private laugh with myself that lasted an hour. I'd gotten my first taste of felony paranoia and I have to admit, I wanted more.

I'm free to sit here and crack jokes about all this. I've never had to live with the fact that one knock on my front door could burn a hole in my life I'd never recover from. In this War on Drugs there are no Purple Hearts. It's dark and it's corrupt and it murders my friends without apology.

Professor Afghani was for a while the pointman on my revolving team of cultivation writers. It was not known where the Professor received his degree, or even what subject it was that he was qualified to teach, but if you wanted to know how to grow high-quality herb, he was your man.

The Professor was tall with a jackhammer stare and a handshake so tight you felt it in your teeth. He had a Siberian husky that he took with him wherever he went. He'd come and go and when you didn't see him for

a while, these stories would begin to surface—he flipped his rental car in
a ditch somewhere in Puerto Rico, the Feds showed up at his mail-drop so
he moved to Arizona, he's living with some stripper and her three-year-old
kid.

Most growers try and live as anonymous a life as possible, but the fight
was an integral part of the Professor's lifestyle. If it was up to him, he told
me, every person in America would have a thriving marijuana garden in
their backyard or on their fire escape. When he wasn't growing, he was
sending vicious faxes and hate mail to the White House, all of which had
a "catch me if you can" kind of urgency to them.

He was a presence, a character who was always interested in what you
were doing (then there were times when he'd be out partying for days and
he'd have trouble talking and the words he did say sounded like they
came from a grave). But when he was in a good mood, he made you feel
like it was your birthday. He'd smoke you out with his killer harvest, then
treat you to dinner and to drinks afterwards. In his own way he was a
prince.

We were friends, not best friends (true confidants are a liability in his
chosen profession) but we always spent some time together when he was
in town. I liked the Professor mostly because I could never figure out his
motivations. He was paranoid, and at the same time took huge, unnecessary risks. The other guys around *High Times* had their shit together. You
could guess where they'd draw the line. The Professor was that free radical that would someday land in the wrong place at the wrong time and
cease to exist.

When I became Cultivation Editor, it wasn't until I was congratulated
by the Professor's wrenching handshake that I really felt like I'd switched
titles. I met him unexpectedly one day in Central Park. The Rainbow
Family was having their annual spring picnic and as I walked through the
crowd of blissed-out hippies the Professor spotted me.

"Heyyy!" he exclaimed with his usual enthusiasm. "What's up,
brother!"

When I told him I was the new Cultivation Editor he laid it out to me
how important the title was—

"You have a *responsibility* now, Chris. You are in charge of the only
marijuana cultivation forum left in this country. Thousands of farmers look
to you for guidance, you *can't* disappoint them."

He was heavy on the movement talk, but I listened because I knew he
had some good shit on him. I sat down with him and two other folks who
shared his same profession, one of whom had a vicious-looking, muzzled
pit bull at his side. With the dogs and the anxious glances, they carried
with them the kind of suspicion generated by people trying to avoid notice.

I could imagine a senior officer pointing to a picture of us and telling his men, "Scenes like this are what you're looking for. Big dogs and dilated pupils—when you see this, don't worry about Miranda rights . . . "

After the Professor assured his comrades that I wasn't a cop, they told me about their operations. When I asked if I could visit one of their rooms, I got the very definitive "fuck no" I was by then used to hearing. Anyone who approached us for a puff was instantly accosted by the Professor—

"Are you now or have you ever been a member of any law enforcement agency, state or federal, or has any member of your family ever been a member of any such organization . . . "

It must have been a line he heard in an old episode of *Dragnet*. It was something he had to say, and once he got the answer he wanted, he relaxed and invited you into the first circle of his multilayered life.

After hanging out with them for a little while I realized they were all whacked on designer drugs. They had pharmaceutical MDMA, stamped and numbered from Switzerland, and a large vial of liquid ketamine which the Professor would occasionally administer to himself nasally with a dropper. The shit would hit him like a taser and he'd bolt off into the center of the crowd, boogying with the hippies, talking to the girls, and generally enjoying whatever small amount of euphoria he could carve for himself at the moment.

By the end of the picnic, the Professor had attracted a little crowd. He was like that, naturally charismatic. When it got dark he dosed me and two young girls with MDMA and then we all went for a tour of the city in his rented Lincoln Continental.

"I am a patriotic American," the Professor told us. Sometimes he spoke in sermons and when he did, I knew not to interrupt. "This is a multibillion-dollar industry I'm a part of. Do you realize the talent they waste when they put us in jail? Why should we be incarcerated when we can be contributing to the Gross National Product like anybody else?"

The Professor liked to party in the war zone. Driving around in a car full of drugs, high as a kite with two girls and a *High Times* editor all tripping on his Ecstasy—that was the Professor. The Yes tape cranking, the unspoken threat of instant incarceration—he enjoyed the rush. He lived a fragile existence. One wrong move and he was out—way out, as out as a person could be and still remain breathing. I understood now why he thought my title was so important. He was entrusting me with a certain legacy. He was saying, Chris, if you don't do your job all this will cease to exist. And as we cruised around Gotham with the E soaking deeper and deeper into my flesh, I realized that Professor Afghani and those like him were out there fighting for their lives.

The Professor lost that fight. As terrifying a waste as it might seem, two years later the Professor piped his car full of carbon monoxide and sat there in the driver's seat for what must have been a strange couple of minutes until he died.

Maybe it was the pressure, the paranoia, the cops, the drugs. Who knows? My guess is it was just The Life. I figure I can at least pass along a few of the things he wanted to tell the world, which can be reduced to the essential idea that people who aren't hurting anybody should be left in peace. Doing what he did, he didn't have that luxury and I suspect that was the big contributing factor to his state of mind. He was a good person whose particular talent happened to be very illegal. I never thought of him as a criminal. He was a farmer, the salt of the earth, and since he left, *High Times* has felt different, wrong—like the Who after Keith Moon died.

But for every Professor they manage to liquidate, ten more grow back in his place; that's the nature of weed. They write to me from all over the country, people with names like Captain Chronic, Max Yields, Bud Fool, the Closet Commandos, Rob the Resinous, King Cola, Leif B. Greene, and about a hundred different Bud Gardeners and Elmer Buds. There's a whole nation of underground farmers out there, and when the law enforcement agencies of this country tell you they're close to stopping them, you owe it to yourself as a taxpayer to check their temples for horns.

Look around, Uncle Sam, you'll see your worst nightmare has come true—our numbers are greater than you think, check it out—

The Field of Dreams

The first *serious* garden I ever saw, before I became Cultivation Editor, back when I was still a lowly freelancer trying to impress the boss, belonged to a guy named the Dirt Farmer. He was a bit of a legend around the *High Times* office—a friendly farmer with his own pot plantation somewhere south of the Mason-Dixon line. People would tell stories of this wild old hick with three hundred plants in his backyard just begging some aerial surveillance team to swoop down and hand out life sentences like bags of candy corn to trick-or-treaters.

Of course I'd seen pictures of these kinds of things in the magazine, but I always imagined them to exist in exotic locations—vast marijuana fields tended to by slaves who were whipped constantly by men in military uniforms screaming, "Faster, infidel! At this rate we'll never destroy the American way of life!" I couldn't envision a crime so blatant being com-

At play in the "Field of Dreams." (Andre Grossmann)

mitted in Uncle Sam's backyard. The senior editors assured me it did indeed exist, and also hinted that a fledgling dope reporter like myself might rack up a few hash-brownie points with the powers that be if he paid the man a visit. I knew they were snickering among themselves—

"Just tell him *Hunter Thompson would do it* and he won't even ask for expense money."

The truth was they knew I'd probably walk a tightrope from one of the World Trade Center buildings to the other if I thought there'd be three hundred plants at the end of it. The "South" part of the deal worried me more than the potential prison term. My perception of the South was based primarily upon old Burt Reynolds movies: *Gator*, *White Lightning*, and the granddaddy of them all, *Deliverance*. Now if they thought Burt was an uppity, good-for-nothing piece of white trash, what would they think of me? And as I drove down the interstate through the woods and the farmlands, past the truckstops and the Quick E Marts, all I could think was that they used to call Ed Gein a friendly farmer before they knew any better.

As I rolled into the Dirt Farmer's driveway, I was greeted by a mad assortment of dogs, cats, and chickens, all grunting and yelping for my attention. He lived in an old farmhouse—the kind of place the Waltons might have stayed in if Papa was a sociopath and a multiple felon. Cows stood chewing the grass and a goat gave me a malevolent stare from across the driveway. I was immediately put on the defensive. I imagined at any moment some grizzly bear eight feet tall was going to emerge from the woods and beat me over the head with a blunt object.

I rang the bell, and before I could say "hello," the Dirt Farmer grabbed me and gave me a big hug. This is it, I thought, this guy's gonna have me squealing like a pig before sundown.

He must have noticed the desperate, road-weary, and underpaid look in my eye because he steered me straight to his plants. Sometimes enlightenment can be the product of years and years of concentration, experience and meditation, and other times it comes to you in one blinding, emotional second. When I saw those plants, I felt like Ben Franklin must have as the lightning traveled down the string of his kite and lit his balls up like Christmas ornaments.

"Forgive me, Father, for I have sinned!" I cried out, seeing the folly of my cosmopolitan ways. "I have seen the promised land!" Hundreds and hundreds of green and purple indica plants stood before me, all lined in rows, imparting upon the air the sweet smell of lollipops. Now maybe I was just stupid, but my fear of imprisonment vanished. I felt as though I were standing in a sanctuary, a little piece of Eden that God spared for himself and then forgot about.

I started to look differently at the Dirt Farmer. Standing there amongst

the plants with his baseball cap and his white hair, he looked like the outlaw grandfather I never had. He scooped up a small white dog and stuck
it inside his V-neck T-shirt so that its head poked out of the front. He
pointed out his favorite plants, the ones with the purplest leaves or the
biggest buds, then showed me a couple sick ones and explained to me
where he went wrong. After thirty minutes with him, I was ready to forsake
my true parents and draw up adoption papers.

"One day I just decided to join the Drug War," he explained. "It
seemed that this side needed some help, so I started growing. If circumstances were different and the other side needed some good people, I
probably would have joined with them." When I asked him if he ever
feared imprisonment, he shrugged and said, "I've been to prison, son, and
I tell you, they need good people there, too."

When we finished with the garden, we poked through the barn and he
showed me his moonshine still, his two off-road vehicles, and his dusty
1929 Harley-Davidson that he had bought new. He showed me his tools,
machinery, and assorted bric-a-brac, sorting through piles of stuff he'd forgotten he owned. Back in the house he showed me his vast gun collection,
with some pieces dating back to the Civil War. I was getting a crash course
in country culture, and without his actually saying it, I could see it was important to the Dirt Farmer that I understood the way he lived.

We climbed aboard his Winnebago and he produced several photo albums. "Most of my life I was a salesman, and a good one at that. I could
sell nudie magazines to blind people at twice the cover price if I put my
mind to it. Half my days were spent apart from my family in strange cities
trying to get people to give me their money. After a while I looked at my
life—my hands shook, my hair was falling out—I'd become a monster.
Then, by chance, I met up with some of the Rainbow People. Fifteen years
ago I went to my first Rainbow Gathering. I couldn't believe it. These people were so peaceful, so friendly . . . I came home, quit my job, and bought
this farm." He had lots of Gathering photos as well as pictures from road
trips he had taken through Mexico and South America. I smoked myself
silly (the Dirt Farmer didn't smoke) and flipped dreamily through an
album filled entirely with pictures he'd taken of the sun rising and setting
over his property. Each photo had a mood all its own and together they depicted the entire spectrum of human emotion—from peace and happiness
to rage and terror. It would be a perfect book to give to manic-depressives,
I thought, or people on bad acid trips. It was a simple reminder that every
day was different and anything was possible.

After a mammoth dinner of chicken, corn, and potatoes, the Dirt
Farmer introduced me to his two farmhands, Jeff and Todd, and the four
of us piled into the Winnebago and headed over to the local bar. Todd was

a younger guy, about thirty with curly blond hair, and Jeff looked like Greg Allman would if instead of becoming a rock star in the seventies, he'd gone to Vietnam. Jeff and Todd were curious about New York and they asked me what we did for kicks. I told them about the clubs, bars, and bands, and they laughed at the fact that everything we did was indoors. I was equally incredulous that they were going out on a Saturday night dressed like Jed Clampett.

"I never had any desire to visit New York," said the Dirt Farmer. "The times I've had to go there or pass through there, I just couldn't wait to leave. I get claustrophobic real fast. I start feeling like a rat in a maze."

We drove up to the "bar," which was little more than a shack with a neon Budweiser sign in the window. It's where Billy Carter would be hanging out, were it not for the tragic fact that he was dead. Inside, the wood-paneled walls were decorated with stuffed trout, pike, and bass. "I caught that one!" Todd said, pointing to a two-foot-long largemouth. "I mean, not *that* one, but one like it."

"Taking Care of Business" pounded out of a jukebox in the corner of the room and a huge poster of Elvis watched over the bar like a patron saint. I knew I couldn't impress anyone in there with my knowledge of hunting, fishing, or college football, but if there's one thing we can do in New York as good as anyone else, it's drink. Jim Beam seemed to be the house favorite. Me, Jeff, and Todd all got shots while the Dirt Farmer smiled, temperately watching.

"I met Rolling Stone," a drunk older man with a beard and a baseball cap said to me. "Rolling Stone himself." He was obviously trying to connect me, with my long hair and leather jacket, to something he could understand. This bold, toothless lie was his way of reaching out. "He shared his woman with me. I fucked her three times and he gave me fifty dollars."

"Oh yeah? You ever meet the Beatles?" I asked.

"I used to manage them. A fine bunch of fellers."

The song "Simple Man" came on and I sat and contemplated my like/hate relationship with Lynyrd Skynyrd. Me and Todd started taking bets on when the barmaid would break down. Not only did she have the impossible responsibility of keeping the peace in a bar full of two hundred-pound men in flannel shirts drunk on whiskey, she had to dodge constant advances from just about every guy in the place, and even a few of the biker chicks. That's the simple problem with alcohol—it makes you plain stupid. But stupid, along with horny and self-inflated, were just local stops along the road to oblivion, which is where I knew me, Jeff, and Todd were to make our beds that evening.

"So what do you guys hunt out here?" I asked Jeff.

"Oh you know, deer, sometimes wild turkey, a lot of squirrel."

"Squirrels? What do you do with them?"

"What the hell you think we do with 'em? We eat 'em."

"Is that just you who does that, or is that a common thing?"

He looked at me like I was a moron. Until that moment I didn't realize there existed a whole squirrel-eating population in America.

In New York when we drink, we usually sit around and try and convince each other how cool we are. This selfless "I'm-just-here-to-have-a-good-time, I-don't-give-a-damn-what-you-think" kind of drinking was new to me. But I can make a fool of myself as easy as any country hick, and by the end of the night I was telling everyone that I wanted to go into the woods and pull a Jeffrey Dahmer trip on the local squirrel population. I told them that in another life I was Marlin Perkins, a man who, regardless of his age, really knew how to beat an animal into submission.

And after the Dirt Farmer drove us home and said good night, me, Jeff, and Todd ate enough squirrel for ten men.

The next morning the Dirt Farmer woke me up early. The four of us ate our eggs and before I could take back the previous night's boasting, the Dirt Farmer was picking out a shotgun for me. Now, I've never shot anything in my life, and to paraphrase Muhammed Ali, no squirrel ever called me a nigger. Worried that I'd come off like a big-city pussy, I kept my mouth shut.

The Dirt Farmer had to tend to the plants and feed the cows, so Jeff, Todd, and I piled into the truck in search of game. To my surprise, we only drove about five hundred feet from the house to a little campsite with a picnic bench. Jeff produced a twelve-pack of Bud and I realized that we were just going to sit there, drink, and wait for something to come to us.

We set up a few cans on the other side of the pond and took some shots at them. We had a complete little arsenal and I started wondering, if by some chance the Feds did sneak up on us, whether these were the go-down-fighting sort of multiple felons you see on "MacGyver." We had a .38 handgun, a .22 rifle with a telescopic sight, and several different shotguns which we kept loading up with these huge, single-shot slugs that probably could have grounded Rodan had he chosen to pass by at that moment. A shootout would definitely have been our only escape. If the Feds had busted in at that moment, they probably would have saved the taxpayers some money and strung us up from the nearest tall tree, passing my press pass amongst the junior officers for their amusement.

A little while later the Dirt Farmer drove up in his Winnebago. He brought us a .44 magnum wrapped in an Old West–style hip holster that tied around both the waist and thigh. He wondered how we were doing, but we told him we hadn't had any luck yet. He didn't join in the shooting, just watched us and smiled, petting his little dog still peeking out the front of his T-shirt.

"Back when I was a salesman, I'd take two days off, call in sick, and come out here to the woods," he said. "I'd tell my wife I wasn't coming home that night and she'd understand. You gotta get back to reality. I'd get so wound up sometimes I thought my head was going to pop off. I'd just come out here and sleep in the woods, do some fishing—anything to get my mind off the job. We're not too fancy out here. We're just a bunch of good ol' boys, you know? I don't worry too much about how big a mess my barn is or whether there's mud on my shoes. I just like what I do and I do it."

I had to ask myself why he invited *High Times* down to see his garden. It seemed a bit of a risk. I'd never met him before my visit, and yet he trusted me implicitly. I came to the conclusion that he really did have a message to bring to people. The plants were just a manifestation of a larger, "you can't catch me" sort of total freedom he felt and was the only way he wanted to live.

I walked with the Dirt Farmer down to a small pond and he pointed out tracks of cows, raccoons, squirrels, and wild turkeys that had been there for a drink. No matter what part of his property we traveled to, there was something he wanted to show me. As we walked back into the pasture, a group of grunting cows started heading toward us. "They're hungry," he said and stuck out his hand for one of them to lick with its meaty tongue. "All these fellers do is stand around, eat, and shit. These cows produce a soil finer than money can buy. That's why they call me the Dirt Farmer, because I got the best." The dirt is where we all end up eventually—cow, plant, and bank teller alike. Laws and time clocks were of no interest to him. Whatever system mankind could devise, it eventually had to answer to Mother Nature.

My last night there I slept out in the Winnebago. When the wind kicked up, I could smell the plants and it seemed unreal to me that this idyllic, starry night could at any moment be raided by a bunch of pissed-off, caffeine-wired, wife-beating federal agents, and we'd all spend the next ten or twenty years behind bars. After all, what's more down-home, Norman Rockwell–American than a farmer sowing a seed? Pushing buttons for IBM?

As I was getting ready to leave the following morning, the Dirt Farmer showered me with gifts: Moonshine, pot, hash oil—it was like Christmas would be if Keith Richards was Santa Claus.

"Wait one moment," he said as he walked over to the Winnebago. When he returned, he handed me the photo book filled with sunsets. "I know you don't see too many of these over there in New York City."

"Man, I couldn't . . ."

"Take it," he said and laughed. "There's plenty more where those came from."

As I was driving up the interstate later that evening, I watched the sun sink in the sky, just like the Dirt Farmer said it would. The bugs splashed against my windshield and I was listening to the evening news on the radio. It was around the time of the O.J. trial and the guilt or innocence of this man that I'd never met and never cared two shits about was all anybody was interested in. Everyday the Juice would fly past us and we had the pleasure of shooting at him like a clay pigeon from the comfort of our cars, desks, and TV chairs.

O.J. did us one favor, though; he showed us we have shitty aim.

When I got back to *High Times* with the herb and especially the hash oil, I found myself to be a popular man around the office. "I told you he was a good writer," Hager said to the editors. We all went to Don Hill's and smoked drippy oil-soaked joints, listened to Iggy on the sound system, and planned the future of the magazine. As I drank my beer and scouted the club for a woman crazy enough to be impressed by the fact that I was now a legitimate dope journalist, I wondered what all those little miscreants I used to teach English to would have thought if they could have seen me there—Mr. S on dope. I think they would have been very proud.

The Dirt Farmer was busted about a year later when one of his associates was looking at twenty-five to life and didn't like what he saw. He's in prison now, even as I write this. He calls me from time to time, just to talk. I asked him once how he felt about being in prison. It was a dumb question; I knew it even before I asked, but I wanted to know.

"Oh well," he said with a laugh. "I'm a talker and the people here, they gotta listen to me, they can't go no place else." He won't be there forever—he got two to five and that was lucky. He grew plants. As far as I can tell, O.J. murdered his wife and a total stranger, nearly decapitating them in the act, and all they did was take his money. If history is written by the winners then that's justice plain and simple. But sometimes, I have to admit, when I'm drinking a beer in Central Park and a cop grabs me and writes me a ticket, or if I jump a turnstile and the Transit Police use that as an excuse to run a warrant check, I think about the nature of this thing they call justice, and I can hear the tap-tap-tap of O.J.'s Bruno Magli shoes dancing on my future grave.

4

Fear of Flying: Inside Potsmokers Anonymous

I think the business side of the magazine was a little disappointed when I failed to get incarcerated at the "Field of Dreams." I'd proven that I was willing to take ridiculous risks for little or no money. Like it or not, I'd become an asset.

At the first couple of editorial meetings I tried not to be noticed. I don't like talking to people much, especially people with jobs. I felt even more uncomfortable in an office than I did in a classroom. It went on like that until one meeting Steve asked me what I wanted to write about. It was my chance to sell the other employees on me, to let them know that he wasn't crazy for letting me hang around and smoke their dope.

I was fucked for something to say. I didn't read magazines, much less *High Times*, and had no idea what would appeal to its readership. The two rags I took an occasional flip through were *Big Butt* and *Outlaw Biker*. They were the only ones I saw as doing something progressive. Then I had the idea to bring that kind of quality journalism to the potsmoking community.

"Isn't there a festival or something where bikers get together every year and do drugs and kick the shit out of each other and the women walk around flashing their tits to strangers?" I asked.

"Sturgis?"

"Yeah, Sturgis. Where is that?"

"South Dakota."

"Yeah, I want to write an article about Sturgis." A week of drugs and violent behavior was what I was looking for at that point in my life. I didn't ride, I just liked the biker sense of humor. Bikers weren't NYU grads who dyed their hair purple in a fit of twenty-something angst and later got jobs doing A&R for Arista; when they dropped out of society, they dropped out for good. A three-hundred-pound man with "Fuck You" tattooed on his chest was not a frontrunner in the rat race. I felt we needed to reach out to our countercultural grandfathers.

My pitch hung in the air like a chicken trying to fly.

"Yeah . . . " Steve said, warming to the idea. "I've wanted to run a biker feature for a while now . . . " The other editors weren't about to object. They had their own fiefdoms to build with *High Times* money, they weren't concerned with how I constructed mine.

"Sturgis is still a couple months away," Steve said. "I was thinking maybe you could write an article about Potsmokers Anonymous. You know, go undercover for us. You think you'd like that?"

I wasn't going to say no, I needed the cash. People in the marijuana movement talk about how you can turn pot into rope and shampoo and paper and fuel, and that's all fine by me, but at that point in my life I was mostly interested in turning pot into money. The problem was that I wanted the money to buy more dope. I saw a conflict of interest. *High Times* asking me to secretly infiltrate Potsmokers Anonymous and undergo a cure was like Kirk asking Scotty to beam aboard a Klingon ship and "go native." I had this image of my counselors asking me why I wanted to quit smoking pot and me answering, "Because it makes my mouth dry . . . "

Then I thought that if I took this assignment, which required me to give up the very substance that was providing us all with our livelihoods, maybe they'd think I was a real tough reporter, a man willing to make sacrifices for his art. I also figured it would be good to know if I could quit in a pinch. What if someday I wanted to join the LAPD and had to pass a urine test before I was given free license to beat passing motorists with impunity? I told *High Times* I was their man.

I'd never been to a rehabilitation meeting of any kind, so I was unprepared for what was in store for me. I felt no shame for my indulgences and I half imagined myself bursting in on the group—making a grand entrance, perhaps a running leap through the air that culminated in a slide that extended halfway across the room, after which I would proudly rise to my feet and say, "My name is Chris Simunek and I am a pot-smoker!"

The meeting was held in a nursery school playroom on Eighteenth Street in Manhattan. I walked inside and recognized the blinding fluorescent lights and dirty yellow walls that are standard decor for any New York City educational facility. It was the holiday season and decorating the walls in obscene combinations of red, white, and green were the children's own finger-painted holiday portraits—Santa Claus standing in a green snowstorm with what seemed to be an ax sticking out of his head and a sled pulled by a random cast of pit bulls and wild boars. Next to it was a more impressionistic piece: a preschool depiction of either a Christmas tree or the right-hand panel of Bosch's "Garden of Earthly Delights." All pigments were swirled and mixed to form one primary color—a muddy purple-black. Together all the pieces would have made a fine coffee-table book called *It's a Rorschach Christmas*.

I was too stoned to be in such an environment. Figuring that this was only the open house and my rehabilitation hadn't "officially" begun, I got myself good and blunted beforehand. Other potential "quitters" started taking seats in the aluminum chairs arranged in a semicircle in the center of the room. Soon Francis Duffy, director of Potsmokers Anonymous, introduced himself.

He told us Potsmokers Anonymous was founded in New York City in June 1978 by psychotherapist Dr. David Izenzon, as a nonprofit educational program dedicated to freeing people from the insidious grip of marijuana, "the drug that quietly undoes your life." Dr. Izenzon developed a nine-week course in which pot-smokers were to gradually decrease their usage while developing "emotional recognition skills." The good doctor had since passed on and the program was now directed by Francis Duffy, himself an ex-smoker.

"It is the nature of pot to subdue your processing of feelings," Duffy told the group. "It's an emotional anesthetic. When was the last time you were truly angry? Happy? Sad? It is impossible to lead an emotionally fulfilling life and still smoke pot . . . it comes to the point where you have to ask yourself, 'Am I smoking pot or is pot smoking me?' "

The group itself consisted of seven people, mostly yuppie career types who had just gotten off work. Notable exceptions were a hybrid Deadhead/grunge-rocker who looked as stoned as I was, and one woman dressed in the Lower East Side's finest: ripped jeans, Doc Martens, and a funny hat.

We were given the "Five Danger Signs" of pot dependency:

1. Nervousness when the supply runs low.

2. Forgetfulness.

3. Fatigue.

4. The "Yes, but . . . " syndrome (. . . yes, but I can stop anytime I want . . . yes, but it's better than drinking alcohol or breathing polluted air, etc. . . .).

5. The Amotivational Syndrome.

The Amotivational Syndrome was by far the most insidious symptom of pot-smoking, explained Mr. Duffy. "It's the 'hidden price tag' . . . the all-encompassing yet invisible inertia in the face of life."

I was guilty of most, if not all, of the danger signs. I started wondering, is it possible? Do I have a problem? Is there such a thing as too much marijuana? I thought back to when I was in college, living next to two Deadheads. Between them they must have had seven hundred Dead tapes and all I ever remembered them doing was smoking weed, eating Ben &

Jerry's, and staring for hours at *Deadbase IV*, as if hidden inside its pages somewhere was the key to the universe. "It'll never happen to me," I said, but who knew what that foul bitch Fate had in store for me?

After the introduction, we were told that groups would meet in two weeks' time and would cost a whopping forty dollars a session.

"It's only a quarter of what you would spend a week on weed," said Duffy, and I wondered just where the hell he got that figure. "It's expensive, but think of all the money you'll save once you quit smoking."

"Mr. Duffy?" I said, moved to speak.

"Yes?"

"How about if we just go through the course and pay upon successful rehabilitation?"

His shrill laugh told me it was going to be a long nine weeks.

Two weeks later I was preparing for my first meeting by smoking up the rest of my stash and flipping between Geraldo and Donahue. Geraldo's topic of the afternoon was "KKK Kids—Children Too Young to Hate," and Donahue had a panel of crackheads—three black, one white. What I really wished was for both panels to be on the same show and for Phil and Geraldo to hand out flame-throwers.

It seemed to me a bad omen. Somehow I knew that once I left my apartment, I would also be leaving behind the ability to entertain myself at the misfortunes of others.

Assembled once again in the nursery room, I was surprised to find that only three other "abusers" aside from myself had shown up for the second meeting. Our counselor Ivan introduced himself. Ivan had been through the program and was so impressed he decided to undergo the six-month training program supervised by Mr. Duffy to qualify as a counselor. He appeared to be about forty, dressed casually in jeans and a T-shirt. When he told us he was a salesman during the day, I wondered if I shouldn't save myself the forty-dollar fee and take my troubles across the street to one of the guys at The Wiz.

Ivan explained that he had started smoking weed in college and had continually smoked for ten years, sometimes dealing in order to pay for his habit. One day he realized he had a problem. "I wanted to get married and my fiancée was worried that I smoked too much pot. She wanted me to go have my lungs and my sperm checked by a doctor. Well, I came back from the doctor with some distressing news. . . . He said my sperm were 'sluggish.' " Personally, I couldn't see what Ivan was complaining about—if anything, I'd like to train my sperm to retreat. "I was really upset and the doctor told me I was smoking too much pot. . . ."

Okay. Now I have a confession to make. I've never told anybody this, but I feel that in order for me to give an honest account of my experience, it must be revealed. It's something that happens to me when I find myself in ugly, boring scenes like this—on the bus or subway, on line at Motor Vehicles—I look around, find the most attractive woman in the room, and lose myself in carnal fantasy. On the surface, this doesn't sound strange at all. It's when you're caught in situations where really, there's no one even remotely attractive and you start daydreaming about yourself and a two-hundred-pound waitress with a gap between her teeth you could fit a dime through, that it enters the realm of the bizarre.

I found my attentions drifting over toward a slightly overweight blonde dressed in yuppie attire—blue skirt, stockings, and the obligatory post-work sneakers. Save for her wandering eye, she wasn't all that bad. She seemed like the type who fifteen years ago used to hang out in the parking lot of White Castle drinking beer, smoking weed, and listening to Black Sabbath. After ten minutes of Ivan and his lethargic sperm, I didn't care whether her eye packed up and moved to Acapulco. I started imagining myself and her up in the rafters at a Blue Öyster Cult concert at Nassau Coliseum circa 1975, smoking a joint the size of a banana, and dreaming about prom night.

"The good news is," Ivan continued, "since I quit smoking, *my sperm's okay!*" Both fists raised triumphantly toward the sky in procreative glee.

Next, Ivan passed each of us a stack of index cards. On each card was written a reason for smoking pot. We were instructed to choose the cards that applied to our particular situation. Once finished, Ivan called upon us to tell a little about ourselves and reveal our cards to the group.

First to go was Scott, the Deadhead/grunge-rocker from the open house. Weed had lost its allure for Scott. Lately, every joint he smoked left him with a heavy dose of the Fear. "It was like the song goes," he explained. " 'Going down the road, feelin' bad . . . ' " His grades were dropping and he figured if he didn't stop smoking and hit the books, his dad was going to yank him out of New York University and get him a job as a real estate agent. He was finding it difficult to quit because he was in a band full of pot-smokers. Among the cards he had chosen from the pile was one labeled "Pot makes music better."

"The thing you must remember," explained Ivan, "is that when you are under the influence of a drug, how can you be sure it's better?"

"I dunno," shrugged Scott. "All my favorite bands did drugs—Hendrix, Zeppelin, the Stones, Aerosmith . . . "

"Yeah, but Hendrix is dead, so are some of the guys from the Stones and Zeppelin. Aerosmith, on the other hand, are clean and sober and they're soundin' better than ever. . . . "

It was right about there that Ivan lost any remote trace of credibility with me. Anybody who would put *Get a Grip* above *Rocks* or *Toys in the Attic* had nothing to teach me.

Next was Chuck. Chuck was tall and skinny and dressed smartly in a corporate suit and tie. He explained that years back, he had fallen in with the wrong crowd at college. Having recently lost his job, all he wanted to do now was piece himself together enough to get a teller gig at Chemical Bank and forget about weed altogether. Pot was a handicap in the rat race. He held up his various cards, the two most notable being, "Pot helps me tolerate being treated like a moron" and "I'm forty years old and I still hang out with teenagers."

My blonde blushed when her turn came. "My name's Barbara and uh . . . I have a lot of cards. . . . " One after the other, she held them up— "Pot makes TV better," "Pot makes sex better," "I can't go to the movies without getting stoned," "Pot helps me deal with my parents," "Pot puts me in touch with my feelings. . . . "

"Jeez," she said coyly in a Brooklyn accent. "I'm so embarrassed."

"There's nothing to be embarrassed about," said Ivan. "We're all here for the same reasons and nothing said here leaves this room . . . and finally, your name is?"

"Uh . . . " It took a moment to realize that he was talking to me, I was still pretty high. "Yeah, uh . . . my name's Gene."

"Any cards, Gene?"

I looked down at my pile of cards and instead of holding them all up, I chose the one that I felt best described my situation: "Pot is my way of life."

"Hmmm . . . " Ivan said, writing something down on a note pad. "Let me ask you, Gene, do you do other drugs?"

"Whattaya mean?"

"Well, do you drink?"

"Well yeah, doesn't everybody?"

"Uh . . . no. Acid, mushrooms?"

"I have . . . "

"Coke?"

"Are you buying?"

Ivan started writing furiously on his pad as the others kind of stared at me and suddenly my function in this group came clear. I was the control experiment, the challenge. I felt like one of Geraldo's daytime-TV patsies. No one in the group had to say it, I could read it on their faces loud and clear: "Hell, at least I ain't *that* bad. . . . "

Concluding the meeting, Ivan gave us our "homework" for the week, comprised mostly of a series of calculations. He wanted to know:

1. The amount of money we spent annually on weed.

2. Any loss of income we've experienced due to smoking weed.

3. Time "lost" per day stoned.

4. The number of tokes we took in a given day.

The "toke count" was the official measurement of pot intake used by Potsmokers Anonymous. It's how progress was measured, much like the "body counts" of the Vietnam War. Ivan suggested what he called the "toke and stroke" method whereby the smoker, upon every toke, was to note it with the stroke of a pen on paper.

"But what if we're smoking with other people in a social situation?" I asked. "If I start writing things down on a piece of paper, they're gonna think I'm a narc."

"No one said quitting was going to be easy, Gene."

As we sat in our semicircle the next week, Ivan greeted us all cheerfully and said, "Welcome to week two—the beginning of our journey to awareness."

Going around the room, we all gave our data to Ivan. The amount of money spent annually on weed by each of us varied from eight hundred dollars (Chuck) to an overwhelming five thousand dollars (Barbara). Barbara blushed again as she revealed the sum to us. The only one of us who figured they had lost any income was Chuck because he was currently unemployed. The time "lost" being stoned averaged from eight to sixteen hours a day and our toke counts ranged drastically from ten (Chuck) to fifty-seven (Barbara).

When I told Ivan that my toke count of twenty a day was basically a guess, he got a little pissed.

"Gene, you have to have faith in the program and use the tools I give you. If I say toke and stroke, I mean toke and stroke! No exceptions!"

With my chastisement out of the way, Ivan went on to explain once again that when we are stoned, we are unaware of our true feelings. He believed the reason we were smoking pot was because we were unable to face certain emotions.

"I don't think I agree with that," Barbara said, beating me to it. "I find when I smoke pot, my feelings are if anything, stronger. . . . "

"And I'm sorry, Ivan," I said, "but I don't think 'Living on the Edge' is anywhere near as good as 'Back in the Saddle.' "

"Huh? Guys, guys . . . let me make my point, then I'll answer your questions. . . . Now, we at Potsmokers Anonymous have come up with a system that will help you come to terms with the feelings that you have been denying yourself while stoned." With that he passed us each a little chart. Across the top of the chart a twenty-four-hour time period was divided into four six-hour sections, and down the side was written the words Fear, Anger, Love, and Pain. "All of your emotions can be divided into one of these four categories. What we want you to do is, throughout your day, when you are feeling one of these emotions, mark it on the chart. We call this the FLAP system. If you are feeling good, happy, I want you to FLAP Love. If you're pissed off at your boss, don't let it get the best of you—just FLAP Anger. If you're nervous, I want you to FLAP Fear. Got it? I can't tell you what FLAP-ing has done for my life, how it has put me in touch with feelings I never knew I had."

We did some practice FLAP-ing where he read us a story about (of all things) Popeye and Olive Oyl being harassed by Brutus. We were to FLAP what emotions we thought Popeye was going through at any particular moment. All the while I kept thinking to myself that FLAP-ing sounded like something I might do after eating too much Mexican food.

Our homework for the next week was to FLAP diligently, every day. We were also to reduce our toke counts by three a day and to institute what Ivan called the "ten-minute rule." This meant we were to wait ten minutes before smoking and contemplate whether it's something we really wanted to do.

"Hey, Ivan," I said. "How about if I keep my toke count the same, but I switch from Kind to commercial?"

"Nothin' doing. And I want you all, if you think you are going to surpass your toke count, to call me first. Okay? And Gene—no guessing this time! And don't forget to FLAP!"

About one hour after leaving the meeting, I reached my toke count with some of the *High Times* crew in front of the No-Tell Motel on Avenue A. I figured that, since it took a while to roll the joint, I'd complied with Ivan's ten-minute rule. But when I finally began refusing my turn at the spliff, everybody started giving me strange looks. I told them I'd reached my toke count and they started calling me a lightweight. Then someone suggested I call Ivan up and see if he'd let me borrow some tokes from next week's count. It seemed like a reasonable solution.

"Hello, Ivan? This is Gene from P.A. I called to tell you I'm goin' over."

"Wait a second, Gene. Let's talk this out . . . "

"I'm up to my limit but my friends here got a joint and it's starin' at me like a goddamn hungry vulture. I'm FLAP-ing some pretty serious Pain. You gotta let me blow one on credit, Ivan."

"Did you do the toke and stroke?"

"Ah . . . no."

"You know, Gene. I can't help you if you don't have faith in the methods of the program. You know, sometimes I get the impression that you
don't want to quit."

"My friends are calling me a 'lightweight,' Ivan. There's a small matter here of my reputation to uphold."

"Well, if they're saying that, Gene, maybe they aren't your friends."

We both agreed that maybe I should start taking the program more seriously. We made an agreement to speak privately after next week's class.

The following week, the only people who showed for the meeting were
myself and Chuck. Barbara and Scott must have bailed and Ivan was
running late. I asked Chuck whether he thought the course was helping
him. He shrugged his shoulders and told me he didn't know what else to
do. We both agreed that we didn't find the course remarkable enough to
justify the forty dollars a week expense. I told Chuck that I had heard
about a free twelve-step program called Marijuana Anonymous that was
meeting in an hour over at the Fourteenth Street Workshop and we both
grabbed our coats and agreed to meet there. As I left the building, I sadly
mused upon the fact that Barbara and I would probably never see each
other again.

Later, at the twelve-step program, I sat in the brightly lit, olive-drab
room and listened to the stories. In a group of nine people, I was the only
one who didn't speak. People talked of money and friends lost due to
drugs and alcohol—of time wasted and opportunities passed over. Some
spoke of the Fear—of being stoned in a room and imagining that all eyes
were focused upon them in judgment. One guy even told the story about
how he was once rushed to the emergency room because he had a roach
stuck in his ear. He was saving it there for later, he explained.

Each story seemed tinged with a small dose of self-loathing. Everybody shook their heads solemnly with each tale of woe and thanked each
other for having the courage to speak up. Some had been sober now for two
weeks, others two years, and for that I too congratulated them. Some were
happy, even satisfied, and who was I to take that from them? The truth was,
though, as I sat there, all I could think about was how I could escape without hurting anybody's feelings. I was restless and I wanted a beer. This
wasn't my scene, not yet at least.

"Now let us join our hands," said the moderator. Before I had a chance
to say, "I'm just doing an article on you guys, can I be excused?" I was in
the center of the room with all the others and reciting the "Serenity
Prayer."

"God, grant me the serenity to accept the things I cannot change, the courage to change the things I can, and the wisdom to know the difference."

With that finished, everyone introduced themselves to me, welcomed me to the group, even commented that they liked my attire. Chuck grabbed my hand, shook it, and said, "I can't thank you enough, Gene, for telling me about this place."

I walked out of the meeting feeling as though I had just witnessed something I wasn't meant to see; like I had just stolen a peek up my mother's skirt or something. By the exit doors, I passed a three-hundred-pound Hispanic woman with an inoculation scar that upon first glance was the spitting image of Richard Nixon. On the phone she said, "Come pick me up, Tony, I just came from the Messy Apartment meeting. . . . "

I hit Fourteenth Street, ducked into the nearest Irish bar, and ordered a pint of Guinness. Who was I kidding when I thought I could deny myself these simple pleasures? As the first warm rush of alcohol penetrated my brain I thought to myself that it was the American in me that drove me on—the frontiersman. The gold rush was long over and Teddy Roosevelt was just a name in a history book. What was left to fill that void?

I'm an Evel Knievel man myself. Sometimes you have to create your own adventure. What was wrong with trying to grab a little glory by hurling yourself into potentially suicidal situations and proving to yourself and the world that you could make it on guts and instinct alone? And if I woke up the next day in some cheap hotel trying desperately to remove the roach stuck in my ear as some three-hundred-pound crack whore snored away next to me in a malt liquor–induced coma, I wouldn't despair. I would simply accept it as a thing of my own doing, the same way that Custer had to accept, for one brief moment, that the arrow sticking out of his heart was his own damn fault.

The beer felt good and I ordered another. I started planning my trip to Sturgis. Fuck Potsmokers Anonymous, I wanted to visit a place where I would be understood. The first thing I needed to do was find some kind of patsy, some gullible friend/sucker who I could talk into accompanying me at his own expense. All my tough words aside, I knew that if things ever got rough with the bikers, I was going to want someone with me who I could offer as an alternate sacrifice. My friend Vlad was the only person I knew who let me treat him with such obvious disrespect. He was living with his mom and collecting unemployment, so I knew he had time and a few bucks to burn. I called him on the pay phone and told him to meet me for a drink.

5

Home of the Brave

I bet if I wanted to, I could convince Vlad to throw a bucket of water over his head and stick his dick in a light socket. He trusted me, and in a strange way, he needed me. He was the type of guy who couldn't order a slice of pizza without assistance, much less plan a healthy, fulfilling life for himself. That's where I came in—I provided a false sense of security. It was an arrangement that usually worked for both of us.

When Vlad walked into the bar his eyes betrayed him. I could always tell when he was in a receptive mood—he had that dog-in-the-rain look that practically begged me to lead him into trouble. With his brown, whiz-kid curly hair and his timid mannerisms, I was surprised he'd made it this far in life without somebody tackling him on the street and stealing a kidney or two for resale on the black market.

"I've been waiting here for a fuckin' hour," I griped as he approached the bar. It was always a good idea to start the night out on the offensive.

"Is that any way to greet an old friend?" he asked sitting down. I'd known Vlad since high school, back in the days before he'd discovered daily showers. He was one of those kids who didn't realize he'd reached puberty

Beer guts and chrome belches; a party on wheels in Sturgis, South Dakota. (Malcolm MacKinnon)

until he graduated, and as a result carried a stink with him as if it were his imaginary friend. Sometimes when I went over to his house I'd buy a pack of orange Tic Tacs and shove a few up my nose as a comfort barrier. When you have no friends at that age, you tend to hook up with other kids who have no friends. That way at least you have someone to walk down the hall with, and the football players don't think you're a homo and beat you up.

"You're lucky I'm even speaking to you right now," he said as the barmaid brought him a Guinness.

"What do you mean?"

"Crossroads."

"Oh."

I must admit, I get mischievous when we get drunk. It's part of the reason we have such a stormy relationship. I start to play with him like he's an action figure someone gave me for Christmas. I put him in impossible situations and then see if I can get him out.

"That silver-haired lunch lady . . . " I said as if trying to remember, but really the image came to me like a photograph. "If memory serves me, you followed her to the bathroom . . . "

"You told me to. You said she was into me . . . "

"I stopped you. You're lucky you have me for a friend."

"If you weren't there the issue would never have come up."

"If you don't purge your suspicions about yourself from time to time they get the best of you."

"Suspicions are all I have left," he said and lit a cigarette.

There's something I call the chip/pang dialectic, my own little psychological theory. It basically states that we are given both a "chip" and a "pang" at birth and they are molded over the years by our own successes and failures in life. The "chip" is that proverbial rock you carry on your shoulder, that beef against a world you feel has wronged you. The "pang" is the chip's internal cousin—the pang of jealousy, the pang of self-loathing—that private burning deep in the heart.

I have a pretty big chip—I'm man enough to admit to that—but mine's a pebble compared to the Rock of Gibraltar Vlad carries on his back. He's like the chip/pang poster boy. Part of my motivation in wanting to bring Vlad to Sturgis was to see that chip knocked off his shoulder. If it had to be done with a hairy fist then so be it.

"So what is Sturgis, some kind of fish?" he asked.

"Sturgis is *America*," I said. I didn't want to give too much up.

"I hope it ain't one of those phony pioneer towns where they walk around in britches and bang out horseshoes all day."

"No, no. Sturgis is a party, man, the biggest in the world."

"Like a Rainbow Gathering?"

"It's more like a gathering of automotive enthusiasts."

"Like an auto show?"

"Yeah, like that . . . " I wanted to save the details for later, preferably for the ride there. "We'll have a great time, just leave it to me."

He stared at me suspiciously, but not suspiciously enough. In my mind, he was already paying for the rental car. I was holding in so much laughter I thought I was going to start bleeding from the ears. I could already see the twisted, confused expression on his face when he saw the first biker in Sturgis with a swastika tattoo on his forehead and started to realize what he let me talk him into.

I fast-tracked the budget for the trip through the money men at *High Times*, insisting on an extra two hundred dollars for "miscellaneous expenses" of the herbal variety. A few weeks later Vlad and I were driving through Wyoming on our way to South Dakota in a rented Subaru.

Ripping through the skeletal cliffs and plateaus of the Badlands at eighty miles per hour, I thought to myself that this was the stuff that postcards were made of. There was more sky than I had ever seen in my life and as we drove past an open field with acres and acres of yellow flowers, I realized that there was such a thing as "America the Beautiful."

"Where's the weed?" Vlad asked. He had this Commie idea that my weed was his weed too and thus far I'd been humoring him because I wanted him good and paranoid for when he got dragged a city block from the rear of an old Softail.

"In the glove compartment," I said and he started rolling one up. So long as he wasn't buying, he smoked them like cigarettes. I called him "Vlad the Inhaler," as his lungs could suck half the life out of a joint upon first toke.

As we got closer to our destination, bikers began crawling up beside us doing ninety without helmets, making the pilgrimage to Sturgis like the Magi following the Star of Bethlehem. We approached a roadside restaurant with a parking lot lined with rows and rows of immaculate customized motorcycles.

"You see that?" I asked pointing to the Harleys.

"Is that Sturgis?"

"It's a big part of it. But Sturgis is also babes, beer, guts, tits, ass, tattoos, drugs, vets, and a lot of people telling bad jokes."

"Tits!" Vlad said with a grin, stoned enough to forget his fiancée for the time being.

As we cruised into downtown Sturgis, I watched Vlad's expression change from stoned intrigue to absolute terror. The small town had been invaded. Everywhere you looked there were huge, bearded men covered in tattoos grinning and making obscene amounts of noise on their Harleys.

Women who could probably kick my ass in the time it took to crush a beer can walked the streets half-naked in bikini tops and leather G-strings.

"I wanted America, not Altamont," said Vlad.

"But this is America—raw, unadulterated America."

We drove up to Main Street. Four blocks were reserved strictly for motorcycle traffic. Hundreds of customized Harleys gleamed in the beaming sun, parked in four rows across the street, the center two forming a vortex around which a constant parade of bikers circled flaunting their hogs, tits, colors, and pride. People stood around with cameras and camcorders recording the madness for posterity. We cruised slowly through the streets, careful not to take down any bikers in what was probably the only Jap vehicle in the city. I pulled over and parked.

"You mean we're getting out?" Vlad asked. "I'm wearing shorts, for Chrissakes."

I laughed gleefully, knowing it was only going to get worse.

For over fifty years the town of Sturgis, South Dakota, had been hosting the annual Sturgis Rally and Races. The event was founded in 1938 when a group known as the Jackpine Gypsies got together with local businessmen and decided to hold an annual half-mile race at the city fairgrounds. It was a chance for the local hicks to swap motorcycle stories—tales of bravery and near catastrophe—the same way fishermen swap fish stories.

The founders of the Sturgis rally were not so much "bikers" as they were motorcycle enthusiasts who actually had contests to find the club with the cleanest uniforms. The earliest riders got into motorcycles because they were cheap in the days of the Depression, where any car that would actually run cost upwards of three hundred dollars. At first, guys fixed up old junkers; later, they graduated to Indians and Harley-Davidsons.

As the years went by and the biker lifestyle became its own subculture, people grew less interested in the events at Sturgis and concentrated on the party atmosphere created around them. Sturgis' one city-owned campground started getting more and more crowded, until a particularly miserable and rainy week in 1982 when bikers started setting Port-O-Sans on fire and lighting off whole sticks of dynamite. A subsequent shootout between the Outlaws and the Sons of Silence also didn't do much to promote the family image of the event the city tried to sell. A petition was passed around the town to stop the rally altogether, which unintentionally caused it to get bigger. An end to the event would have destroyed the local economy, so city officials and local businessmen decided to make it "professional," with more advertising, police, and large, privately owned campgrounds outside of town.

As we walked down Main Street I was at first scared to gape at all the scantily clad biker women. Eventually I realized that staring was considered a compliment to both the woman and her mate.

We stopped and watched the hog parade. One biker and his old lady rode by with huge condom hats on their heads. Another rode by with his old lady in full bondage gear, including a leather mask that covered her whole head. There was an Indian biker in full warrior regalia and headdress, an old man on a bike constructed to look like the starship *Enterprise*, and several female bikers that made you wish the body stocking had never been invented. The time these people put into their bikes was downright inspiring. Some were works of art. That was the whole point. The characters were diverse—from yuppie executives to whole families to psychopathic killers—but they all shared one thing, an almost religious devotion to motorcycles.

Figuring I had an article to write, I gathered the nerve to start talking to some of these freaks. I approached one grizzled man with hair down to his ass sitting casually on his bike. I told him I was reporting on the event for *High Times*. He told me his name was Squire and that he had no job, no permanent residence, and the last time he cut his hair was 1975.

"You know, I ride my nuts off to get here and there's people who actually trailer their bikes here," he said. "They drag down the street making all kinds of noise, destroy their bikes, put 'em back on the trailer and drive off. We call 'em 'R.U.B.s,' Rich Urban Bikers. They're the reason you can't find a bike nowadays. These guys buy 'em, ride 'em for three years, and put five thousand miles on 'em. Me, I got a '92 All-Star at home that I put ninety-five thousand miles on in three months. I have a '91 I put forty-five thousand on in thirteen months. The one I got now [a '94 Ultra Tour Guide Classic] is sixteen weeks old and I've got twenty-four thousand on it already."

Obviously the physical act of riding your bike was a responsibility not to be shrugged at. When it was, a case had to be made. There was no shortage of casualties at Sturgis—scarred and limbless bikers were a frequent sight and were accorded the proper respect. Squire's bike was his world and he looked at poseur bikers the same way a survivor of the Tet Offensive would look at a draft dodger.

Cops were everywhere, harassing the bikers. From the differences in their uniforms, I gathered most of them had been imported from neighboring counties. I watched as they chased a guy holding up a sign that read SHOW US YOUR TITS—a no-no now that the event was trying (none too successfully) to clean up its image. Police harassment was always an issue in the biker world. It's no secret that bikers tend to have a Jesse James–style interpretation of the expressions "life, liberty, and the pursuit of happiness," not to mention "the right to keep and bear arms," and certainly cops don't have to worry about citizens' groups bemoaning the lots of the poor oppressed bikers.

Vlad and I popped off the crowded street, and went down a flight of stairs to a dark bar with walls covered in graffiti. A tall, ratty biker started talking to Vlad about visiting Mount Rushmore, or as he described it, "those four assholes on that mountain." I left the conversation to get beers and when I returned, the guy was extolling to Vlad the virtues of his Bowie knife.

"This is my tracheotomy knife," he growled. "This way I can choke a guy to death, open 'em up with this thing, and say, 'There. Now don't say I never did you no favors!' "

"I needed it last night," said his girlfriend. "I was choking on it, honey!"

I introduced myself and Vlad and told him about the article we were writing.

"Man, you fuckers 'er from *High Times*?" he asked, excited. "I got a question for you. I'd like to know what the fuck happened to all the pill presses? Fifteen years ago you'd buy crosstops all the time. Methamphetamine sulfate. Now they don't bother putting it in the pill press anymore, everybody just snorts the shit. I mean, fifteen years ago if you were to pull out your crosstops, crush 'em, and snort 'em, people woulda thought you were nuts."

"What happened to that good fifty-pill sulk?" his girlfriend asked with a drug-freaked cackle.

"Where are you guys staying?" he asked and I told him the Buffalo Chip campground. "That's where we are!" he laughed and Vlad looked like he'd just been punched. "My name's Buster," he told us and shook our hands.

There were a lot of campgrounds in and around the town of Sturgis, but Buffalo Chip had the rep for being the party capital. In its heyday, I was told, girls used to stand on its stage in front of hundreds impaling themselves with cucumbers, bike parts, and other like-shaped items. During the upcoming week, entertainment was to include Black Oak Arkansas, Blue Öyster Cult, and Mötley Crüe.

"I tell ya," said Buster. "Me and my buddy Kovac got high one year and stayed up all night, and not five minutes goes by where you do not hear a mill turning. We consciously listened and the longest time it was quiet was a minute and a half. God, I love motorcycles."

As Vlad and I drove through the gates of Buffalo Chip I figured the bikers would probably kick our asses on general principle alone. But as the sea of chrome, denim, leather, hair, and flesh parted for us to pass, no one said a word. They were waiting to see where we pitched our tents, I figured. If they nailed us right there it would've been over too quickly. It was a week-long rally after all, and it was bound to have its slow moments.

The camp was sited in a field just outside of the hills where *Dances With Wolves* was filmed. The tents were all pitched on a hill overlooking the stage, wrestling arena, and food stands. There was no real shade outside of people's makeshift canopies, and I noted that if the weather ever got really hot I would need large amounts of alcohol and nitrous oxide to remain comfortable.

I found an empty lot and parked. I looked to my neighbor's camp and saw a red, white, and black swastika flag flapping in the wind above his tent. It seemed that the standard flag—the insignia in a white circle on a red background—was insufficient to convey the intended message, because this one was supplemented by an Iron Cross in each corner.

I'd never gone camping before in my life and I had to borrow all my equipment. Before I left I asked Steve Hager if he had a tent I could borrow and he said sure, he had a great one he took to all the Rainbow Gatherings. As I began unfolding it, I discovered that he'd given it a Gathering-style custom paint job. The thing was covered in peace signs, little psychedelic swirls, and very big, pink hearts. I looked back at my neighbor's campsite and figured there was no way around it, Vlad and I would fall beneath a flurry of pool cues and ax handles sometime within the next few days, perhaps the next few hours.

Vlad fumbled with his camping equipment, cursing in such a manner that begged me to ask him what was wrong. I wouldn't take the bait. I knew I'd find out anyway.

"FUCK!" he yelled and then threw his backpack against the car. "I left my fucking tent poles back in New York." He said that in such a way that begged me to ask, "What are you going to do?" But again I didn't oblige him. It would be easier to refuse the next logical question if I showed I had no sympathy from the start.

"Hey, man, how big is that tent? Is that a two-sleeper?"

"Let me get this straight," I said. "You want to sleep with me, here, in Sturgis, in this little tent with the peace signs and the pink hearts on it?"

"Yeah . . . I guess that wouldn't look right. Fuck it, I'll sleep in the car. At least I can lock the doors." He threw his bag back in the trunk, elated that he didn't have to expend the energy it would have taken to set up his tent. "Ah! the real America!" he cried out, staring off at the Black Hills. "Home of John Wayne! Gary Cooper!"

"More like Billy Carter and Richard Speck," I said.

"Purple mountains majesty, man!" he said and took a deep breath. He closed his eyes and unfolded his arms like this was orientation day at the local Est chapter.

"Are you trying to get us killed?" I asked him. "You're supposed to act tough at these kind of events."

"Smell that air," he said. "Amber waves of grain!" He didn't know what the fuck he was talking about.

With my one-man hippie commune now in place, it seemed best if I put as much distance between me and it as possible. Something down by the stage snagged Vlad's eye—the California Women's Oil Wrestling, "America's Sexiest One-Ring Circus."

"You're a journalist, Gene. I think it's necessary to explore all aspects of this event. I suggest we start there, after of course a little herbal inspiration for the artist in you, no?"

"Why not?" I said. "Staring at nude women is an activity that normally transcends any sociopolitical classifications, and I will certainly need to be properly objectified in order to assure that my story is the absolute, unbiased truth!"

As Molly Hatchet's "Flirting With Disaster" cranked through a cheap stereo, we found seats and watched the girls fondle the crowd for tips. One blond biker with a black swastika beret and a patch on his jacket that read "Crazy Joe" let it be known right from the start that not only was he the biggest degenerate in the bunch, he had the wad of singles to prove it. Hurricane Heather jumped on him, cramming her tits into his face and accepting the bill from between his teeth without the aid of her hands. It wasn't long before he was laid out on the ground with a five-dollar bill sticking out of his mouth and she crouched down, effortlessly plucking it from between his clenched jaws with her remarkably dexterous buttocks.

Afterwards, I talked with Crazy Joe and his friend Big Rich, a burly, bearded Grizzly Adams sort of guy in a cutoff denim shirt. When I told them I was from *High Times*, they told me they hadn't seen the magazine in fifteen years. They also told me they didn't smoke or drink anymore. As Joe put it, "There's nothing like waking up with a tattoo of your name on your dick to make you quit drinking."

I spent the next day approaching any biker over the age of forty that looked like he might not kill me if I asked him what this biker shit was all about. Not always the most articulate bunch of people, the first half a dozen men I talked to said something along the lines of "It's about motorcycles, what do you think?" and gave me a stare that dared me to ask them another stupid question.

The first generation of what became known as "outlaw" bikers—the real badasses—were basically good ol' boys who'd fought in World War II, came back, and figured if they made it through that, they could make it through anything. The downside was that postwar America gave little opportunity for a natural-born hellraiser to prove his bravery in any way constructive. Compared to bomber runs over Germany and the South Pacific, life back in the factory felt sterile to say the least. On the weekends they were out getting drunk and stoned, fighting, looking for girls, and racing their bikes in the street.

"The feeling was," Mike Parti explained to me, " 'I done my bit for my country, now it's *my* country and I will do as I damn well please, and if that means going one hundred miles per hour through downtown Hollywood, then I think I'll just do that.' " Now sixty, Mike was an ex-member of the Galloping Gooses. The Gooses formed in 1946 in Los Angeles and were— along with the Yellow Jackets, the Booze Fighters, the Compton Moonshiners, the P.O.B.O.B.s, the Market Street Commandos, and the Hells Angels—among the very first outlaw motorcycle clubs. Mike joined in the early fifties and was a member for eleven years.

"You use the word 'counterculture' and that's just what it was. We would just have more fun than the law allowed. Maybe the police didn't think riding your motorcycle through the front and out the back door of a tavern was a good sport but we did, and maybe trying to outrun them wasn't funny to them, but to us it was. We were a bunch of crazy hillbillies that liked to fistfight. One of the rules of the club was you could turn down no fights—anybody and everybody, any amount, anytime. Fights usually started when people took exception to our language or to our emblem, which was the 'galloping goose,' or the finger. We never thought we had an attitude; we figured it was the rest of society that had an attitude. We didn't give a damn what they did, why should they care about us?"

Fifty years later, personal space and freedom was still foremost on the biker consciousness. The movie image of the biker as an extremely violent drunken White Power maniac was as misleading as the stereotype of a black pimp in a fur coat with a .45 tucked in his pants. Of course there were assholes and psychos in any crowd, but I felt safer in Sturgis than I would have at the Super Bowl. I wouldn't have wanted to have the thankless job of being the local Harley-Davidson repo man, but the prevailing ethic seemed to be, "Don't fuck with me and I won't fuck with you." The hair, the leather, the swastikas, and the "Sheep Don't Tell" shirts were an extension of the Teddy Roosevelt maxim, "Speak softly and carry a big stick" (or a nine-millimeter semiautomatic, as the case might be).

Back at my tent, I saw that we had new neighbors. Each looked as if he could pick up his bike and carry it on his back if circumstances demanded it. On their cutoff denim jackets, they wore the Confederate flag colors of the Southern Gentlemen. I went over and introduced myself and, rather than split my skull with the nearest blunt object, they shook my hand, gave me their business card, and offered me beer. After sitting and bullshitting with them for a while, I asked them how they felt about the way the media stereotyped bikers as drunken brawlers.

"We're like anybody else, easygoing. But you step on somebody's toes, they gonna get you off," said Go Willa, a member of the West Virginia chapter. "You're supposed to have respect for anybody doesn't give you a reason not to. It's not as crazy as it used to be—things have changed. You even have yuppies now."

"Nowadays everybody's got a Harley," added Big Ron, a brother from North Carolina. "You ain't a biker just because you got a Harley. The lifestyle is different. For us it's like having a woman, being married. We ride ours every day, everywhere, work our asses off so we can get the money to go places."

"Like yesterday we were in Wyoming," said Go Willa. "It was beautiful, wide open . . . there's no curves, them motherfuckers just keep on going. Everything's so spread out . . . we rode around three hundred miles yesterday." Road trips in and around South Dakota were a large part of the experience. When I asked him what his favorite part of Sturgis was, he told me, "The ride there and the ride back."

"We came back last night and we were doing ninety or one hundred," said Big Ron. "We slowed back down to eighty and it felt like we were hardly doing the speed limit. The sky was like a blanket with big stars just spread out. It looked three-dimensional, 'cause as you rode they just stayed there, like a metallic paint job."

As if suddenly reminded of just how good it felt, the two thanked me, climbed aboard their hogs, and in one grand movement, kick-started them and drove off. I read the business card: "Southern Gentlemen M.C.: Wars Fought, Governments Run, Uprisings Quelled, Assassinations Plotted, Stud Service, Bars Emptied, Tigers Tamed, Orgies Organized—LORD HELP THOSE WHO DON'T HELP US!"

As word got out that *High Times* was around, growers approached us and turned us on to some super-crystallized homegrown biker bud. We were even invited to a wedding right in Buffalo Chip, and were smoked out by the groom, the best man, and the preacher who performed the ceremony. All smoking was done discreetly. This was one dope journalist who didn't want to share a jail cell with a biker just regaining consciousness and realizing he didn't have the money to make bail. Many of the bikers I talked to had quit partying altogether, realizing that you could only get hammered, fight, and drive drunk so many times before your ass wound up in jail, in a wheelchair, or riding that big Harley in the sky.

Regardless of their warnings, Vlad and I were still burning the torch of self-destruction as we stood waiting for Blue Öyster Cult among the long rows of Harleys by the Buffalo Chip stage, sucking on a balloon filled with enough nitrous to drop even the baddest Nam vet in the lot.

"The land of the free!" Vlad said, sucking more than his share of the nitrous. I wondered which definition of the word he was referring to. Thus far nobody had yanked the teeth from his mouth with a pair of rusty pliers, and he was visibly grateful.

Vlad handed me the balloon and I sucked down hard on it. As the gas soaked its way into my cerebellum, I had a fatal image of me falling over and sending a hundred bikes crashing to the ground like chrome dominoes—a faux pas of the highest order. Someone on stage yelled, "I want you all to do me a favor. I want each and every one of you right now to flip me the bird!" With that, the opening band went into a soulful country ballad called "Sleeping with My Butt to the Wall," about a guy who was concerned about the funny looks he was getting from the fellow he happened to be sharing a jail cell with.

Blue Öyster Cult took the stage shortly thereafter to the thunderous roar of a thousand idling Harleys. A guy wearing a shirt that said, "Real Bikers Don't Wipe Their Butt," asked for a hit off my balloon. B.Ö.C. rocked on, the soundtrack to my chemical lobotomy.

"Is it Mothra?" Eric Bloom asked.

"NO!" the crowd screamed back, their engines belching like seven-hundred-pound steel locusts.

"Is it Rodan?"

"NOOOOO!"

"It's GODZILLA!" Eric screamed and ripped into a tune that was as representative of seventies stadium rock as laser shows and cocaine addiction. As they segued from "Godzilla" into "Don't Fear the Reaper," the roar of the bikes came to a furious climax and I sucked down superhard on the balloon. I heard a "whoosh" as I temporarily lost control of my motor functions. "You let it go!" I heard Vlad yell as nitrous stars flashed in front of my eyes—my mind once again thrusting its fist forward into space, reaching like a jackass for that cosmic carrot of total enlightenment. When I came to, Vlad was holding the limp balloon.

"I would've took a bullet for that balloon," he said sadly.

"You know what they say in America, 'If you love something, set it free and if it comes back, it's yours forever . . .' "

B.Ö.C. closed the show with an extrametallic version of "Born to Be

Wild," the "Ave Maria" of Sturgis. Later on we went backstage and talked to them. They're family men living on Long Island now. At one point Buck Dharma said, "Man, you look fucked up!" When Blue Öyster Cult start worrying about your health, it is time to rest. The week of nonstop partying had juiced me dry. The only thing keeping me awake at that point was the smell of the latrines.

As Vlad and I stalked off in the direction of my hippie tent there suddenly appeared a huge explosion, a burst of fire and light right in the center of the crowd. It was the "Honda Meltdown," and a whole pile of Jap bikes was being reduced to lava by an enormous jet-fueled torch. Flames reached a hundred feet into the air. It was one of the most dangerous, ridiculous, fantastic spectacles I'd ever seen in a public place.

Out of nowhere a man wearing a T-shirt that read, "He Who Dies with the Most Toys Just Dies," decided he was gonna fly through the center of the flames like some biker Superman. He took a running start, got within fifteen feet of the thing and ran back screaming and laughing. I imagined the guy standing at the Pearly Gates like a slab of overcooked bacon, trying to explain to God how he'd managed to cancel himself out of life. But I guess some people had to go crazy to stay sane, and if God couldn't understand that then we were all doomed.

Framed by the Black Hills and the stars, the inferno reached upward toward the heavens like an offering. Where previous cultures sacrificed food and slaves to appease their deities, it only made sense for us in the last gasp of the twentieth century to offer our machines.

"You were right, Gene, this is the real America."

"I shit you not, Vlad. This is the last bastion of that take-no-shit American spirit that got us kicked out of England in the first place."

"And I always thought America was a cheeseburger you never had to leave your car to buy."

"Actually, Vlad, there's a theory that bikers discovered America. It is said that the Vikings who visited before Columbus used to roam the countryside in search of wine and plunder on self-propelled two-wheeled vehicles—crude machines by all accounts, but apparently street-legal."

Damaged from the gas, Vlad nodded his head.

As the flames died out and that semi–brain-dead postnitrous syndrome began to overwhelm me, I thought to myself that sometimes you've gotta piss on death's doorstep and let him know you're not afraid. And whether death was toxicity of the blood, a Honda Meltdown, or an eighteen-wheeled semi heading straight for your Harley on a dark country road, there was no denying that life-affirming feeling you got down your spine when you gave it the finger.

In the morning Vlad and I packed up our gear and smoked the rest of our
stash with the Southern Gentlemen. After a week of Vlad sleeping in the
car, the thing had acquired a cheesy, funky smell, and I was in no real
hurry to start the twenty-four-hour drive back to the Denver airport. Vlad,
me, Big Ron, and Go Willa all watched casually as a drunken biker chased
after his wife with a large monkey wrench. She locked herself in the cab
of a pickup truck and he started slamming the hood with his tool.

"Dumb fucker," Big Ron said. "That's an American car, you don't
treat it like that."

After a few warnings, campground security came and gave the guy the
beating he deserved. We all shared a laugh and I exchanged addresses
with the Gentlemen (you never know when you might need someone to take
care of an uppity *High Times* editor). With the dope now gone, I'd run out
of excuses to be there. I thanked the Gentlemen.

"What the fuck you thanking me for?" Go Willa said. "It was your
dope."

"Sorry, just a habit," I said and jumped into the car.

"Let's cut through the Rockies on our way back," Vlad said, waving
good-bye to a few of the bikers as we drove towards the gate.

"Don't fuckin' do that," I said. "This ain't Disneyland, these people
are not being paid to be nice to you."

"So what about the Rockies?"

"All right," I told him as I pulled out to the road. "I just want to buy
some orange Tic Tacs first."

6

In Search of Tuff Gong

When the Potsmokers Anonymous piece came out, I received my first couple of hate letters almost immediately. They told me how irresponsible I was and how, with people like me in the movement, marijuana would take a thousand years to be legalized. They talked about me the same way my high school guidance counselors used to. I would sit in the 4:20 room, *High Times'* unofficial smoking lounge, and pass them around with a bit of arrogance. With my first published article I was pissing people off. I'd finally made it as a writer.

There were other things that told me I had reached a new level of success. The kids at my local video store found out I wrote for *High Times* and started giving me my rentals for free. The hippie woman at Starbucks no longer charged me for my morning iced coffees. When American Trash, the bar down the street from my apartment, made it a habit to give me my first few drinks for free, I knew I'd hit some kind of scumbag jackpot.

Trench Town, Jamaica, where Bob got 'im start. (Brian Jahn)

Free booze north of Fourteenth Street; I never knew such a thing existed.

Soon I was bumped up from freelancer to part-timer and was given a desk at the office. I was a little unsure about this Park Avenue marijuana movement, but it was refreshing to have a level surface to roll my joints on. It wasn't long before the down-and-out rock stars who regularly visited the *High Times* offices started remembering my name. Benevolent bartenders, sycophantic video kids—I was a made man in the Hemp Mafia. For the first time in my dope-smoking life I was being treated with respect.

In the 4:20 room one afternoon I met Mort Todd, former editor-in-chief of *Cracked* and then editor-in-chief of the Marvel Comics music line. Mort was telling us about a recent trip he had taken to Jamaica with writer Charles Hall. Marvel was planning a four-part comic series based on the life of Bob Marley, and the two of them went down to Kingston for "research." They talked about Trench Town, the ghetto where Bob grew up, and about some guy with no legs named Tata, who had taken Bob under his wing in the early sixties and was now apparently living in Rita Marley's tool shed. The way Mort told it, Kingston was filled with friendly, contemplative Rastas always willing to offer advice to curious white boys with cushy jobs.

Steve Hager had the idea to build a whole special issue of *High Times* around what would have been Bob Marley's fiftieth birthday. At the time I didn't know anything about reggae or Rastafari, but Steve suggested I go down to Kingston in search of the "real Bob." At this point in my career I'd reached a certain level of confidence (or pomposity) and I not only accepted the assignment, but told everybody that I was the only guy at *High Times* who could possibly do it justice.

High Times Music Editor Steve Bloom introduced me to photographer and author of *Reggae Island* Brian Jahn. Bloom had enough sense to see that my complete ignorance demanded I bring someone with me who actually knew something about the subject. I bought a few Bob Marley records, read through a couple biographies, and spent the whole night before I left congratulating myself on all the preparations I'd taken for the story.

At the Kingston airport we were met by Carl, a cab driver that Brian had met back when he was researching his book. Carl loaded our bags into his black-and-yellow taxi and Brian directed him to the home of reggae legend Earl "Chinna" Smith, who had invited us to stay with him during our visit. We pulled out of the airport parking lot and I watched the Blue Mountains in the distance, my vision marred slightly by a billboard showing Colonel Sanders' smiling face inviting Jamaica to smell his fingers.

Chinna, I was soon to learn, cut his teeth making records with Lee Perry's Upsetters. He was one of Jamaica's premier session guitar players, recording with Burning Spear, Big Youth, Culture, Bunny Wailer, and Bob Marley. Currently he was Ziggy Marley's guitar player. It was like being asked to write about punk rock while staying at Dee Dee Ramone's house. All I had to do was interview a few of Chinna's friends and I could spend the remainder of the trip sipping Red Stripes on the beach.

As our cab crawled through the dusty streets of Kingston, I watched the shantytown ghettos pass by one after the other—rows and rows of shacks constructed from zinc and wood, strung together by clotheslines. Brian is a quiet guy, not one to ask me what I thought, but if he had I think my answer would have had something to do with the heat. I felt like I was the only one in Kingston who noticed it. Kids in polyester school uniforms ran down the street and buses were packed to capacity and spewing diesel fumes in the air as they brought people from one end of their lives to another.

Looking out through the tinted windows of our cab I was overcome with a sense of otherness unlike any I'd ever experienced before. At the time I still hadn't spent much time outside of America. I'd been to a few places in Europe which to me could have been hidden sections of Queens. In Jamaica there was no escaping the feeling that I was just a visitor, and I started to wonder what chance I had in even understanding the life of your average Jamaican, much less the "real Bob."

When we arrived at Chinna's place, a modest single-story ranch house, we were greeted by a heavyset Rasta named Bigga. We told Carl we'd meet him later, and followed Bigga into the house. Chinna wasn't home so we sat in his living room with a few of his brethren. We asked Bigga to cop us some herb and he returned with a couple saran-wrapped balls of ganja, each enough for one spliff.

I got stoned and soon after that I got the Fear. As the visitor, I felt the need to make some kind of conversation, but my attempts were all met with either monosyllabic responses or wordless, knowing smiles. One Rasta, a percussionist who worked with Chinna, was fooling with two metronomes, trying to get them to synch together in whatever rhythm it was he was hearing in his mind. For a half an hour we all sat there listening to the two machines going in and out of time.

"So, uh . . . " I asked the drummer. "You ever meet Bob Marley?"

"Yeah, mon."

"Yeah . . . and?" It made me so nervous I thought my heart was going to rip through my chest.

Carl returned, and our research started at Bob's old house on Hope Road, now the site of the Marley Museum. Mort had told me to talk to Neville Garrick, the museum's curator, about finding Tata. Neville was busy, but invited us to join a museum tour with a group of Germans. We wandered through the estate checking out Bob's platinum records, clothes, and other personal items. The young tour guide couldn't hide a giggle as she showed us Bob's old blender and explained that Rastas were vegetarians.

The "real Bob" had left Hope Road a long time ago, but it was still a good place to start our search. Bob's brethren gathered at the museum regularly, so it was like going to Graceland and seeing Priscilla, Lisa Marie, and Charlie Hodge hanging out in the Hawaiian Room. I figured I'd just drink a few Red Stripes and wait for the story to come to me.

After the tour I spotted Rita Marley getting into her four-by-four. I ran up to the car but was intercepted by a bodyguard who explained she was too busy for an interview that week.

"*High Times* . . . " I said, holding up the magazine. "You know what that means? She *has* to talk to me . . . " I was ready to tell the guard about the respect my position commanded in the world, about the free movies and all that, but the car pulled away before I got a chance. After that I watched Ziggy Marley and his band kick around a soccer ball on the front lawn for a few hours. I looked pleadingly at his manager, wondering when I was going to get my interview, and he nodded his head to me as if to say, "Give it time." I left that day without talking to anybody.

We spent a few days at Chinna's house making phone calls and eating Bigga's homemade porridge. For the equivalent of one American dollar I could walk to the corner stand and buy a Red Stripe and enough herb for one joint, and that kept me sane in those early days of the trip. At the house I was introduced to some of Jamaica's reggae superstars—from Rasta greats like Ras Michael to up-and-comers like Yami Bolo. When I asked them if they wanted to say a few words about Bob, the stock response was "Maybe later." Inevitably that "later" never came.

Chinna would watch over the scene and encourage us. I was shy around him and a bit intimidated. He lived the life I'd always wanted to. He was a music legend, he owned his own record store, and all I ever saw him do was play guitar, smoke herb, and sleep.

"Don't worry, mon, it will all come together . . . " he told me when he saw me stressing out.

"I've been here five days," I'd say with desperation.

"You'll find what you are looking for . . . soon come, soon come . . . "

The next night we decided to catch an Al Green show at Kingston's National Arena. As I sat in the audience listening to one of the opening acts mangle the theme song from *The Bodyguard*, I scribbled some notes that were of no use to anyone—

find someone to blame for failure . . .
maybe pay a local a few bucks to tell me what I want to hear?
figure some way to tie Al Green into all this . . . IMPROVISE!
IMPROVISE!

I needed to get my alibi straight for when I came back without a story.
I finally calmed myself at the press bar. As they gave me free rum I was
relieved to think that somebody thought I was a journalist.

When I sat down again an old Rasta punched me playfully and asked,
"Are you on drugs?"

"Not enough to cope with a Caribbean-flavored 'How Deep is Your
Love?' " I answered but I don't think he understood. As an afterthought I
asked him—

"Hey man, you ever meet Bob Marley?"

He smiled and walked away.

The house lights dimmed. Al Green's band took the stage and played
the version of "Thus Spake Zarathustra" that Strauss would have written
had he been the support act for Siegfried and Roy at the Tropicana.
Al strutted out in a white tux, did a Tom Jones–style 360° spin, and
knocked the mike from the stand to the floor. This sent the members of
Third World, sitting a few rows to my right, wiggling across the seats in
hysterics.

Al did a high-pitched "I'm-Still-The-Bad-Mutha-You-All-Know-And-
Love" scream which made it worse. He was staggering a bit. I think the
good Reverend was juiced. He ran to the back of the auditorium and
wrapped his arms around a woman in the bleachers, hoping to save his act.
He segued from "Amazing Grace" into "Let's Stay Together" and the crowd
softened up. Even the Third World guys clapped their hands.

After the show we decided to have a few drinks at the Pegasus Hotel.
If there were slot machines and a couple of Confederate flags hanging in
the Pegasus, I'd have thought we'd walked into a Vegas casino with a Dixie
motif. Black youths in starched white shirts tended to the needs of overweight white tourists. I sat at the pool with my piña colada thinking I
might as well have been looking for Bob Marley on the Jersey shore.

"Is it always this hard?" I asked Brian. I needed to know if it was me
who was fucking up here or Jamaica. Thus far Brian hadn't shown any concern about our lack of progress and I wondered whether it was because he
knew better, or because he was getting paid no matter what kind of story
we got.

"I came down here with a guy from *Vibe* for a story and we got the thing
finished in a weekend."

"Uh hunh," I said. It wasn't exactly the answer I was waiting to hear.

"But you weren't asking them to tell you crusty old stories about a guy who died thirteen years ago."

"No, nothing like that."

I broke down and called one of the *High Times* editors from the hotel phone. It was after six so I had to call him at home. I explained the problems I'd been having with the article, hoping he'd tell me I'd already worked harder on the story than the magazine had a right to expect. Instead, he suggested that I walk around Trench Town until I got shot or seriously wounded and then he'd take my notes and write it as a news story. He promised to throw in a few words about what a cutting-edge journalist I was and the prosperous future I would have had.

The next morning Chinna drove us back to the museum. I guess he figured if he didn't help us "find Bob" we'd be stuck at his house forever. He introduced me to some of Bob's old brethren. He wanted me to talk to the Rasta elders, the people who not only knew Bob but taught him the mystic ways of Rastafari. Chinna spent fifteen minutes laying it out for me just how heavy these guys truly were—

"I cannot pimp them to you, ya unnerstand? These men don't care about being in the papers. They have nothing to gain. They see a white man with a camera and they think CIA. Maybe they will talk and maybe not. But this is the real thing, ya unnerstand? These are the people who really knew Bob and taught him . . . and stop calling them 'dudes.' "

Properly humbled, I approached an older Rasta named Georgie with graying dreads and a gray beard. Georgie was one of Trench Town's most respected Rastas and is mentioned by name in Bob's "No Woman No Cry." I explained where I was from and what I was trying to do. He looked at the *High Times* I'd given him and then stared at me. For a moment he actually considered it, then shook his head "no" and waved me off.

After that I just hung around the museum for a few hours, smoking herb and drinking soursop juice. I finally talked with Bragga, a soft-spoken older man who was Bob's soccer coach when Bob first moved to Trench Town at the age of thirteen. He told me a bit about Bob's early days.

"Trench Town is a college of knowledge," said Bragga. "You have to know how to live amongst people. Sometime you have a pot cooking out dere and a man come and take away your pot. It's a place, they call it a dungle—where they dump things, where they bring the rubbish. Well, a certain amount of peace of mind is there because you people hardly come there. There's a certain amount of contentedness there. You meditate.

"We was young so all we want was food and things. There wasn't a fantasy about a car or this . . . as youth. Because we know it's not in our reach. So we never really want this or want that, we know time will give you everything. With time we have life. Experience teaches wisdom.

"In that time the music couldn't be played on the radio because it was more imperialist and more victimization, apartheid. It was a Babylon civilization. It's when young Rastas start to come and show people different ways to Babylon teaching. Bob see our brethren who is Rasta move freely, forceful, so it gave him a strength. People are born to be Rasta. If a man became Rasta and look back over him life and see the things that he used to do, him can see Rasta. He never really used to molest people and do wrong things. It was Rasta from the start. There's an inner power that rests within you, the power of the Almighty. Politicians can't admit that Rasta is truth or them not have a job."

Trench Town is still the spiritual Mecca of the Rasta faith. In its smoke- and music-filled yards Bob learned that Haile Selassie was the prophesied messiah of the black people, Lord of Lords, King of Kings, and Conquering Lion of the Tribe of Judah as confirmed in the book of Revelations. He learned that the Rasta's true home is in Ethiopia and that, until he was repatriated to the birthplace of his people, he was never truly free. I knew that a visit to Trench Town was essential, but it wasn't the sort of place you visited without a local to show you around. For days we'd been trying to reach Tata, Bob's spiritual mentor, but had had no luck yet.

Chinna was going to take us down to Trench Town after our trip to the museum, but when we got back to his house, he realized someone had stolen a case from his jeep containing every important document he owned—passport, credit cards, title deed of his house, everything. He wasn't too distraught. He walked outside with his Telecaster to where he had a few Fender amps set up for the local youths to come and use, plugged himself in, and played guitar for the rest of the day. I'd stop and listen to his lyrical jazz phrasings and arpeggios, transcribe my notes and tapes, and then come back and watch some more. The phone would ring, people would come and go, but he'd just play and play and play.

The next day Chinna told us to go to Trench Town ourselves and look for a singer named Massive Dread. "He's a soldier," he promised, "the real thing."

At first, our taxi driver didn't want to take us, insisting it was not a good time to be visiting Trench Town. Two weeks before our visit a police station was shot up by a gang in a neighboring section called Denham Town. Four were killed and nine wounded. That's how they treated the cops, the driver told us, they had even less respect for journalists with expensive camera equipment. We sat there debating while the cab filled with diesel exhaust. Finally, he gave up and we took off.

When we got to First Street, we asked the driver to pull up in front of a group of about ten Rastas sitting under a tree smoking ganja. We told them Chinna sent us to find Massive Dread and someone went to look for him. The cabbie didn't want to leave us there and actually got out of the car to make sure we were safe before he drove away.

Massive Dread appeared with two other singers, Knowledge and Formula. They greeted us and took us for a tour of the area.

Trench Town and its surrounding communities comprise Kingston's most volatile area, a large ghetto locked indefinitely in a political struggle between the socialist People's National Party and the conservative Jamaica's Labor Party. Corruption within those parties creates ongoing struggles over who gets the lion's share of jobs, housing, contracts, guns, and cocaine. Trench Town was a maze of houses and shacks, constructed out of cement and rusted, corrugated zinc. From what I could see, there was no running water, plumbing, or electricity.

Massive took us to Joe Higgs' old yard where Bob and the local youths used to practice and sing, and to the house that Bob and Bunny once lived together in. As I cut through the yards and the alleys, past people washing their clothes and kids running around playing ball, I felt a bit closer to the "real Bob." Massive and company led us through several Rasta yards where people hung out and smoked spliffs and cooked food on wood-burning stoves made from modified oil drums. Trench Town had been preserved almost exactly as it was before Bob left. "Cold ground was my bed and rockstone was my pillow" was as relevant a lyric at that moment as it had been twenty years before.

"This is where Bob make 'im start," Massive explained and we all sat down on Tata's porch. Tata's house was one room, connected in a row to several other separate dwellings. In front of it was parked a gutted Volkswagen bus, its windows broken, its engine rusted with time and neglect. Bob used to sleep in Tata's "kitchen" (a five-by-five-foot space separate from the house) when he first came to Trench Town, and together he and Tata wrote "No Woman No Cry" right where we were sitting. The kitchen was no more than a crumbled foundation now.

"Bob Marley was like a sleeping giant," Massive said. "It's like you have a bomb, and nobody knows about it until it explodes. The world wants to know about reality. What they were showing the world was a false reality. So Bob come now with the real reality. Bob did things in Jamaica that are unbelievable.

"When Bob live in the country, the suffering wasn't so bad like it is here. Trench Town was the place where he get the inspiration. That's the legacy we get from Bob Marley—take care of the music. All we do is just deal with music. We feed the people with music."

"All the feelings come through the music," said Knowledge. "If you tell a man something, he'll hear it. Put it on a record and he'll *listen*."

"Trench Town is bigger than Bob Marley," added Massive. "Bob Marley is the spiritual chapter of this time, like Moses. He lived amongst the people, helped the people, and told the story of the people like Moses. Bob established Rasta to the maximum. What he sing is our lifestyle. It is a joy to hear somebody sing about how you live. Whether a white man or a black man, any man, it don't really matter. Because the Almighty God come to man any way. He come to you, He come white. He come to me, He come black. Ya understand? It's not a partial thing."

We ended up at the Trench Town Reading Center—a small, one-room library with about six shelves of books. The walls were decorated with framed pictures of Bob, Haile Selassie I, Marcus Garvey, and a Rastafari Last Supper with a Selassie Christ. On top of one of the shelves was the first guitar Bob ever owned. I asked if I could see it and Massive took it down and handed it to me. It was beaten and warped and someone had stuck a "Property of Trench Town Reading Center" sticker on it. As I stared at it, thinking I was finally earning my paycheck, Massive picked up another guitar that was leaning against the wall and began to sing. The others, joined now by Ziggy, a Rasta who sang for a while with the Wailing Souls, chimed in on the harmonies while I rolled spliffs in fronta leaves.

I must live and let others live,
I must give not only to receive . . .

People walked in and out of the library, smoking spliffs, joining in. These guys weren't singing for fame or money or girls—all the things that encouraged me to pick up my first guitar—they were doing it because they had to, because they had something inside them they could not contain.

Back at the house, Chinna held court in his driveway with a few of the local youths. There was a kid behind the drums who looked to be about eight and another kid on bass who was about fifteen. They were rehearsing a simple rhythmic pattern, and Chinna was coaching them through the changes. I walked in and Bigga told me that someone had returned all of Chinna's papers. The only thing that was actually stolen was the case he carried them in.

From inside the house, I could hear the kids singing—

I don't want to be nobody,
I'd rather be a Rasta music man . . .

We finally managed to connect with Tata. If I were to liken this trip to *Apocalypse Now*, Tata would be our Colonel Kurtz. Tata met us at the Marley museum and promptly gave us his demands. He needed fifty U.S. dollars before we left so he could buy all of Trench Town lunch, and then another fifty upon our return. He was the big time, and he wanted us to know it. With the transaction out of the way, he told me to buy him a warm Guinness. I was a little wary of returning to Trench Town with a man with no legs as our guide. Massive and his friends were healthy young guys. In a life or death situation, Tata might just cry rape.

My concerns were unnecessary. As we wheeled him down First Street, people ran out of their houses to greet him. Tata was like the ambassador of Trench Town and people were so surprised to see him they didn't notice his two guests.

"Long time me not come to your house and get it!" said one woman, laughing. "Where is it? Where did it go?" she asked as she started searching Tata's person.

We wheeled Tata back to the porch where we had sat the other day, but instead of the peaceful, mellow talk we had with Massive and company, the whole town came to greet us. Our visit was an excuse for a party. Tata spread around some of *High Times'* expense money, buying cheese puffs and soda for the kids, and ganja, Red Stripes, and fish with red beans and rice for the adults. After Tata told the townspeople we were friends of his here to tell the truth about Trench Town, I had a whole town trying to talk to me.

"Bob sleep right dere!" Tata exclaimed proudly, pointing to the kitchen. "Rita Marley get her first nice love dere! Come over here," Tata led me out behind the kitchen. There was a skinny tree and the ground around it was covered in shit and toilet paper. "Look at dat!" he exclaimed. "Take a look! This used to be nice! This used to be a plum tree and at nighttime when people sleep, we'd rehearse on a bench, me and Bob. Here them write songs. It was clean and the pipes used to work."

"Trench Town is a community with lots of talents," said Lancelot, one of the Rastas. "We need exposure. We need help from outside. Nothing is going on for youth except guns and bullets. It's just hand-to-mouth. When they're sixteen, seventeen, you have three children. They can't find no work, and work in a factory. Three-fourths of the youths here leave school before time and get involved with certain systems that they don't really love because the system is a fraud."

"A set of vampires is trying to conquer I and I community," a man named Raphael added. "I and I don't get no benefit out of nothing, politics, nothing. All the superstars who come out of here, we don't get nothing. It somewhat shocks you."

"When a minister win, we always lose," said Massive.

At one point an argument ensued about Island records founder Chris Blackwell, with Raphael calling him a "vampire" who did nothing but "spoil and spy," and Tata defending him, claiming: "Bob make him a star and he make Bob a star."

Massive told me about other times the press had visited Trench Town, how film crews had come down claiming to be making a documentary and the footage ended up in music videos. Other crews have depicted them as miserable and poor. Such an idea belittled their pride.

Brian and I walked out to First Street so he could take some pictures. While Brian took his shots I watched a few kids burning a garbage can across the street.

"All the people who live here have different talent," said Roger, another Rasta with long dreads and sunglasses. "There's ones who can dance, who can run, swimmers, netball, football, you have all kind of people in the community. They've never really sent us nothing to help the youth from outside. Them not really put up no training center, nothing progressive for the youth."

For a community that has produced artists like the Wailers, the Heptones, Rita Marley, Alton Ellis, and Ken Boothe, Trench Town has never seen the rewards that, say, Nashville or Memphis did. Here, the ripe fruit was picked from the tree, while the tree itself was left to starve. There was a plan to build a million-dollar Bob Marley Community Center in the heart of Trench Town, but local street gangs were already fighting each other over who had the right to extort the developers, delaying the project indefinitely. Chinna produced a compilation of Trench Town artists, called *Trench Town*, that was to be released on Ziggy Marley's Ghetto Youths United record label and distributed by Tuff Gong International. Proceeds from the album were to go toward the center, but thus far it hadn't been released.

"There is a natural mystic blowing through the hills," said Derek as myself, him, and Roger watched the sun set over First Street. "You get up in the morning and you see there's nothing there for dinner. . . . I never had a boss in my whole life. Friday comes and I have to get up and pay bills never yet. I have a family to take care. I don't know how mystery reaches you, but we're not looting and shooting. We're not walking and grab nobody's chain. That's the mystery of Almighty God, I and I."

When it got dark, we said good-bye to everyone and wheeled Tata over to Spanish Town Road where we hoped to catch a cab. The bright, full

moon above looked like a single light bulb in a deep blue room. Even the
cemetery across the street seemed at peace with itself. Cabbies don't like
to stop in Trench Town, afraid they'll be robbed, so we stood there for over
an hour. When we did find one, a girl ran up to Tata and started hugging
him and we had to send the car away.

"You can tell people you were at Trench Town at night," said Tata.
"You hear what they say about us, about how we nyam off people's face and
when you look all you see is his skull. . . . No, no. We are not talking about
white or yellow or pink or blue. We are one. We make God pleased."

The week in Kingston left me with a drained kind of satisfaction. The otherness I'd felt upon my arrival had dissipated enough for me to realize what
a privileged fucker I was. I wasn't sure if I'd found the real Bob Marley,
but I'd found a few reasons why a person would work hard at becoming Bob
Marley. Having seen the space in Tata's kitchen where Bob used to sleep,
it wasn't hard to imagine a fifteen-year-old kid dreaming about becoming
a superstar.

There was another side to Bob's music, though, an almost saintlike
passive resistance in the face of oppression. If Bob was so ambitious,
why didn't he just become a gangbanger like so many other Kingston
youths? There was a spiritual side to the man that I knew I'd only find in
the country.

Bob was born and now rests in Nine Miles, a small village in the St.
Ann's province of Jamaica's "Garden District." Brian and I encountered
the usual hassles trying to find someone to drive us there, and after we
were taken for forty dollars by a local driver who thought we wanted to
drive "nine miles" out of Kingston, we convinced Carl to take the day off
and be our personal guide. Carl had grown up in the country and was glad
for the chance to leave Kingston.

For two hours we bounced over decrepit roads in Carl's black-and-
yellow-taxi, listening to dancehall DJs growling rhymes over the radio and
smoking spliff after giant spliff of Jamaican-grown Alaskan herb. Sometimes a vista would open up on the side of the road and we'd park and look
down over small farms and hamlets where people grew coffee, ganja, and
assorted fruits and vegetables. By this time Brian and I had gotten used to
the fact that neither one of us was much of a conversationalist and instead
we connected on a rudimentary "Wow, check that out" kind of plane. Occasionally Carl pulled over to snag a particularly ripe avocado or papaya
from a tree hanging over the road.

When we got to Nine Miles I sat in a small bar and listened to one of
Bob's uncles tell me what the man was really like. He looked to be about
sixty, wearing a boy scout uniform, and as he talked he smiled wide enough

for me to see both sets of gums. I didn't have the heart to tell him I didn't understand a word of his conversation. We sat with the obligatory Red Stripes and herb, and as I was listening to Bob's uncle, Brian pointed to a ten-year-old *High Times* calendar hanging on the wall and made me laugh.

We met Donovan, a young Rasta with short dreads who took us for a tour of the village. There were no paved roads, no sidewalks, no modern buildings—most everything there was green and still alive. Donovan led us past one-room Rasta shacks painted red, gold, and green, through herb fields and vegetable gardens, and to the tree which was planted along with Bob's afterbirth fifty years before.

Finally we were brought to the mausoleum, a modest room painted in Rasta colors. I walked into the tomb, filled with notes, drawings, herb, records, and graffiti left by other travelers, and when I was finished I went and sat with Donovan on an adjacent hillside. Donovan passed me his joint and told me that this was Bob's favorite place to sit and meditate. Green hills extended out to the horizon in all directions and every time a cloud passed the sun, the mood of the scene shifted. I finally understood why everything took so long to get done in Jamaica. You don't want to miss the subtleties.

Donovan told me about country life, about walking four or five miles to school every day. When I told him that must have been rough, he disagreed and told me that you often got a ride, but even if you didn't, you just walked at your own pace, picking fruit along the way.

"In the country, you live closer to Jah," he said. "Here you don't pray for money, but for rain to fall because you know things will grow. I remember skipping school and going with my friends to visit the herb fields. It would take two days to get there and there'd be huts you could sleep in along the way. The farmers used to get together and plant four or five acres worth. Now you have to hide it or the government will come." He pointed to some clouds of smoke in the distance, the government burning someone's ganja field.

From this little village, where a thunderstorm was enough news to last a week, Bob Marley worked his way into the global consciousness to the point where *Legend* ranked next to the first Boston album and *Led Zeppelin IV* for the most overplayed album at frat parties across the United States. I thought of all the times I'd heard "Three Little Birds" at parties in college and thought, Birds on my doorstep? Everything's gonna be all right? *What's this guy on?*

It took ten days to realize it, but the "real" Bob Marley thrived somewhere in the middle of all those contradictions and mysteries that regularly sent me reaching for oblivion. Bob had what I always wanted, the ability to find freedom in captivity, peace during war, hope in distress. What gave

Bob his power was his ability to see that reality was in the eye of the be-
holder.

When it came time to hit the bumpy road back to Kingston I was almost afraid to leave. Chinna's house was one step closer to the airport and
I was worried that trying to take the "real Bob" back with me to America
was like trying to mail a snowball from the North Pole to Miami Beach.

I spent my last day in Jamaica sitting in Chinna's driveway, going
through four hours worth of interview tapes with one of his daughters.
Since I'd spent the majority of my interviews shaking my head politely and
wondering what people were telling me, I enlisted her to help me translate
what I'd been missing. With the exception of my interview with Tata, which
neither one of us could understand, I managed to recover just about everything that had been said.

I came across the first interview I did at the Marley museum with
Bragga. There was something he said which nailed it for me. I was glad I
could at least take his words back to Babylon, even if I had to leave those
green hills back in Nine Miles where I'd found them. He wasn't talking
about Bob Marley, but he summed up those contradictions I was talking
about, and why I shouldn't be so concerned with them.

"We've reached the fast ages," he said, "the Modern Age. You can
want everything you see, but you can't always get it. Some people, them
can't satisfy. But one word can change things. One man says South Africa
is free, and it is free. You have to look for miracles every minute of every
hour. Miracles don't happen, and then one does. Then you come around
and see that everything is so simple and sudden."

7

Fear of a Groovy Planet

I grew up in the eighties; for me there was no Summer of Love. When I was a kid I had a few summers of Swanson's frozen dinners; I remember a summer when everyone walked around with Batman logos on their clothes, but that liberating season full of golden-haired, bra-burning nymphomaniacs only ever existed for me in Channel 13 documentaries. Summer in New York City means three months of alcoholism and claustrophobia. So when the good folks at *High Times* asked me if I wanted to come along on their annual Rainbow Gathering excursion, I went home, listened to CSN&Y's "Almost Cut My Hair" a dozen times, and talked myself into it. I knew there'd be a truckload of drugs there, and after hanging out the past year and a half with rednecks, bikers, and Rastas, I wanted to go somewhere where *I* could feel like the tough guy for a change.

A nature excursion seemed like just the thing I needed. I'd get in

Groovy Planet: The lack of sterile water sent a few of the Rainbow folks into states of delirium. (Gabe Kirchheimer)

touch with my primal self, maybe even find God. Little did I know just how hard it is to find peace when you're surrounded by ten thousand hippies.

The idea for the first Rainbow Gathering came when a large group of environment-minded people, refugees from the splintered peace movement of the sixties, gathered in Portland, Oregon, in September 1970 at the Vortex I celebration, a "biodegradable festival of life." There they named themselves the Rainbow Family of Living Light. Now that they had a name, they had to find something to do—like maybe hang out and get high. After two years of planning and word-of-mouth publicity, the first Rainbow Gathering convened July 1–4, 1972, in an area in Colorado called Strawberry Lake. Every year since, the Family has gathered somewhere on public land in the United States and practiced their own peculiar brand of communal living. Police harassment follows them to every Gathering, but regardless of that the event goes on. At the center of their ceremony, every July 4, is a communal prayer for peace.

The drive from the Albuquerque airport north up Route 25 to Taos, New Mexico, confirmed my belief that this was going to be the easiest assignment of my dope-reporting life. I sat in the back seat smoking our "miscellaneous expenses," feeling like a psychedelic Edward R. Murrow. The Allman Brothers were playing on the radio, and as I watched the tumbleweeds blow through the New Mexico desert, I half expected to see the Roadrunner dropping an anvil on the Coyote's head. As we drove further north, the desert gave way to tall, tree-covered mountains and the temperature started to drop. There were storm clouds on the horizon as we approached the site of the Gathering, but I didn't anticipate a problem. I was ready for a vacation, with an emphasis on the vacate part. I wanted to vacate my body, mind, and soul, and just dig some campfire-type fun.

We drove up to the gate, where a big sign read "Welcome Home." A couple of Rainbow People greeted us and gave us what they called the "Rap 101," in which we were asked to respect the trees, the animals, the meadows, etc.—all very reasonable requests. We drove deeper into the Gathering, passing old cars, Volkswagen buses, school buses, and even a converted Greyhound. Every person we saw flashed peace signs at us and mouthed the words, "Welcome Home." Even at that early stage I couldn't help thinking to myself that any "home" of mine would have to include a flush toilet.

The site was a cow pasture that sat in a lush valley divided by a small stream. Towering over us were mountains covered with huge pine and aspen trees. We came a day early, but the hills were already spotted with little camps. This used to be Apache territory, I was told, and I was both awed and a little frightened by its beauty. This was not civilization anymore, this was nature, and nature moves forward in an unalterable path, chalking the roadkill up as fertilizer. I'd have to watch my back if I planned to live through the week. As I walked with my pack the other campers greeted me, their smiles and salutations cheery enough to make even the Osmond family look like manic depressives.

Five minutes after I set up my tent it started raining and didn't stop for three days. I hadn't thought to bring any raingear whatsoever, so I spent most of those first couple of days cowering in my tent and watching the sky attack the earth with mammoth bolts of lightning that reached down and punched the trees.

Occasionally I'd venture out to secure a bowl of rice and beans from the Rainbow folks, who for the most part seemed unperturbed by the rain and cold. These people were survivors, there's no doubt about that. I was a consumer, born to die in a hospital bed while medical bills soared and a rerun of "Growing Pains" flickered on a TV screen in the corner of the room. I wasn't proud of this but evolution's a one-way street, and once that tail falls off your ass there ain't a glue in the world strong enough to stick it back on.

When I could sleep I had a recurring dream that I was surrounded by dreadlocked white people with acoustic guitars singing "Love the One You're With," while Bigfoot slapped me on the ass and told me to squeal like a pig. From my tent I could hear the constant, foreboding beating of drums. Even in the foulest weather there was some idiot out there jacked up on acid and risking pneumonia just so he could piss me off. With no TV to occupy my time, I instead stared up from my wet sleeping bag at the space between the rainfly and the mesh windows on the tent ceiling and watched spiders trap and mangle lesser insects. It seemed to me a warning, a reminder of Darwin's first commandment, "Only the strong survive."

Once the clouds parted, the penises started making their way into the public sphere. Overweight men with beards walked around in the raw inventing new and exotic ways to get sun poisoning. The marshy atmosphere left by the rains provided an excellent breeding ground for vicious winged insects, and, though I soaked my skin with my trusty Deep Woods Off!, a halo of mosquitoes followed me wherever I went.

My first forays into the Gathering left me feeling confused. The Rainbow People seemed friendly enough, but if there's two things I can't stand, one is being called "brother" and the other is being hugged by people I don't know. I couldn't find fault with the general message of the Rainbow Gathering—peace, love, and respect for Mother Nature—but the passivity of the thing was unnatural.

In my efforts to get down with the Rainbow people, I struck up a conversation with a white-haired man named Dancing who was in semiregular contact with extraterrestrial beings. He hadn't always been a shaman, he explained to me; he used to be a roadie for Iron Butterfly. He was with Richard Dannely, the author of a book called *Sedona: Beyond the Vortex*. Though Richard hadn't met any aliens yet, he was a believer, and I imagined that it wouldn't be too long before his advanced aura was spotted by some little gray men and contact was made.

I also met a man wearing nothing but a burlap sack and a Timex. Around his neck he had a sign that read "Deviations From the Norm." Norm would go from an almost comatose passivity to an inspired state of poetic ecstasy, pulling pieces of unadulterated id from his brain, like the one he called "Drug-Oriented Suicide Art With Bad Words In It," which went:

Inkwells link well with pigtails,
here's mud it must have been made to fly,
shoot heroin underneath your fingernails,
drop cocaine in your eye . . .

On and on he went, bouncing around like Robinson Crusoe on DMT.

Near the Main Circle, I was introduced to Plunker, who wore a cowboy hat, glasses, and a hemp vest with a pot leaf over an American flag on the back. Now Plunker was no newcomer to this lifestyle. A Vietnam veteran, he'd been there from the beginning. As we sat out on the grass and talked, I found his manner to be instantly disarming—he had a broad smile and talked simply and straightforwardly about his way of life, genuinely hoping to impart some form of understanding upon me.

"The human condition is in such trouble right now. We can't help people who are out there in the darkness, we just hope that they'll come home. When we're home here we can help each other. The human condition is that kind of darkness and confusion that causes people to do dumb things."

"I do a twelve-pack of dumb things almost every night."

"We've all done dumb things. But we all walk, stumble, bounce, and slide back home. We teach each other respect here. Pretty soon they carry that out into the world; they have a little more respect for what's going on. We better the human condition.

"I'd like to go to the black gangs—big tribes like the Crips and Bloods and take them peace belts and recognize them for what they are—vast tribes of people that work together, men, women, and children. I'd like to see these people come here, bring representatives, and do peace with us."

Certainly that would be an interesting experiment. Could you imagine a bunch of inner-city gangbangers ripped on acid and wandering into the Krishna camp? In the meantime, there were more earthbound concerns to be dealt with. Plunker told me he was going to go speak with some forest rangers who were complaining about one of the old-timers, a man named Kalif, who had been cursing them out as they tried to drive in through the gate. Out of respect for the Rainbow Family, the rangers wore windbreakers over their guns.

Plunker is a natural diplomat, talking to the rangers, telling them he'll speak to Kalif, and did they know by the way that the Rainbow Family just had their first Catholic Mass? And that they said prayers for the rangers who are out there doing their jobs, and also for the Hispanic logging community, who also had a couple problems with ten thousand people converging on their local national forest? The cops were charmed. Plunker started telling them that he smoked marijuana every day, that it helped him with the post-traumatic-stress disorder that he had suffered from since the war. By the end of the conversation, the rangers were agreeing with him that marijuana should be legal.

As we parted, I thanked him for letting me see Rainbow diplomacy in action and told him that he handled the situation well.

"Well," he said, "I guess I've had a lot of practice."

Back at my camp, a crazy-eyed, self-proclaimed shaman named Moses got me higher than I'd ever been in my dope-smoking life. He was a white guy in his late forties with dreadlocks that stretched well below his ass. He kept turning me on to his own homegrown, mind-bending strains that were smuggled back from Amsterdam, like Jack Herer and SuperSkunk and one totally out-there strain he grew himself called MoseSkunk. He lived in Oregon.

"I should do an article on you!" I said and his eyes widened at the idea of being profiled in the pages of *High Times*. I had an ulterior motive. A few months before, *High Times* had done a photo shoot for a possible Sturgis cover. For models we contacted the local strip club and they sent over four girls who were quite happy to pose on a Harley in their underwear. Three of them were typical plastic surgery cases, but there was one there who didn't fit in. She lived in Oregon, she told me, she was just in New York to work for a few weeks at one of those huge sex supermarkets in Queens where a girl could clear a thousand a night.

She told me she hated New York and wanted to get back to Oregon. We exchanged addresses and I was surprised to get a letter from her the next week, telling me to come visit her. When I met Moses, all sorts of schemes started forming in my head. As we parted company, I told him I'd try and work out a trip to see him and his mighty gardens. Call it joy, call it mutual self-interest, but before we parted, we were both moved to hug.

One of my responsibilities that week was to build the *High Times* "Hemp Booth." The following morning I figured I'd throw down some hippie drugs for inspiration and build a booth that would get me a seat in the Rainbow Hall of Fame right next to Squeaky Fromme. At the Sun Dog camp (by far the best in terms of food and vibe) I was given a little handful of mushrooms by a smiling Mexican. He'd been eating peyote straight for a few days now, he told me, and from his grin and happily mischievous eyes I guessed he had some good shit. I swallowed my lot and headed back out to the Main Circle where I would begin my masterpiece.

By now the Gathering was packed and swinging. I walked over to the trading circle where people sat on blankets trading trinkets, jewelry, hair wraps, pipes, dope, books, and probably lice, crabs, and influenza. The mushrooms I'd taken were starting to erupt and for a moment I felt like I was in Calcutta as I watched the girls walk around barefoot and topless, wearing Indonesian-style dresses and jewelry that chimed with every step. The men too were topless, most looking like grungerock Jesus/Manson hybrids with long dreadlocked hair and beards.

Someone started playing a flute and suddenly I felt like I was trapped inside a Jethro Tull song. I began to feel *very* crowded. Claustrophobia overwhelmed me as the mushrooms started doing their thing. I couldn't build my hemp booth in this condition, so I set out for a hike in the opposite direction.

The Gathering was flanked to the west by a steep hill. It seemed like a good vantage point to sit and contemplate the scene in stoned isolation. I hiked up, and by the time I found a comfortable rock I realized that I was extremely stoned and dehydrated. A few seconds after that, I realized I left my canteen back at the camp. The mushrooms started turning my brains into compost, and as I looked out over the happy people drumming and singing, the trees danced in mockery of my stupidity. Fuck 'em, I thought, at least I'm alone.

At the bottom of my hill I could see a dark-haired guy walking in my direction. It's a big hill, I thought, with room to share, but as he got closer I realized that he was coming to visit me. I watched him climb slowly toward me until there was no doubt. When he finally reached me he said, "Hey brother," and tried to hug me. I gave him a healthy shove and he sat there looking like a mangy puppy that'd just been kicked. All I knew was I was in the middle of a pharmaceutical miscalculation, trying to keep my head above the psilocybic waters. The last thing I needed was to be manhandled.

"Do you have any water?" I asked him. I was on the verge of drinking my Deep Woods Off!

"No water, man, but I got some pot."

It felt like a Cheech and Chong movie—one of the later, really lousy ones. Adding to my dilemma was the fact that I'd temporarily lost the ability to speak coherently and could only communicate my needs to him in a rudimentary sign language.

He torched up a joint and told me he used to work for an alternative radio program, but that compromised his integrity so now he "just lives on planet earth." Unfortunately for me the part of earth he was currently living on was the sad little rock that I had hoped I could sit in solitude on for twenty minutes, or at least until the trees stopped laughing.

He started inviting even more people to my rock to share his soggy joint and I had to leave. My need for water had reached crisis proportions and was demanding my attention.

Back down in the confusion of the Main Circle, people were waiting on this huge line, in the broiling July sun. There were so many food lines at Rainbow I expected Stalin to jump out at any moment with an acoustic guitar and sing "For What It's Worth."

I made it over to one of the kitchens and in a cracked voice pleaded with a fat guy behind the counter for a cup of H$_2$O.

"We waited for ours just like everyone else," he said pointing to the line.

"Oh," I said and started on the long journey back to my camp and all the water I could steal from the gullible *High Times* employees.

I had been rained on, starved, poisoned, groped, laughed at, and reprimanded to the point where I just wanted to leave, but unfortunately our rental car was stuck in about two feet of mud and I didn't have the strength left to hike all my gear up the steep mountain and out to the road for a lift to town.

After nearly a week in the woods I felt no closer to nature than I had before I left. All I knew was that I was cold, hungry, and very easily agitated. What's more, I found out that I had camped on what must have been the forest toilet. Every day some new and exotic form of turd appeared at the door of my tent like a burning cross placed there by Mother Nature herself. Now I'm no expert when it comes to the outdoors but I've seen "When Animals Attack." I knew it wasn't Bambi or Kermit the Frog running around, excreting with hate and vengeance. At any moment I could have been raped and gored by some rabid deer while the Rainbow People stood around me in a circle trying to stop the carnage with an "Om." I longed to be back in New York, back to the relatively generic fear of murderers, cops, and ex-girlfriends.

I didn't give up. All I needed to do was to commune with the Great Spirit. I needed an exorcism, something to make the trip worthwhile. It's a curse to see through everything and sometimes I see through so much I find myself in an invisible world. I'd heard about a "peyote sweat" at the very end of the Rainbow in the last camp—about a six-mile hike. I was down for the walk and hoped this might provide the breakthrough that I was looking for.

The sweat was run by an old Cherokee man. He sported a long gray beard and an old Rasta-style knit hat and welcomed everyone to his "anarchist" sweat (meaning you could come and go as you pleased and he wasn't going to stand over you and preach like some wannabe Timothy Leary). I sat out on the grass and drank his tea and waited for the trip. After a while the others headed toward the sweat lodge—a makeshift little cabin where rocks were heated until they glowed and then brought inside, roasting the inhabitants. The thought of perspiring with strangers—most of whom hadn't showered in days—did not appeal to me and I opted to stay outside and talk with the old Cherokee medicine man instead.

"I've tried doing set rituals with churches or whatever and never got anything out of it, yet I can eat just one button and get a whole lot out of it." As he talked, he stirred a cauldron of peyote tea. I felt like I was hanging out with the old guy in the gatefold of *Led Zeppelin IV.* "I can't describe what I get out of it because it's an inside thing and you can't describe things that don't have words. It tunes you up with the whole universe. And of course there's its actual medicinal uses, too. It's an antiseptic, antibiotic, analgesic, and antihistamine.

"I don't believe in traditions, really. I believe in evolution. My second-grade science book on the first page said, 'Nothing in the universe is ever lost, it just changes.' I figure if I just change enough each time, I'll never be lost."

He talked about Oneness, of being one with the universe, saying it with a laugh as if it was such a simple concept even an idiot like me could understand. After a while I walked off by myself and tried to grasp the Oneness thing. The peyote gave me a mellow glow, like I was looking at life through a stained-glass window. Certainly I understood the Oneness concept—that the earth was really just a single living being, composed of all living things the way a human body was composed of a multitude of living cells—the problem was I just didn't feel it. Maybe if theme music had suddenly filled the air and Lassie had come bounding out of the hills, I could have found the words in my emotional vocabulary to convince my brain that I had some place in this nature scheme. There would be some shock of recognition. But as it stood, it just looked impenetrable, foreign, and terrifyingly beautiful.

July Fourth finally came. While the rest of the country was celebrating the birth of the Psychopathic States of America by sitting in parks with coolers full of Budweiser and throwing M-80s at the ducks, the Rainbow People were sitting in silence and praying for peace. Only I didn't know you should be silent and came babbling my way down to breakfast with my usual complaints about the cold, the discomfort, and everything else.

People glared at me silently. I poured some coffee and started asking people what their plans were for the day. Again I got "the look"—the one that asked, who is this asshole? I figured they were still pissed at me for stealing their food. I went to another part of the camp and started talking. "It's nice to get a break from them drums," I said. "Nice to get some peace and quiet for a change." Again it was eyes everywhere saying, who invited the schmuck? Fine. "Well, fuck you, too," I finally said and walked out of the camp.

Down by the Main Circle, people were gathered around the totem pole. I met Steve Hager and he hipped me to the fact—using pen and paper—that everyone is silent on the Fourth until noon. I walked over and sat down in front of the pole. At its base, people had placed an assortment of items—pipes, buds, a picture of a family, a mahogany staff with a face carved at the top, and a copy of *Sedona: Beyond the Vortex*. There was also a poem that read: "We would like each of you, as you walk on earth, to speak to the blades of grass, the grains of sand, the petals of flowers . . . and to state your presence . . . allow the land, the living library that is alive with the love frequency, to move into your body."

I was surrounded by people—a pretty young woman, topless with flowers in her hair; a tall man in a long purple robe with his dreadlocks shooting out of a purple crown; a sloppy, overweight man carrying a feather, naked save for a psychedelic T-shirt and an umbrella hat. There were also mothers, daughters, squatter punks, road dogs—a cross section of the extended Rainbow Family.

Suddenly an "Om" started and people were on their feet. The topless girl next to me was chiming in, singing the "Om" in various keys. People were in a trance, eyes closed, arms around each other, going through some sort of metamorphosis. A guy right up front started freaking out. "Don't touch me!" he yelled as the dreadheaded gypsy tried to calm him. The guy with the umbrella hat walked over and waved his feather around the acid casualty. People were Omming and Omming. I felt a hand placed on my back. I looked over and it was Deviations from the Norm. When our eyes met he removed his hand from my back like he'd just placed it in a frying pan full of boiling Crisco.

The "Om" went on and on, everybody was sending out their prayer for world peace and unity and all I kept thinking was Man, I gotta get out of here. I didn't get it and I didn't want to get it. I was just glad that no one I knew was there to see me in the middle of it. Breaking through the chain of attached arms was difficult. Again I got those looks. What kind of asshole breaks out of the "Om" on the Fourth of July? After a short, heated struggle, I was on the outside—a freak amongst freaks—a situation I'm used to.

Someone blew a conch and the place erupted. People were screaming, laughing, singing. Some guy started singing "Zippity Doo Dah" and the whole crowd joined in. "Zippity doo dah, zippity yay, my oh my what a wonderful day. Plenty of sunshine, heading our way, wonderful feeling, wonderful day!" Now I have never, in my life, been happy enough to understand the kind of mind that would even dig a Paul McCartney song, much less an abortion like "Zippity Doo Dah." I was overcome with that same kind of fear and distrust a little kid feels for Santa Claus. And what's more, there was some woman running around pissed off screaming, "We must honor the children by sitting down and covering our heads!" and trying to get everyone quiet again.

The song changed. "All we are saying is give peace a chance!" Over and over, the chorus refrained. Everybody was ecstatic, dancing and singing. "All we are saying is give peace a chance." Some guy walked around on stilts, covered in balloons and singing, "All we are saying, is give peace a chance."

Give peace a chance. Why not? But to that I'd like to add a quote from another one of the Fab Four and say, "It Don't Come Easy." Not this easy, at least not for me. Looking down at the people gathered in a circle singing for world peace, I was reminded of the end of *The Grinch Who Stole Christmas*, after the Grinch had done his deed, taken all the presents, all the food, all the decorations, and is on top of the mountain waiting to hear the pissed-off moans of all the Whos down in Whoville. But no. There are no moans, no whines, no cries. Only a song. There he is with everything, and there are the Whos in a circle singing their Who Christmas song like there's nothing wrong.

Even as a kid I thought the ending of *The Grinch* was bullshit. Really, if it was me down there in Whoville and someone stole all my toys, I wouldn't be singing, I'd be saying, "Man, we know who did this, we know where the fucker lives, let's find the bastard and string him up by the balls." Because if Christmas means "Peace on earth and goodwill toward men," then it was stolen from us a long time ago and no one's ever going to give it back no matter how loud we sing.

I found Hager, blissed-out, digging the scene. Actually, I think that out of all the ten thousand people there, I was the only one in a foul mood.

"Hey! Let's smoke some of this organic DMT!" he said.

"What, are you crazy?"

"What do you mean? This is the perfect place! Feel the energy!"

"The only energy I want to feel is that of an internal-combustion engine taking me away from here. I'd absolutely lose it if I did that."

"What do you mean? It only lasts five or ten minutes."

"That's about how long it took to bomb Hiroshima," I said and wandered off toward my tent.

By the time darkness fell, I was back up at my camp, clutching my gut in pain and praying for death as my entrails shot out of my body in fast, furious spurts. Somewhere along the line I'd eaten some bad food and was now paying for every hippie joke I'd cracked over the week. I'd found God all right—not the friendly guy they talk about on the "700 Club," but the Yahweh of the Old Testament. I pictured myself dying right there at the Rainbow Gathering. I imagined trying to explain myself to St. Peter, how and why I'd wandered so far from God's path. I think he would have kicked me in the dick before sending my soul screaming down to hell to spend eternity with the likes of Hitler and my eleventh-grade gym coach.

As the drums thundered throughout the forest and my intestines became the host of a dozen nameless parasites, I finally managed to guilt the *High Times* people into driving me back to town. Enough beans, enough drums, enough spirituality. What this boy needed was a cheeseburger and some cable TV. As far as finding God goes, I figured I'd made the first move. If He really wanted to talk to me, He knew where to find me—at the local Holiday Inn nursing a six-pack of Guinness and watching "America's Funniest Home Videos."

8

Born to Lose

A Harley screamed past the T-shirt booth and I watched Bundy's eyes open, booze-soaked and even slightly repentant. A groan worked its way through his skeletal cheeks, and with his long blond hair and beard he looked like a speed-freaked Colonel Custer.

"Why these motherfuckers wake up so early, I'll never understand," he said lying there in the dust among the cigarette butts and the empty beer cans, staring up at the blue tarp that covered the booth. His voice cracked like a stick, he was so dehydrated.

I was similarly wooden. I'd been up all night, exploring the campground, but when the sun came out I came back here to Bundy's booth before the last of my bodily fluids left me. After a few days awake on speed, your muscles freeze up and your veins feel like there's Drano running through them. It feels lousy, but not lousy enough to make you stop doing it.

"Wanna beer?" I asked, reaching into the cooler next to me. I wanted water but that was all the way across the campground. I threw him a Bud Light, which he caught and popped. I grabbed another, took a swig and pretended to feel better.

Somewhere in my mind,

The town of Sturgis was kind enough to provide orientation guides to welcome newcomers. (Malcolm MacKinnon)

buried under a thick layer of drugs and beer, was the idea that I should do something. This thought wasn't exactly nagging at me, it simply had a presence. Back in New York I'd told *High Times* that, if they sent me back to Sturgis, I'd set up a vending booth where I'd sell hats, T-shirts, Cannabis Cup tickets, calendars, back issues, etc., and basically spend the trip spreading the hemp gospel to our Harley-riding brethren. Since the merchandise never arrived at the post office box it was supposed to, I bailed on setting up the booth and wandered around the campsite until I met Bundy and his crew late one night at a party they were having. Bundy sold "Fuck You" shirts, Harley-Davidson patches, motorcycle boots—accessories for the biker everyman. I checked the post office box once a day, but aside from that I spent most of my time sitting in front of Bundy's booth watching the other bikers, feeling like I'd finally found that thing that my life had always lacked—namely, methamphetamine.

Before I came to Sturgis, I also had plans to write an article about the first generation of bikers, the World War II vets who started the whole thing, but when Bundy gave me my first-ever taste of crank, any plans I had to write went up my nose and out the back of my head like a shotgun blast. Like I said, there was this theory somewhere in my mind that I should be doing some kind of professional journalist-type thing, but I figured I had the rest of my life to do things like that. The story here was in my veins.

Bundy talked to me about Vietnam, drug-running, jail—the kind of subjects that don't come up in conversation in Park Avenue offices. I don't know how much of it was true—bikers tell lies like McDonald's sells cheeseburgers—but like most stories, the art was in the delivery. He told me about pimping and ripping off crackhouses, and with my crank-fueled mind breaking the sound barrier, I came to the conclusion that Bundy and his friends Tucker and Billy were the coolest people I'd ever met in my life.

They told me that back in Gainesville people called them the Good, the Bad, and the Ugly. Tucker was the Bad. He was more beast than man, really. When he stood up, which was not that often, his hairy gut hung out of the bottom of his T-shirt like a bear cub that had lost its way. With his dark hair and almost black beard, he looked like a low-rent John Bonham. He bragged that he'd done time in every single state, including Alaska and Hawaii, and though I knew that was an exaggeration, I also knew it wasn't much of one.

Billy was the Good. He slept out back. No doubt he was out there in his tent dreaming about God knows what. Probably that he could walk again. Even Bundy dreamed that Billy could walk again, he told me, at least once a week. When he did he said it felt good because it meant that there was still something human about him.

Bundy was the Ugly but he never told me why.

"Tucker, wake up," Bundy said, nudging the hairy lump next to him. There was no way he was going to feel this shitty this early by himself. Tucker's eyes opened without even a grimace. It took more than a hangover to make Tucker groan. For him to show any sort of emotion it took an *event.*

Next to Bundy, snoring away in a chemical coma, was an Esplendido that had been hanging out the night before. The guy wasn't a club member yet, just a pledge with a reputation to make. Once he got his patch, and he would, he was going to be one scary motherfucker. He was a scary motherfucker already—skinny, young, crazy—stalking the campground like a dog on a leash that was still too long. When he drank—which was all the time—you could see his bent little Mexican mind overextending itself, reading your insults, your fears straight from your brain, picking up on the thoughts you were too chickenshit to say.

Suddenly the tarp was pulled open at the front and there was a flash flood of daylight, followed by Jodi, Bundy's girlfriend, who was maybe the loudest person I've ever known.

"Dammit, that asshole's still here?" she asked, pointing to the Esplendido.

"He's an *Esplendido,*" Bundy said, as if that explained everything.

"He's an *asshole* and a *crazy* asshole at that."

"We're all crazy," Tucker said.

"I know we are but that asshole's crazier. Spic-crazy. There's a goddamn difference and you know it." Jodi walked over and kicked the Esplendido in the side. "Get up! Go home! The party is *over!*"

The Esplendido woke like a startled animal, like he was never really asleep to begin with.

"Oooh shit, baby," he said with a laugh. He laughed all the time and you had to interpret that laugh and whether it meant he was happy fucked up or readying himself for a bit of blood-pumping violence. "Shit, baby, I got a *job* for you . . . "

"Bundy, you gonna let him talk to me like that?"

"How 'bout it, Bundy?" laughed Tucker.

"Jodi . . . "

"What?"

"Shut the fuck up." I could tell by the look in his eyes that as soon as he said it, Bundy knew he shouldn't have. Tucker and the Esplendido laughed loud.

The scene was making me nervous, then I remembered I'd basically been nervous for days and was somehow enjoying it. There was something funny about the ability to hear someone *think* you're an asshole from across the room.

I sucked my beer and hoped I wouldn't get sucked into this one. Jodi liked me and I liked her, but sometimes she'd flirt with me, I guess because I was fifteen years younger than Bundy and she liked to piss him off whenever she could. Bundy knew what time it was and never acted like he gave a shit, but there was always the chance a crazy fucker like that might change his mind. Jodi was cute in her own kind of way, but I liked the Esplendido's fifteen-year-old daughter, and I didn't know what to do about that.

As I walked out of the tent I could still hear Jodi screaming. She had a mouth like a chainsaw. The other venders were opening up for the day, pulling the tarps off their booths, brushing the dust off their clothes. The venders always slept in their stalls with a gun—the only sure way to prevent theft.

I drove my rental car into town to get a dose of the madness, and to give Bundy and Jodi time to resolve their troubles. I knew they wouldn't, but I had to let them try. Between the sun and the crank, I thought I was going to have a stroke as I stood and watched the Harleys circle Main Street like steel panthers. On the way back to the campground I picked up a few cases of Bud Light and one Coors, just for variety.

Bundy had set up his tent while I was gone and was now trying to act like a salesman. He had a small stock of leather clothes—pants, boots, and chaps—that he always tried to push. When I entered the tent he was talking to a guy about the chaps, which went for a hundred-fifty dollars, one of his more expensive items.

"But are they waterproof?" a biker asked him.

"All you need is to waterproof them like you would a pair of boots," Bundy said but the guy walked away unconvinced.

Tucker sat in a lawn chair in front of the booth, occasionally whistling at the girls, and Billy sat in his wheelchair yelling "Light 'em up!" to every bike that rolled by. Any biker who heard him and looked over and saw the guy—a cripple who couldn't ride but would if he could—was happy to burn a little rubber for him before leaving the campground. Whenever Billy saw the dust kick up and the engine roar, his blue eyes looked like they were either in a state of total joy or ready to burst into tears.

As Tucker told it to me, Bundy met Billy when Billy was riding with the Arrows, a sober bike club, and the rules were no booze, three strikes and you're out. Billy'd had about two dozen strikes in the two-and-a-half years he rode with them but never got kicked out. Bundy met them sometime in the eighties as they pulled into a truck stop he was flipping burgers in. He and Billy clicked, and Billy offered to sponsor him in the club.

Bundy needed to get a lot of shit out of his system and thought a sober bike club might do it. It didn't. He couldn't hold a job. If he couldn't deal he'd starve, so he quit the club, but kept in touch with Billy the whole time after.

"What's happenin', Billy?" I asked as I took the seat next to him.

"Wanna buy a joint, Chris?" he asked and then held up a cardboard display of little joint pendants. That was his favorite joke. I never saw Billy without a smile on his face. Out of the three of them, he was the one with the least chance and the most hope. "Man, look at all these bikes. Where are they going? Deadwood? Mount Rushmore? The Badlands? So much to do when you got a bike."

"Which T-shirt's better," I heard one customer ask his girlfriend. "The one that says 'Show Me Your Tits' or 'Die Yuppie Scum'?"

"I like that there Confederate flag that says 'If I'd Have Known This Was Gonna Happen I'd Have Picked My Own Damn Cotton,' " she answered with a country twang.

The sun was kicking the shit out of all of us. Bundy was sweating like a twelve-year-old trying to cop his first feel. It was running out of his scalp, down his long blond hair, down his scraggly beard, down his neck, and into his black Harley shirt. He looked at me and I kind of knew what he was going to say.

"Chris, I'm gonna go out to the van for a bit."

He walked off and I watched Tucker's wildcat eyes follow him from behind his shades.

"Hey, Chris," Tucker said, laughing in his indiscretion, "I'm gonna go take a piss out by the van, you wanna come?"

"Sure," I said, and as we walked out of the camp I heard Billy yell, "Light 'em up!" and a few seconds later I heard the roar of a Harley.

Jodi was about my age but looked older, as if something had happened to her in her life that caused her to grow up fast. She had long, straight blond hair, and was just heavy enough to be considered sexy rather than overweight. Jodi was actually the one with the meth. She brought it with her to make sure this whole trip didn't lose money. She rarely did the stuff herself, she was just the only one out of the four of them with any business sense. Seeing the first night that I'd taken a liking to the speed, she offered to trade me a gram for a whole bunch of *High Times* products, a deal I accepted before she could change her mind. (Even though the mother lode of products hadn't arrived, I'd brought a bunch like I do on all my trips, just to hand out.)

She wasn't so generous with Bundy and Tucker and rationed them both out what they considered to be a paltry amount of crank. That's where I came in, a wooden bridge between hand and mouth. I basically had more than I could use, so I didn't mind kicking it over to my newfound friends.

We walked behind the booths to the van. They had a blue and silver Econoline, with blue carpeting and a mattress in the back where Jodi and sometimes Bundy slept. Bundy jumped in the driver's seat and Tucker in the back. I jumped in the shotgun seat and pulled the sweaty little plastic bag out of my jeans. When the cleaning solvent smell of the meth hit my nostrils, my insides started rearranging themselves. I broke off a piece of the rock and laid it on the tray between the seats.

"A little more than that," Tucker said.

Chet, an old-timer I met the day before, walked over to the van. Bundy greeted him as he cut out a line for me. Tucker put the rest in the dome of an upside-down Bud Light can and mixed in a little water.

"Mornin', Chet," Tucker said. "Wanna smoke a joint?"

"Sure," Chet said and climbed into the back. Chet seemed like a nice enough guy. I wanted to interview him for my article on old-time bikers, but I'd only met him once. I reached for my herb but Chet stopped me and said, "I got some of the good stuff."

I did my line and winced.

"I dunno," said Tucker. "Doin' drugs' about the only thing I'm good at anymore."

Chet lit the joint and watched over the proceedings with a bemused smile that showed a big gold tooth right in the front row.

"Which one's yours?" Tucker said, holding up two needles.

"I dunno," said Bundy. "The one with the blood in it, I guess. Want some?" he asked Chet.

"No, no—just some reefer for me. The rest of it I gave up a long time ago."

Looking out the window at the crickets flying through the tall grass and breathing the clean Dakota air, I found it strange but somehow understandable that I was spending so much time sitting in a van doing hard drugs. Sturgis was like a Russ Meyer rewrite of the Garden of Eden. Get high, talk about guns, feel good—it didn't seem that weird a way to live your life. Bikers weren't so much a part of nature, but a confidant—like a rusted hubcap from an old Chevy dug into the mud for years until it looked like it belonged.

"So when did you start riding?" I asked Chet.

"Oh, I'd say sometime in the fifties."

"Chris works for *High Times*," Bundy said, drawing fluid into his needle from the well on the beer can.

"*High Times*? Damn, I used to read yer magazine . . . shit, twenty years ago it must've been. I tell ya, I've been growin' marijuana on my farm since the sixties."

"I was thinkin' about doing an article on the old-time bikers, the first guys, back from World War II."

"You should've talked to my daddy before he passed away. He started ridin' Indians in the thirties."

Bundy jabbed his needle in the center of a swastika tattoo on his left arm.

"Lookit that," Chet said, admiring the tattoo. "Y'know I been a member of the Klan now for thirty years."

Suddenly Chet didn't seem like that nice of a guy anymore.

"People are afraid of joinin', of havin' that newsletter sent to their house, but I tell ya. There's a lotta things in that newsletter you don't hear about on TV . . . like did you know the Jews are monopolizing the aluminum industry? Now they already got the banks—that's theirs, and that's fine. All right. They own the entertainment industry and that's theirs, too. But now they're moving into aluminum?"

A few minutes before I was under the impression that Chet was an old farmer who just wanted to ride his bike and watch the corn grow. Where he pulled this white racist trip from I just couldn't see, but I guess that's the secret of evil, its commonness.

"Thanks for the company," Chet said, finishing up the joint. "See you folks later." The three of us sat in drugged silence as he walked off.

Bundy's eyes were stuck on something and I looked and saw Jodi up at the concession stand.

"Man, I don't know why you put up with that bitch," Tucker said.

"Dammit, Tuck, you know she's pretty."

"Pretty goddamn annoying with three annoying kids to boot. And ain't none of 'em yours. I mean, I used to own better women than that . . . used to sell their asses to horny football teams . . . Think about it, Bundy. If Billy was still able to get a woody she'd be spending *his* paychecks on Big Wheels and Baskin-Robbins and them little fuckers'd be callin' him daddy."

"He can't and she won't," Bundy said.

"Man, you ever wonder why that fucker was in such a hurry, he'd drive ninety miles an hour the wrong way down a one-way street?"

Tucker liked to shred Jodi's character at any available opportunity. I liked Jodi, but Tucker was such a balls-out horrible human being that he made me laugh anyway. Over a few lines the day before he told me how Jodi met Billy only two weeks before his accident at a party at Bundy's house. She'd only been with Bundy a month and he was being his usual moron self, giving all his drugs away to anybody he thought was bad or cool or whatever, and Billy was there drinking Coke and not talking to anyone. Jodi invited him to her son's first communion. According to Tucker she had a bit of a crush and somehow the accident made it more of one.

"Fuck it," said Bundy, staring off into his own personal drug dream. "Let's get back to the booth, Billy's there by himself."

I followed Tucker and Bundy to the booth. Jodi was sitting with Billy, and as we approached she glared at Bundy like she was ready to poke his eyes out with a screwdriver.

"I'm almost ready for a joint," Tucker said, reaching into the cooler and pulling out beers for everyone.

"Right here," said Billy pulling out a bag. He picked up the cardboard with the fake joints on it, turned it over, and started rolling.

"Where you two been?" asked Jodi.

"I had to take a shit," said Bundy.

"And you, Tucker, what'd you do, wipe his ass?"

"Listen, Jodi, I ain't gotta answer to no one around here."

"C'mon, Jodi, gimme a kiss," Bundy said, going towards her.

"Don't gimme no 'Gimme a kiss.' "

"C'mon," said Bundy, grabbing her around the waist.

"Get your fuckin' hands off of me," she said, only half serious.

"C'mon," he said, kissing her.

She resisted, then gave in. "There, you happy?"

"How 'bout giving me a kiss," Billy said, grabbing his crotch. "Come 'n get it."

"Oh yeah?" Jodi smiled and bent down over him. When she undid his fly and started making kissing noises, Tucker laughed almost too loud and Bundy snapped, "You guys sell anything?"

"What?" Jodi asked, zipping Billy up.

"You sell anything while I was in the bathroom?"

"There ain't hardly anyone here yet, Bundy."

"Well, I want to make some money this time. I'm tired of leaving these things poorer than I came."

"No problem," said Billy. "Watch this . . . . Hey man, wanna buy a joint?"

Jodi sighed, stood up, and said, "I'm goin' shopping." She gave Bundy one last look and then walked away.

"How you gettin' there?" he called out after her.

"With this ass?" she yelled back.

"I'm just sayin', Bundy . . . ya' know?" Tucker said, plopping himself back into his lawn chair. We all watched as Jodi climbed on the back of some guy's Harley. "We gotta take ourselves more seriously. This T-shirt shit is for losers."

"I know it, Tuck, I know it. You know me, I been an outlaw all my life."

"Shit, me too. Just think of the shit we been through together . . . fuckin' Ajax—"

"Ha ha!" Billy laughed. "Fuckin' Ajax man, now *that's* an outlaw!"

"We were doin' this rip-off, and Ajax had the shotgun on his arm like this . . . " Tucker explained to me, resting one of his arms on top of the other. "And we said if anybody moves, we're gonna shoot. So somebody moves and the gun slips off his arm and he fires—blew his fuckin' arm off," he let out a throaty laugh and Billy passed him the joint. "What I'm sayin' is we gotta start getting serious."

"I know."

"Dammit Bundy, I'm a *businessman*."

"Me too."

"I'm not talking 'Fuck' shirts here. I mean . . . I've run whorehouses, crackhouses—you name it and I done it. And the last thing you wanna do is cut some loudmouth mommy of three in on a million dollars. Next thing you know, she'll be sending them kids to college and you'll be asking her for money to buy a six-pack."

The heavy-metal engine sounds mixed with the white noise in my head—churning, expanding, one steady wavelength of sensation snaking its way through my mind and body. I was not taking in separate images or stimuli, it was all just one single fascinating, powerful force of energy. I sat and watched a biker and his ratty girlfriend walk past the tent like Adam and Eve in denim and leather. The loudspeaker was playing "Rock You Like a Hurricane," and Tucker started rolling another joint.

Bundy went to drop off his Harley with a customizer to get a picture of Woody Woodpecker painted on the fuel tank. "Me and Woody understand each other," he told me before riding off into town. In an effort to keep Billy away from the beer, Jodi took him to the track to watch the hill-climb. That left me and Tucker alone to watch the booth and discuss the issues of the day with amphetamine bravado. The crank had obliterated any kind of tactical screening process in our conversation, and we both agreed that this gave our words credibility. Tucker had sold a pair of Harley boots and thus had an even higher opinion of himself than usual.

Tucker never gave two shits about motorcycles in his life, he told me. He had a Harley once and eventually traded it for a pound of rock with which he started his own house in Houston. Cars were the only thing that could even attempt to house his personality. A Cadillac's got size and girth in addition to chrome and paint. Tucker was a guy who took up space— the more the better.

"Most of these yahoos with their brand new leather chaps and their polished right-out-of-the-showroom chrome are just weekend warriors playing Cowboys and Indians in front of other yahoos. Even the fuckin' club guys, they all answer to somebody and follow rules and go to meetings. Following someone else's rules is just something you shouldn't be proud of. Bundy don't follow anybody's rules. Bundy was in 'Nam and it don't take a genius to see the cracks. If there's one thing I never have to worry about, it's Bundy going straight on me. The Ugly—he'll always be that.

"I never pulled much with him. That rip-off with Ajax. I tell you, though, he did his job. While Ajax was blowing his fuckin' arm off, Bundy hit right on target and he didn't hardly blink and you know why? He'd seen it before. Now this bitch has got him selling T-shirts for almost three years now. Three years watching yahoos drive around in circles while the real dudes avoid him like the plague unless it's to fork his speed up their nose or flirt with his girlfriend. Man, I can count the girls in my life like the red Xs on my old math tests—mistakes most of them, and even if they weren't it don't matter 'cuz they're all gone now."

Esperanza, the Esplendido's fifteen-year-old stepdaughter walked past the booth in cutoff denim shorts and a light green tank top.

"Hola muchacha," Tucker called over to her instinctively, his sunglasses hiding his felonious eyes.

"Hellooo," she said with an impish smile and came over.

"Hey, I got this for you." Tucker reached down next to him and handed her a hemp *High Times* hat that I'd traded to Jodi for crank.

"I don't like *High Times*," she said and looked at me.

"Whaddaya mean?" Tucker asked.

I knew what she meant. The day before we had done a photo shoot with some of my *High Times* products. I figured I'd get a couple of the campground girls to model some *High Times* clothes. Maybe the magazine could use the pictures, maybe not. I didn't give a shit either way, really, I just had to do something besides sit in a lawn chair, stoned off my ass. I asked Esperanza. It was only after we did the shoot, and she posed in all sorts of suggestive positions wearing the *High Times* logo, that I thought to ask for a photo release. I told her it was just a legal technicality, but I needed her to sign and say she was over eighteen. "Is it okay if I'm fifteen?" she asked and I got the sudden image of her father and three of his closest friends tying my limbs to their bikes and driving off to the four corners of a very small world. She told me she could get her parents to say it was okay, blah blah blah, but as far as I was concerned she was out and I told her so.

"You looked great yesterday," said Tucker. "What's the problem?"

"He said I can't be in the magazine." She pointed to me.

"I'll talk to him," said Tucker. "We'll put you in. We'll talk to the boss."

Her smile lit up and I looked at Tucker like he'd just murdered me. He chuckled and she started dancing around singing "I'm gonna be in the magazine, I'm gonna be in the magazine . . . " gyrating her hips, looking at me, and laughing.

This wasn't good. I didn't want her psycho stepfather to even know we took pictures of her, much less think we were going to print them. Ever since the photo shoot, Tucker and Bundy were telling every girl they met they were going to put her in *High Times*, even though they had nothing to do with the magazine. I'd already told Esperanza to take her Traci Lords trip somewhere else, and Tucker sold me out for the fun of it.

Esperanza told me she'd see me later "about the details" and was still singing "I'm gonna be in the magazine" when she left. I looked at Tucker and he smiled at the situation he had created.

"What the hell are you doing, man?"

"What?"

"We took pictures of that crazy psycho's stepdaughter humping motorcycles."

"Oh, fuck that guy. What're you worried about him for? I would fuckin' cut that guy to pieces if he tried any shit. I ain't afraid of that motherfucker, I'll go over there and fuck his wife *and* his daughter if I want to. Man, I did it for *you*. You see the way she looks at you? What're you, some kind of faggot?"

"She's fifteen, man."

"If there's grass on the field you can play ball."

"That kind of shit sounds good when you say it, but—"

"Look, forget it. I tried to do you a favor. Hey, is that Bundy coming?" He motioned towards the gate. "My vision's not that good."

"Yeah. Over there by the entrance."

Tucker shot up and over to the cash register. He opened it up, saying something about beer money, and picked out a few bills. He saw me looking at him and said, "Don't tell Bundy about the boots," and shut the drawer. "I'm gettin' fuckin' tired. You wanna go back to the van?"

"Who's gonna watch the booth?"

"Fuck it, we'll get that fuckin' Esplendido to watch it. Nobody'll steal anything from that crazy fucker."

As Tucker crouched down in the tall grass behind the van and shot his drugs into his arm, he suddenly got self-conscious.

"Uh . . . I don't care if you watch or nothin' but . . . "

I realized that I didn't care if I watched either, so I decided to get a pork chop two inches thick. Before I left I asked him something, not be-

cause I wanted to know the answer (I knew he would lie anyway) but just
to see what he said: I asked him if he ever killed anybody.

"Well, uh . . . " He looked at me and winked. "You know . . . you never
admit to a thing like that." Figuring he gave me the answer I wanted to
hear, he went back to his vein search. When it came to his legend, Tucker
liked to paint his picture thick.

Actually, I don't think he was lying, though.

Anyway.

Someone came by and traded five hits of windowpane acid for three
shirts. Billy took one and Tucker and Bundy each took two. I didn't want
to see what these people looked like straight down to their bone marrow,
so I passed on the doses and instead helped them kill two cases of beer and
get started on a third. Even without the acid, the evening was strange.
Some guy had stabbed his girlfriend in the bathroom and word was getting
around that Jerry Garcia had just died. It seemed like a good excuse for a
party. I went out and bought about six more cases. It was pretty packed in
the booth and Jodi and Billy and Bundy were actually selling a bunch of
merchandise.

Jodi asked me if I wanted to come back to the van, she felt like having a blast, it being Saturday night and all. "Just don't tell the boys," she
warned as we walked the familiar path, overtall grass that we'd managed
to stomp into mud over the past week. By now the van was such a familiar scene, I felt like I was part owner. Jodi yanked the slide door open and
I climbed over the makeshift bed into the passenger's seat. She chipped
off a large chunk, almost a gram, and began smashing it up with an empty
Miller bottle. When she was done she offered me a rolled-up twenty and
I snuffed up my two lines, by now used to the pain.

Jodi did her line and told me she had read my article on the last rally
and she liked it. "Where's your friend Vlad?" she asked. "Is he comin'?"

As the powder soaked into my gray matter, Vlad's whiz-kid face burst
through my mood like a shrapnel grenade. It was the first I'd thought of
him since he wrote me off a few months before, in the middle of an argument that had something to do with drugs. He wanted to cut the cord, he
told me. I was holding him down.

"Vlad? Vlad's lost . . . He's living in a youth hostel in Seattle, sharing
a room with four other dudes for three hundred dollars a month. He
weaseled out of his wedding back in New York and his fiancée filed a pa-
ternity suit against him. That sent both the chip and the pang into orbit."

"The chip?"

"The chip and the pang are these things that you're given at birth—

but the *point* of it is, I treated the little mutant like a son and the last time
I saw him he had his face in a pile of coke and told me I was patronizing
him . . . as if you can do anything *but* patronize that little cretin . . . "
I could have talked about Vlad for an hour, I was getting so wound up
about the creep. Jodi stared at me confused and then climbed over the
seats into the back of the van to change. "It's fucking 1995, Kurt Cobain
is *dead* . . . " I continued in a tone that implied true urgency.

"I want to bring my babies next year," she said. I could see her
through the curtains, tearing through her suitcases as she talked. "I think
they need to do more boy stuff, after all they ain't got no father and Lord
knows Bundy ain't no daddy either."

"Where are their daddies?" I asked. The curtains weren't really
closed, and looking over my shoulder I caught a good eyeful of flesh. It got
me thinking.

"Who knows and who really cares? My firstborn's daddy is José
Cuervo and the second's is Jack Daniels." Jodi laughed at her own joke,
then screamed, "For fuck's sake! Them fuckin' bastards! I almost sat my
ass down on this rig!" she said and handed me a needle. I threw it in the
glove compartment. "I sure know how to pick 'em, don't I?" she added,
climbing back over the seat. She'd changed into a pair of short-shorts.
They hugged her body with a serpentine sexiness.

"Goddamn!" I said.

"You like 'em? I got 'em on Main Street today."

"Looks good," I said. "Especially for this place where most of the
women look like retired Evel Knievel groupies."

"Let's get back to the camp and show the guys."

When we walked back to the booth Billy and Tucker both whistled like
they would to a classy whore. For Billy it was the culmination of a great
day 'cuz he'd already managed to get three different girls to lift their shirts
for his camera, and now he snapped a couple of shots of Jodi.

"C'mere," said Bundy, vicious as a rat, pulling Jodi to the back of the
booth by her arm.

"What?" she said, forcing a laugh.

"Take that thing off."

"Why?"

" 'Cuz I don't need every swinging dick in the campsite taking photos
of your fat ass, that's why."

"Oh, you're jealous, is that it? Tell you the truth, I didn't think you had
it in ya. Sometimes I think you don't give a shit what I do."

"Well sometimes I really don't, Jodi."

"You really are a sonofabitch, Bundy," she snapped. Bundy, realizing his mistake, grabbed her by the arm, and she screeched, "Get your hands off me!" and walked out of the booth into the camp. She was almost out of sight when I saw some old man with a camera say "Show me your tits," to which she smilingly obliged and then disappeared. Bundy was having a little trouble walking at this point and spilled his beer in his effort to grab a seat next to Billy. Tuck stood out in front of the booth drinking a beer wrapped in one of those foam rubber things to keep it cool, talking to a fat redhead wearing a black T-shirt that read, "Death or Glory."

I walked out in front of the booth feeling like I had panzer tanks running through my veins. The August night wrapped itself around the Black Hills like a familiar blanket, and bike sounds swirled around us all like an undulating net. The grass was starting to brown, and when the wind kicked up it brought with it the scent of engine fumes and fresh hay. I felt like I was the center of the universe, like I was chosen by some higher being to be right there, doing exactly what I was doing, as if my actions had a significance on this earth so important, the gods were afraid to tell me what it was.

"Hey, Bill—" Tucker yelled over. "Got your camera ready?"

"Sure do."

"This here's Marla," Tuck said and then yanked up the fat woman's shirt. She had nipples as big as silver dollars and a gap-toothed smile that burnt my eyes.

Billy snapped the shot and then said, "Wait, that one didn't come out." Marla pulled up her top again and Billy took another. "Wait, that one didn't come out either." Marla rolled up her shirt and Billy's flash went off five times before he said, "Damn, I don't know what's wrong with this camera."

"I can't stand here all night with my tits hanging out . . . " Marla said and then—"Oh, you fuckers . . . " as she finally got the joke and Billy, Tuck, and Bundy all laughed for a whole minute. Then Tuck and Marla disappeared in the general direction of the van.

"Light 'em up!" Billy screamed as a bike passed by the booth, ignoring his plea. "Man, I'd like to get a whole fucking row of 'em to light up at one time, just like we used to do. Remember that, Bundy? When all of us used to be on the main drag of some bullshit town and we'd all light 'em up—all of us—burn rubber and freak them motherfuckers *out*. Remember fuckin' Ajax?"

"Fuck yeah."

"Me and Ajax went to this disabled bikers benefit once. It was really nice, man. They had a barbecue with steaks and lots of beers. I remember I was helping this one guy who was crippled from the neck down, pourin' beers down his throat. Bikers helping bikers. Man, it was beautiful."

Bundy spilled his beer again, and I saw Esperanza walking towards the booth, looking too good to be hanging out with losers like us.

"Hey, man!" I said. "Whus up!"

She looked at me like I was an idiot and strolled into the booth, examining some of the T-shirts.

"I'll take the Angels lighter, the 'Show Me Your Tits' shirt, and that bumper sticker that says 'Honk If You Speak English,' " I heard someone say to Billy.

I figured if I just stood outside, feeling like Superman in the face of the huge black sky, Esperanza would come over and start talking to me, and then it wouldn't be my fault. My luck, I was right.

"Hola, Señor," she said. She had been trying to teach me Spanish the night before, but I was too drunk then to remember anything now. I just smiled. "Here—" she said, opening my hand, placing a piece of paper in it and shutting my fingers around it. I looked down, and her name, address, and phone number stared up at me like a smoking gun. "You keep this and tell me when I'm going to be in the magazine. You can call me anytime, you know, just to talk or something?"

I looked down at the crumpled wad of paper, then back at her fifteen-year-old eyes and thought, of all the amphetamine psychoses in the world, she had to walk into mine.

"Hunh?" she asked.

"Sure," I said.

Across the camp there was a biker cover band playing shit like Charlie Daniels, Van Halen, Blue Öyster Cult, and when they started playing "Gimme Back My Bullets" I saw Jodi dancing with three bikers who were hooting for her to show them her tits and that was fine by her I guess because she did.

I could also see the crazy Esplendido hanging out with a few other club members in the tent next to ours and they were all looking pretty lit. The Esplendido was laughing and stomping around in a crouched-like position, spilling his beer, and generally not giving a shit about anything.

The idea just slipped out, at the time I didn't think I had malicious intentions, me being an ex-teacher and all. The campground was crowded, and I realized I hadn't spent any time over by my tent which was nestled away in a somewhat secret spot at the bottom of a dried-out riverbed. I asked Esperanza if she wanted to take a walk and she did.

"So where are you from?" I asked as we cut a path behind the T-shirt booth into the dark fields where all the camps were. "I don't even know anything about you."

"Oh . . . it's boring."

"Where is it boring?"

"El Paso. I used to live in San Diego but my mother fell in love with my stepfather. I miss my friends."

"Sounds rough."

"It's okay, I guess. Where's your tent?"

When we got over to my tent, she started doing cartwheels.

"Can you do this?" she asked, tumbling around in the grass.

"I don't think so," I said. I could hardly move, my muscles were so constricted. As she bounced from her hands to her feet to her hands again, her skirt kept jumping up, revealing her pink panties, and my heart started pounding so hard I felt like it was going to fly out of my mouth and run a few laps around the field. I thought it even then—

You are suicide.

I laid down in the grass, staring up at the star-streaked dome exploding above us. I was waiting for someone or something to tell me what to do. Esperanza walked over to me, breathing heavily from the exercise.

"Phew," she said waving her hand over her sweating face. When she sat down next to me I smelled her perspiration, and I knew everything that was going to happen from that point on. I knew she was going to move a little closer to me, I knew she was going to say something about the stars.

"Sometimes when I look up I wish I could just leave the planet," she said. "I wish that they'd just come down from space and take me away from El Paso. I'd go, too, I wouldn't even think twice about it."

"Me too," I said. "Some things are worth the risk."

"Yeah," she said and looked over to me. "This is nice."

It was. It was really nice. I felt better than I had in months—clean air, open sky, hard drugs, jail bait—I'd won some kind of lecher's lottery. Each part of my psyche had a different opinion about what was going on. My heart was falling for her, my soul was saying she's too young and if she's interested in me it's probably because she's a basket case, my loins were telling me that whatever happened was certainly not my fault so long as I didn't make the first move, and my brain was very quietly saying, Hey, asshole, don't you know it hurts to get the living shit kicked out of you by several members of a notorious bike club?

"So are you going to call me?" she asked.

"You know . . . I like you a lot and all but you're fifteen years old." I said this in such a way that begged her to come up with some reason why this shouldn't matter.

"I'm not a virgin, if that's what you're worried about. I mean, I've had boyfriends and stuff."

"You have one now?" I asked but she didn't say anything, just stared up into the void. In the distance I heard some gunshots, followed by howls and yelps of laughter—just some good ol' boys having fun with firearms.

"I don't know why, just 'cuz you're fifteen, everybody thinks you're a kid. I *hate* it," she said. "It *really really* sucks."

"You're telling me."

"Don't worry about anything. Here—" She pulled a hairpin from her head. "I want you to keep this, you know, to remember me." She put it in my shirt pocket. Just the touch of her fingers lightly against my chest was enough for me to get flushed. She pulled another one out of her hair and ran it over my lips.

"I bet someone's looking for you," I said as she put the second clip in my shirt pocket. "We've been away now for almost an hour."

"I said don't worry." She pulled another clip from her hair, which now fell very long and gorgeous onto her shoulders. "Now I don't want you to lose these," she said and very slowly slid one into the front pocket of my jeans, not so subtly brushing up against my cock.

Now I don't know where I got it from—a strong-willed man I simply am not—but from somewhere deep inside me I gathered the resources to stand up and say, "I bet someone's looking for you, we better get back to the booth." I said it with a certainty that implied there was no room for argument on this matter. She stood up, brushing the grass off her skirt, and I was glad she understood. She walked over to me and on her tippy toes, gave me a peck on the lips. It felt good. Then she gave me another and the second time, I gave back.

We stared dumbly at each other for a moment, the hum of Harleys muffling through the woods. Then I said, "You think maybe, after your folks are asleep, you could sneak away and come back here?"

"Sure."

"Yeah . . . " I said. "You could just cut your way through the weeds behind the entrance gate."

All this time I was thinking, I've done dumber things than this in my life and I'm still here. People in movies do shit like this all the time and get away with it. Maybe it was the full moon, more likely it was the speed, but at that moment I felt it was time for me to take control of my fate and make it do what I wanted it to for a change.

"We should go back separately," I added. She walked off to the booth, me over to the van.

Tucker was sitting in the van with a just-banged crank-eyed grin on his face.

"Evenin', dude," he said to me as I approached.

"Got a beer?" I asked.

"They're back at the tent, you can have some of mine, though." He

handed me his can. I could hear Jodi and Bundy screaming at each other
back in the booth—

"How could you let him? Right there where I gotta sleep tonight?"

Bundy whimpered some kind of apology.

"What the fuck's goin' on over there?" I asked.

"What do you think? She's cuttin' his nuts off. Soon as they grow back
she grabs the scissors."

"What happened?"

"Oh, she caught me fuckin' Marla in the back of the van. I told Marla
I'd give her a line if she made me cum, but the joke was on her—couldn't
no one make me cum after all the crank I've had tonight. I gave her one
anyway. Call me Mr. Softy."

*"You know someone left a rig out and I almost stabbed myself in the
ass?"*

Tucker laughed at that one. "Je-he-he-hesus Christ. Oh man. I tell you
I'm gettin' sick of this whole scene. Sick of Bundy, sick of T-shirts, sick of
all this shit."

*"When you're fuckin' dead, dead from all that shit, I'm gonna squat
right down and piss on your fucking grave!"*

"If I had a dime for every time I heard that one," Tucker said and I
handed him back his beer. "You married?"

"No."

"I'm married to two of 'em. My last one's from Omaha. I spent nine
months there—six of 'em in jail waiting on a RICO charge. They got our
whole crew. When I got off I split with my best whore down to Mexico and
did heroin straight for six months before she returned to San Francisco and
became a Moonie. That was number two. Number one is living in Little
Rock with my son, and I gotta go force a custody battle there in November. *Zero.* The number stares at me in my mind just like it stares at me from
between their legs. I like that Marla, though, isn't she pretty?"

"Yeah, man." Actually Marla looked like my crazy aunt Rona from
Queens.

There was a smashing sound, like a bottle thrown and missed at someone, and Bundy came storming out of the booth back towards me and
Tucker.

"Howdy, partner," Tucker said as Bundy approached.

Bundy stood stiff and stared off into space next to the van. He was
looking at the tires as if he was waiting for them to do something.

"How's that acid treating you?" I asked.

"I tell you," Bundy said, coming out of his coma. "I'm a good person."

"Fuck yeah," said Tucker.

"I been a rebel all my life."

"I'll say fuck yeah to that, too."

"We are rebel motherfuckers. You write that down in your magazine, Chris. I been an outlaw all my life and when I die, it ain't going to be on no goddamn loading dock or no fucking welfare hotel. Fuck the government."

"That's right, fuck the government," echoed Tuck.

"You know, Tuck, I got a good heart, you know that."

"It's too good if you ask me."

"You might be right, Tuck, but that's the way it's gotta be. When I die I'm going to heaven. I'm going *up*."

"There ain't no heaven, Bundy, just hell and we're there right now. After this you feed the worms."

"Fuck it."

I noticed some more screaming, this time it wasn't Jodi. "Who the fuck's that?" I asked.

"Oh, that's probably that crazy spic," said Bundy. "Hey, was that you who left with his daughter?"

"Yeah," I said. "Why?"

"Well about ten minutes after you split, her old man came around looking for her."

It didn't seem possible, but my heart started beating faster.

"Whattayamean?"

"I mean that fucker was pissed off, man. He started yelling in my face. I told him I don't know where the fuck your daughter is. I look like her pimp?"

"Jesus. Is he lookin' for me?"

"He's lookin' for someone."

"Shit."

"You do her?"

"No . . . but I told her to meet me later."

"So fuck it, meet her later, just don't let him find out."

"Shit."

"Don't fuckin' worry about that asshole," said Tucker. "You're with us."

"What'd he say exactly?"

"Oh fuck," Bundy said. "I don't remember. Ask Jodi."

"Uh . . . I just might . . . " I said and wandered off towards the booth.

"Get some beers while yer at it!" Tucker yelled.

I walked past Esperanza's booth and looked in through a separation in the tarp. The Esplendido and Esperanza's mother both sat interrogating her.

"We didn't do anything!" I heard her scream and I decided at that moment to break our date. Quietly, I slinked off to Bundy's booth.

The customers were gone but nobody had shut down yet. Billy and Jodi sat in front of the booth talking. I slipped in and over to the cooler, where I silently removed six cans of beer. Jodi's face was puffy like she'd been crying, and I didn't want to start asking her about Esperanza. Billy looked overwhelmed. Maybe it was the acid or the pot, but it was the first time that week I'd seen him anything but happy.

"You're bein' too hard on him," Billy said, his fist bouncing up and down on the armrest of his wheelchair. "Sometimes you gotta accept people for what they are. Ain't nobody perfect, and besides, who else would take a cripple like me all this way, pay him some change to mind the store . . . who else?"

The argument next door had switched from English to Spanish and who the fuck knew what they were saying? It sounded something like "What I cannot kill with my hands will die by the sword" or "The grass will feast on the blood of the defiler." I don't know. Whatever it was, it had a booze/speed/Latin/violent urgency to it like Ricky Ricardo meets Mussolini. As I slipped back between the tents, certain that my death would occur in the next hour or two, I sighed at the fact that my last beer on this earth would be a Bud Light.

"Light 'em up!" Billy shouted.

Suddenly the screaming next door stopped and the Esplendido stormed out into the center of the now almost empty campground. He picked up a full garbage can, lifted it over his head, and slammed it onto the ground.

"Hey, you fuckin' asshole!" Jodi screamed.

"Uh . . . why don't you just let him alone . . . " I started to say, but he screamed "Fuck you!" back to Jodi and she screamed "Suck my fuckin' clit!" to him and he stormed off. "Fuckin' asshole," she muttered.

I started off towards the van. It seemed like the safest place.

"You gotta remember," I could hear Billy telling Jodi, "and you know it—deep down Bundy really loves you."

Back at Billy's tent, Bundy and Tucker were tag-teaming Marla. They told me to whistle if I saw Jodi coming. By now I'd drank enough beer to realize that all I had to do was sit in the van, behind its locked doors, until it was safe to leave. Over by the showers I could see the Esplendido sitting on a cinderblock, drunkenly swearing and swatting at insects. My rental was parked about ten feet away from him, so for as long as he sat there, I would have to sit in the van.

I was thinking about something Tucker had told me that didn't sit very well with my own personal view of what's right and what's wrong, something he had heard the Esplendido bragging about a few nights before. At first I called him a liar, which he certainly was, but you never know with a guy like that. I told him he must have misunderstood, that the Esplendido was crazy but not that crazy.

"It's his *step*daughter, not his daughter," Tucker said. "What's so hard to believe?"

Watching the Esplendido, with the bottle of tequila between his legs, reeling around and from time to time cursing at someone who wasn't there, I thought maybe he is that crazy, and maybe the world is that sad, and maybe it was time for me to leave Sturgis. I'd already packed up my tent and moved all my shit from my dried-out little riverbed, I just had to load it into the rental. Somewhere in Rapid City there was a motel room with twenty hours of sleep waiting for me. Between Sturgis and New York there was still a bit of grace.

And then everything was quiet. It was the first time I'd heard silence since I'd been there. No music, no motorcycles. Just the trees rustling in a slight wind and a few crickets. It was moments away from sunrise and the silence of the bikes officially announced the changing of the day. It lasted no more than ten seconds before someone turned over their hog and announced to the world it was Sunday.

"Light 'em up!" I heard Billy yell from across the campground. His plea was followed by the sound of Harley wheels tearing up ground where buffalo used to graze. I didn't have to see his face to know he was laughing.

The Esplendido started passing out. He stopped cursing and stared glumly at his booth, as if he thought he was the victim in this Mexican standoff. He looked down at his bottle as if he'd forgotten what it was used for, then took one more long slug and I knew I would be able to leave soon.

Bundy stepped out of Billy's tent, and then stood in place like a wooden Indian, looking dumbly into the morning like he'd never seen it before. Earlier I had watched him pop a few Xanax and my guess was they were catching up to him. Marla's laugh cut through the cool Dakota air, erasing any sense of innocence the morning might have contributed to the moment. The Esplendido stared at his booth, I stared at Bundy, and Bundy stared at something I hope I'll never see.

9

Killed by Death: Whatever Happened to Heavy Metal?

When I was a kid, about eleven years old, I used to go to the local Path-mark and carry old ladies' grocery bags to their cars for fifty cents a pop and then grab my earnings after six or seven hours and blow them at the local record store. That started in the summer of 1980 and lasted about two years until I figured out how to run a lawnmower. I bought vinyl like it was going out of style and when you think about it, I guess it really was. Like most kids with a brain at that age, I hated my junior high school and everyone in it. Rock 'n' roll was my only outlet, and it was enough.

It was in Pathmark one day that I saw a special "Heavy Metal" edi-tion of *Creem* on the magazine rack. The term "Heavy Metal" had been around for years—applied to everyone from Black Sabbath to REO Speed-wagon—but this was the first time I'd ever recognized it as a separate genre. Judas Priest's Rob Halford was on the cover, covered in chains, leather studs, spikes, and, if memory serves me right, carrying a police nightstick. I don't know what it was about ol' Rob that I found so much more offensive than KISS or Alice Cooper. He looked more like one of the Village People than a rock 'n' roll star. I decided never to buy any Judas Priest albums and went back to being the beast of burden to any septua-genarian who would have me.

I couldn't see it then, but that was the beginning of the end of rock 'n' roll as I had always understood it. MTV soon appeared on the scene, the perfect marketplace for these kind of schtick-heavy rockers. For the next decade, Metal *was* rock 'n' roll—proof positive that indeed you can fool all the people all the time. It's a joke now, but to a young grocery slave such as myself it was depressing. I was looking forward to a life of sex, drugs, and rock 'n' roll, and what I got was AIDS, the War on Drugs, and MTV.

Nearly two decades later I was sitting in one of those trendy Upper East Side bars—the kind that charge eight dollars for a martini and peo-ple sit around smoking cigars and lamenting the day Ronald Reagan left office—telling my friend Larry about how the music industry basically de-stroyed my life. He was an ad man for a major record label, and I was drunk enough to think he might give a shit. He agreed with me that rock 'n' roll was a dead art form for which they hadn't yet chosen a tombstone, but as long as he earned enough money out of it to support his cocaine habit, he was content with the status quo.

"The fuckin' eighties," I snarled; by then the martinis had me at their mercy. "They were the nadir of the twentieth century. And the nineties are even worse—they're nothing more than a sequel, the *Robocop 2* of decades."

"You loved the eighties," Larry said as he clipped the end of his Cohiba and struck a match. "You loved hating the eighties. It ain't that bad anymore, you just miss the hate."

"I miss the *clarity . . .* " I said, copping a line from *Three Days of the Condor.* "Back then it was *us* and *them . . .* "

"If David Geffen offered to put your record out or to publish your book you'd sign in a second."

He was right, the prick. I'd have blown Ed McMahon for a spot on "Star Search."

"Well, there ain't much chance of that ever happening," I said, proving I could be right, too. "At least I know what I hate. That's gotta mean something."

"It usually means people ignore you."

I asked him how his wife was and he checked his wristwatch and told me he had to go home. Just when I thought I'd found someone who might actually have understood the larger forces working against our lives, he had something better to do. He put his suit jacket back on, pulled his belt back up to his bulging waistline and motioned to the bartender for his bill. He was one of those friends—always happy to disappoint.

"You fucker," I said, grabbing his lapel. "You drag me out of my apartment to keep you company while you stare at skirts imagining you're cheating on your wife, too chickenshit to go for that bathroom coke fuck you're dreaming about . . . "

"Look at you," he said, yanking his jacket out of my fists. "Bitterer than ten men—"

"Bathroom coke fuck—"

"You're going to have a stroke someday—"

"Bathroom coke fuck—"

"Listen," he said, laying his corporate Mastercard on the bar. "Knowing you and the way you love to hate things, you should talk *High Times* into sending you to Foundations Forum next week. It'll be like morphing back to your local shopping mall in the year 1985."

"I haven't a clue what you're talking about."

"Foundations is *the* music convention for Heavy Metal bands. It's wall-to-wall poodle-haired Heavy Metal freaks out looking for their big break. The joke is, Metal is dead. Dead dead dead. They'll all be there getting fucked out of their minds on hard drugs and then kissing up to yours truly when their supply runs low."

A Cheshire smile spread across his face. He was trying to convince me to go on a business trip. More than anything else in this life he was a salesman—not by default like most of them, but deep down where no one else could see. The image of me there in Los Angeles, drooling after his drugs while he bored me with his conservative view of the universe, managed to keep him at the bar for another hour. He told me stories of booze and powder-influenced mayhem and debauchery, of crawling around the bar on his hands and knees and biting unsuspecting females on their spandex-covered asses. The way he described it, Foundations was like a lost weekend with the Third Reich. Thinking about it made him cackle like a rabid dog remembering the first time he jumped a girl scout.

"It's in fucking *Burbank*," he said. "You'll be so full of angst, you'll feel like a teenager again."

"I'm not like you," I said. "I'm no skull-fucking industry hack."

"Suit yerself, pot boy—while I'm out there knocking a few of the lousier years off the end of my life, where will you be?"

He had a habit of explaining things in such a way that the only logical choice I had was to do whatever he told me. His invitation gnawed at me for days. Finally I realized that the money he was asking me to spend was not my own. I'm still not sure how I convinced *High Times* to send me on a story which had nothing to do with pot. Something really good going around the office that day, I guess. Larry played his hand well. If Heavy Metal was dead, he knew I was going to want to see the body.

When I think about Burbank, I think of game shows and Johnny Carson. Burbank is to Hollywood what JCPenney is to Saks Fifth Ave. It's a vicious little town where reality gets processed and pasteurized and human idiocy is looked upon as an infinite resource, more valuable than gold or oil. As I drove down Beverly Boulevard past the identical tract houses, I felt haunted by the ghost of "Love Boats" past. I felt like Burt Convy was reaching down from that talk show in the sky to warn me I was headed to a party so bad he wouldn't stay long enough to piss in the punch bowl.

Unlike other music conferences, which usually take place in clubs around whatever town they're hosted in, the Foundations Forum happened exclusively at the Burbank Hilton. You'd think they were trying to contain a virus. The Hilton was your average mid-priced hotel with small rooms, cheap furniture, and walls thin enough to hear the guy next door snorting coke and lamenting the day KISS took their makeup off.

As I walked in, the lobby and registration area buzzed with the excitement of music industry clods finally allowed to wear T-shirts to work. Since the first day they walked into that college radio station in search of an identity, they'd been dreaming about an all-expense paid trip to an industry seminar where musicians came from across the country to kiss their ass. For those lower in caste—namely musicians and fans—Foundations was like a support group, a place where they could all meet and lament the fact that their worlds were getting smaller by the day.

"I see you made it," Larry chuckled when he saw me at the registration booth waiting for my papers to go through. He already had a multi-colored selection of laminates dangling from his neck. He was home.

He steered me to the hotel bar, and we made a game of spotting rock heroes of yesteryear killing time with double scotch-and-Cokes. At one point we saw in the same room, Peter Criss, founding member of KISS; the aforementioned Rob Halford; and Carmine Appice, drummer for Vanilla Fudge, Cactus, and Jeff Beck before he reached for Metal greatness with the glam band Blue Murder. Carmine's most distinguishing characteristic was his hair (well, maybe not his hair per se), a flowing mane of brown locks sitting on top of a face that looked like it should have been flipping burgers in a Greek diner.

"You wanted bodies?" he asked me with a cocaine grin. "Pol Pot couldn't offer you as much."

"I feel naked and ashamed," I said. "I never knew I was the car-crash curious type. Where's your coke?"

He snickered and for a moment I thought he was going to take the game a step further and deny me, but he'd won this first battle of morals and didn't yet feel the need to gloat. He led me to his room where there were already a couple members of a recently dropped band waiting for his Bolivian charity.

The first seminar I went to was titled "Active Rock Radio: Alternative to What?" Part of the problem Metal was having was that it just couldn't get airplay anymore on radio or MTV. With so-called Alternative bands inspiring every kid and his girlfriend to start their own band, who wanted to listen to long-hairs growling about eternal damnation? Even Beavis and Butthead, the Pontius Pilates of rock 'n' roll, were laughing at them. The first half of the seminar was a roundtable discussion on the current slump in the Metal market. From a fan's point of view, it seemed like Metal was being snubbed by the very industry that gave it life. After much scape-goating and fingerpointing, a record exec at the front of the room showed mercy and told the crowd, "Don't worry, Metal will be back before you know it."

"But admit it, man," said one fan in the front row wearing a Quiet Riot

Tour '82 shirt. "We're all to blame. I mean . . . how many people in this room bought the last Dokken album?"

The silence in that room was louder than any Van Halen concert, with or without David Lee Roth.

Flipping through the Foundations literature, I could see there were still enough bands to satisfy any Metal fan's thirst for self-indulgent guitar solos. There was Death Metal, Black Metal, Grindcore, Industrial Metal, Doom Metal, Classic Metal—Metal wasn't really dead, just dethroned. The only camp that seemed legitimately gone were the glamour boys like Poison and Cinderella, and if anybody was upset about that, they kept it to themselves.

Most of the seminars were designed to teach musicians how to fall from grace, if not with dignity, then with a little beer money. "College Radio 101," "Underground Press," "Marketing: Doing More with Less," "The Japanese Market"—if there was any milk left in the Metal tit, Foundations promised to teach you how to squeeze. There was almost no discussion about the fact that maybe a lot of Metal bands sucked to begin with and what we were currently experiencing was a simple Darwinian survival of the fittest.

In all the seminars I asked just one question. It went like this:

HIGH TIMES: Is Satan still a marketable commodity in
                   the nineties?
CROWD (in unison): FUCK YEAH!

"I'd just like to see Metal get taken seriously," said a fan when I asked him what he would like to see in an article about Heavy Metal. Fat chance you'll see that here, fella.

I reached my corporate bullshit boiling point at the "How to Get a Record Deal" seminar, chaired by a lawyer named Joseph Lloyd Serling. With his shiny head and hooked nose, Serling looked like Mr. Burns from "The Simpsons." After receiving a professional lesson on how to brownnose your way onto the charts, a nervous guy stood up in the audience to ask a question.

"I'm working on my second degree in business at the University of Oregon, entering an accelerated MBA program. I've been managing a band for two years now. I've pretty much done everything to the letter that you guys have talked about . . . I'm as cool as you can possibly be. Once a year we set up showcases, do three shows throughout L.A., spend thousands of dollars on publicity, and no one will come out to the show. It really makes me wonder what A&R is doing . . . " He pled his case like it was a math equation that didn't add up, and wanted the teacher to tell him where he went wrong.

"Let me ask you a question," Serling said. "You said nobody will come see what you have—well, what do you have? In the context of what a record company would want, what do you have to offer?"

"What do we have?" The guy seemed a bit perplexed. "Well . . . we got a tape which we passed out about eight hundred copies. We got college radio, especially around the Northwest, and a considerable amount of press. We're being championed by program directors at KUFO, Portland's biggest rock station, and ZROCK, Eugene's biggest rock station . . . "

Serling sat and added it all up in his head and then said, just as confused, "Sounds like you're well on your way, you're doing good stuff . . . " and then asked for the guy's business card.

It might as well have been two dogs smelling each others' asses and deciding to go for a dry hump for all that it had to do with making good music. What do you have to offer a record company? It sounded like a sacrifice to a pagan god. As a wise old fag once said, "This ain't rock 'n' roll, this is genocide."

I started feeling a little sympathy for all the deluded musicians wandering around dazed and wondering where their next free drink was coming from. Who was this used-car salesman who decided what was and what was not rock 'n' roll? Nobody even talked about music. It was just an orgy of corporate egos, where the squares loosened up their ties long enough to show the kids who was still boss. It was enough to make me think that if Ozzy really had balls, he would have left the bats and the birds alone and bit the head off of his A&R man.

After the seminars the industry folk sat around in front of piles of coke and talked about limos from the airport and being backstage with Neil Young. They didn't give a shit that Metal was dying because their ass was covered—if not by Ratt, then by Alanis Morrisette. Either way there was an expense account, so why not party?

Back at the bar were the usual selection of hairpiece rockers and over-the-hill coke whores with plastic tits and deviated septums looking to fuck guys in bands or just guys with coke or, well, maybe even my friend Larry. Several times I was approached by windbag publicists who'd found out from Larry that I wrote for *High Times.* They'd buy me a drink and then tell me about how much pot their shitty band smoked and how *High Times* should put them on the cover. After a few hours I had enough promo tapes, CDs, and business cards to start my own label.

Somebody shoved in next to me and ordered a Jack Daniels and Coke. I turned to see who the obnoxious fucker was and was confronted by the awesome presence of a semisuperstar. He stood there looking like a cross between Jesse James and Sonny Barger, dressed in black with an iron cross around his neck and white leather boots. Around his waist he wore two belts—one with studs and another with more studs. It was Lemmy Kilmister, the subsonic genius behind Motorhead.

I introduced myself and told him I was doing an article on the current state of Heavy Metal for *High Times*.

"*High Times*? All you guys write about are faggot drugs like Ecstasy and marijuana. You never tell the truth about speed!"

Journalist that I was, I suggested that this was the perfect time for the truth about speed.

He invited me up to his suite, and we sat down at a table near the window that overlooked the hotel pool and a massive industrial complex across the street. He poured us both water glasses full of Jim Beam and delivered his amphetamine manifesto.

"Speed's a very maligned drug. It used to be given to housewives to avoid depression—and it works. I don't recommend the drug to everybody—some people can't handle it and go twitchy, sending themselves out windows and all. It certainly never killed anybody I know. Whereas heroin killed everybody. I wish people would stop doing smack. They keep coming back to it every fucking year. Everybody's dying again. It's become the in-thing to look fucked up and be in pain every morning. I can't see it myself."

With the truth about speed and dope out of the way, I asked him about music.

"What was the record that changed your life?"

" 'Lucille,' " he answered. "And 'Good Golly Miss Molly.' Little Richard was my boy. That changed me. I was breeding horses in Wales. Had a farm and everything. I just heard him and that was it. I sold it. Gone. Bye. I was on the road with me guitar in my hand. You know, I thought it was all going to be instant stardom."

I told him I thought Motorhead were the prototype for Heavy Metal because they did the speed/thrash thing first. To that he insisted that the MC5 were doing it, slightly less distorted, before them. I asked about other bands who influenced him and he mentioned the Ramones.

"Me and Joey understand rock 'n' roll because we love it. It's our life, our religion or whatever. It fills every gap you got. I ain't got a wife and kids, but music is all right for that. You can sleep with it, you can fuck it, you can lick it, you can prod it, roll it, taste it, anything you want. Music will always be there for you, and if you're lonely in the night, you can just put a record on and everything you had comes back. That's another great thing about music: It's memories incarnate."

"What do you think MTV has done to rock?"

"Almost killed it. It'll come 'round again, it always does. It was like this before the Pistols. It was like this before the Beatles. I remember all them cycles coming around, so I don't panic like these motherfuckers. 'Oh, that's it! Rock's dead.' It's not dead, man. It's asleep. It'll be okay. There's a lot of good bands around now. I don't know what's the matter with people."

"Rock has always come in cycles," I commented.

"Always. First we got Fats Domino, Chuck Berry, Little Richard, Eddie Cochran, Buddy Holly, all in two years, and gone. And then we got Bobby Rydell!" Lemmy said, cracking up.

Recent bands that had the Lemmy seal of approval included Offspring, Nirvana, and Soundgarden. I asked him what he thought about Alternative bands usurping Metal's throne.

" 'Alternative to what?' is what I say. Sounds like the old stuff. People are so dumb. They got to have a label on everything or they don't know if they should buy it or not. People say, 'Well, it's not Heavy Metal, I can't listen to that.' I say what's the fucking matter with you? Music is there for all people; you can listen to anything you like. As long as it pleases you, that's the only criterion. Anything else is bullshit. And if your friends don't like seeing it in your rack, put it in the cupboard and play it later. I don't know how bad your fucking peer pressure is to forego musical joy. Fuck that."

"Do industry seminars provide any useful information to bands?"

"It's an exercise for business to tell itself how well it's doing. You can learn more from watching the band you like play, the band that sends a shiver up your back, than studying a million fucking probability charts and studies. Because they aren't gonna tell you shit about the music. That just tells you about the business and what they're selling.

"You hear that panel I was on? You never heard such a load of waffle in your life." The day before I caught part of the "Touring" seminar Lemmy chaired. He stuck out like a rhinoceros at an AT&T shareholders' meeting. Sitting next to him was some record company stiff who condescendingly prefaced all his responses to what Lemmy said with "Well, from an industry standpoint . . . "

"Let's have a look at that. What is the industry standpoint? 'Well, we sell everything to everybody, and we don't care what it is.' Fucking brilliant. Integrity, out the window. All you got in life is your honor, man, your own self-image, your own self-respect. If you lose that, or if you give it away or if you sell it, then you ain't got it no more."

"That's what rock 'n' roll was always about from the very beginning!" I said.

"Basically, 'Fuck you!' That's what rock 'n' roll is."

"It's that feeling that makes you want to change your whole life when you see someone up on stage."

"Like being thrown in a pool full of cold water! Who needs a fucking bio? It's more fun to find out than be given it. I don't want to see a fucking press kit. Fuck me, I don't want to see no press kit."

"Do bands have to play the game?"

"Nirvana never played the game, did they? They came out of nowhere, bingo, number one. The record companies shit themselves because they hadn't predicted it. And they immediately went to Seattle and signed everything that moved, right? Everybody cleans up off bands, man, and then they get treated like shit. Everybody pays their bills with the bands' money. It's fucking incredible.

"I went to the Grammys. We got one in 1990, for *1916*, and I went over there to Radio City in New York. And I'm sitting there, and I've got me denim jacket on and the Iron Cross on the bare chest. I figured, 'I was dressed like this when I was writing the song. I was dressed like this when I was playing the song. It seems to me I should dress like this when I'm gonna get an award.' About five or six bands walk in, long hair and the dickie-bow, hired tuxedos that didn't fit, sleeves too long. I said to a couple of them, 'What the fuck are you doing, man? You come to their dance and you dress as the enemy? Why don't you give them a blow job while you're at it? Because they are your enemy.' "

I felt a lot better. It's always nice to have a rock star you can bring your troubles to. Before I had a chance to ask him for a hands-on lesson on amphetamine use, Lemmy turned off the tape recorder, took out a plastic bag from his coat, and laid a pile of crank on the table large enough to give Joe Walsh a heart attack.

"Don't worry," he said. "It's not all for you." He dabbed a bit with his finger and put it in his mouth, leaving me with what was still a pretty huge pile. I dabbed at it cautiously with my finger until Lemmy yelled, "Jesus Christ, man, it's not gonna kill you! Clean it up!"

We talked more about music, how Lemmy used to work for Jimi Hendrix, and how speed rotted his teeth and now he wore dentures. After that I started railing on about *High Times*, Trench Town, and Larry's interest in Cuban cigars, until he asked me to leave. Lemmy was a rock 'n' roll dinosaur, but proud of it. He might not have had as many teeth or as many brain cells as he did a few decades before, but he could still teach Soundgarden a few things about the word "grunge."

Lemmy got up at one point and looked out the window. I asked if he saw any girls by the pool.

"Nothing. Load of guys in big shorts. These people in the merchandising companies only have to make one size shirt, now—XXL. They

make these big fucking shorts, they look like your father died and you got
his off-duty trousers, his gardening smock. These people with their hats on
backwards, they look like nerds. I'm sorry, but that's what we used to call
nerds in my time, the fucking village idiot. And that's exactly how it should
be."

"What do you mean?"

"I should be offended by it. Because if I'm not, then they're not doin'
it right. That's how rock 'n' roll works. It obeys no set rule. As long as we
got that, then keep the shorts on, boys. As long as you're doin' that, that's
good. Although I would like the chicks to wear something a little tighter,
you know?"

I spent the rest of the night sleeplessly listening to my thoughts degenerate into cartoon sound effects. The following afternoon I hooked up with
Larry in the bar. He was sweating, his face was covered in blotches—he
looked like Willie Loman on crack. With him was this little muskrat of a
publicist whose nose dripped into her fruit salad as she announced that
she'd done more coke in her life than anyone else at the table—pretty bold
talk in the present company.

"I got a great interview with Lemmy," I told Larry.

"Who's Lemmy?"

"Lemmy, from fuckin' Motorhead. They're playing tonight, you wanna go?"

There was still enough life left in him to drawl a sarcastic "Puh-
lease . . . " and order another double Stoli.

I left everybody and went down to the Junior Ballroom to watch Rob
Halford receive a lifetime achievement award from the Foundations
Forum. It provided me with the closure that I'd been looking for since that
traumatic day I saw him on that cover of *Creem* fifteen years before. Seeing Rob up there, minus the leather, the studs, the spikes, the chains, and
the majority of his hair, eased my mind. He was being put out to pasture—the industry had sucked him dry and was now giving him a big
grassy field upon which he could graze forever. I felt the same satisfaction
when I heard that Ronald Reagan had Alzheimer's disease—this man
who was once such a formidable enemy was now talking to his soup and
shitting in his pants. That sort of thing gives you hope. It reminds you that
there are certain irrevocable laws of physics which supersede both fame
and fortune, namely that whatever goes up has got to come down.

Unfortunately that kind of logic worked two ways. The same thing
happened to your heroes and that's a much harder thing to watch. I'd already heard about the upcoming Sex Pistols reunion and had pitched it as
a story to *High Times*. The magazine had such a long and ruinous history

with the Pistols—basically, the band hated us—that it was an entertaining idea to send me to write a story about them and destroy whatever possible relationship we might have had left.

The next day I saw Larry in front of the hotel with his bags packed, and he asked me if I wanted to share a cab to LAX, so I ran upstairs and grabbed my luggage. When I came back down I told him my whole Ronald Reagan theory. He got pissed off, insisting that Ronny was the greatest world leader since Churchill, so I started attacking his character instead.

"Don't you feel a little guilty?" I asked him. "You're a part of this monster, you deal in the dirty business of dreams."

"If God wanted me to be a saint, He wouldn't have given me a dick, two nuts, and an unquenchable thirst for oblivion."

"Our methods are different," I said. "But our motivation comes from the same place."

He pulled out a joint and said, "Smoke 'em if you got 'em."

We stood there for twenty minutes, smoking Larry's herb and watching musicians passing the last of their promo kits to strung-out industry folks. Then a stretch limo pulled up to the curb.

"Here we are," he said.

"A limo?" I asked. "How very, very droll."

"You ain't paying for it, your musician friends are," he said as the driver grabbed his bags. "Are you getting in?"

I stared at the car. Larry smiled like the snake on that famous tree, offering Eve a tall, cold glass of apple juice, and telling her that her boyfriend was an asshole. When I handed the driver my bags and sat down in the back seat, I think I made Larry very happy.

"I bet I live my entire life and never hear you tell me this ride to the airport was a mistake," he said. "I bet you fifty bucks—think about it, you can't lose."

I sat there and didn't say another word. Larry thrived on these kinds of situations. He was never truly comfortable unless he was compromising someone else's integrity. I don't know whether it was his sincerity or his wretchedness, but there was something about him I admired.

I was laughing at the situation, too. I knew he'd probably die before me anyway, so the day would come when I'd be able to tell people I won that bet and he wouldn't be able to say shit about it.

10

Never Mind the Sex Pistols, What's Your Fucking Problem?

The idea was for me to follow the Sex Pistols on the first few dates of their Filthy Lucre comeback tour. I was supposed to go to Finland for the first show, but that date got canceled because Johnny was sick and coughing up blood. Since my nonrefundable ticket to Helsinki had a stopover in London and it was too late to book a later date, I arrived nearly a week early for the band's first show in England in nearly twenty years.

High Times and the Pistols have had a strange relationship over the past two decades. We were the first U.S. magazine to put them on the cover and, against their wishes, *High Times* founder Tom Forçade bankrolled a film of their only American tour, *D.O.A.*

Tom's special talent was for nurturing the seeds of discontent. One of his projects was the Rock Liberation Front. Formed in 1970, the RLF demanded that the corporate promoters of large Woodstock-type rock festi-

Johnny Rotten raids David Bowie's wardrobe again. The Filthy Lucre tour hits New York, 1996. (Bob Gruen)

vals "turn the receipts over to the Movement whose culture they're ripping off or let everyone in for free." Ex-Yippie that he was, he wanted to put rock 'n' roll back in the hands of the People.

When six years later the Pistols started screaming about "Anarchy in the U.K.," Forçade saw the fulfillment of his RLF dream—a band of the People, for the People. He wanted to be a part of them, but never considered that they might not have wanted to be a part of him. During the Pistols' American tour in 1978, Forçade's film crew and the band's road crew clashed repeatedly. The Pistols were planning their own movie—*The Great Rock and Roll Swindle*—and saw Forçade as a liability and a saboteur. At one point (so the story goes) Forçade kidnapped a drug-hungry Sid Vicious, promising to cop him heroin, and refused to give him back until the Pistols allowed him to proceed with his movie without the road crew smashing his equipment. Those kind of ultimatums tend to piss a band off. A year later, after the band broke up, Forçade shot himself and never saw the film's release.

Whether or not this history had anything to do with the Pistols not responding to our requests for an interview I do not know. It was twenty years later and I bet if I had the money, I could hire the Pistols to play *Carmen* at my cousin's first communion. The band's publicist, Tresa Redburn, told us she would try and interest them, but hadn't succeeded before I left for London.

As a journalist, even a dope journalist, it's good to approach a story with some kind of "wish list" in mind. On this list are things you *hope* to find out about your subject and things you *have* to find out. These questions should be in your head until you hand the baby in. If you are doing your job right, these things are making you nervous, keeping you up at night.

I had no such list prepared when I went to cover the Pistols reunion. I had one wish: to be *far away.* Far away from New York, far away from the office, far away from nightclubs, Larry and his Bolivian poisons, and the girlfriend I had just split with for reasons I won't go deeply into here, except to say that for months I'd been slowly withdrawing into myself, compounding my thoughts, personality, and emotions into one solid brick that made hanging out together an uncomfortable experience for both of us.

When I arrived at my friend Richard's flat in London, he pulled out a wad of aluminum foil and said, very amicably, "I figured I couldn't have a New Yorker come and visit and not offer him some coke." And certainly, I couldn't visit London and refuse the gifts of my host. That night I couldn't sleep, but it wasn't the story that was keeping me awake, it was that brick. It hung over my head like a wrecking ball, threatening to smash my brains into Richard's futon if I stopped thinking about it for more than ten seconds.

Maybe at that point I should have stopped doing drugs, but the next night Richard wanted to take me to my first rave. I wanted the experience, even though I knew I wasn't going to like it. We went to the Solar Boom Room, a dark club near London Bridge. I ate my pill like a good little soldier and achieved the only goal of my trip: I was *away*, as far away as I'd ever been.

Whatever I took that night made me feel like Plasticman, as if you could grab my arm and run across the room with it. The lights flashed around in twisted patterns and the music was repetitive and irritating. Instead of bringing me to a grand, empathic state, the Ecstasy haunted me. It lit up the abyss that existed between myself and the rest of humanity in a myriad of different colors.

Across the room I saw a drunk woman sitting by herself on the floor. She had blond hair with dark streaks in it and wore a black velvet jacket and tight red jeans. She kept looking over at me and then slugging down beer like a pirate. Several times she got up to go to the bar, only to return to her private spot and stare at the dance floor with a fresh beer in her hand. She, too, was far away, and I took that as a signal that she was the girl for me.

Richard was dancing, doing what I call the White Boy Shuffle—that timid head-bop and arm-swing Caucasians do when they don't want to be noticed. I went to the bar to see if I could cut the E-trip in half with some booze, and also to make eye contact with the blond queen still sitting by herself as if she wanted someone to talk to her.

"What's your name?" I asked, but it was hard to hear her answer. She wasn't English but German. I told her I thought techno music and Ecstasy were part of an international plot to keep the youth of the world interested in a synthetic culture that could at any moment be altered imperceptibly to the needs of a totalitarian regime. She told me that I sounded like I was fifty years old. That ended the conversation.

On the dance floor, beautiful, faultless women like living magazine photos twisted in their own little drug dreams. I'm not the kind of person who is afraid to dance. When I'm really loaded I can bust some epileptic James Brown–type moves that are not exactly graceful, but entertaining to watch. This was a different kind of scene—distant, reserved, very English. With the E drowning me in waves of self-consciousness all I could manage was a tight-assed Shuffle.

I bumped up to Richard.

"What's up with these folks?" I asked him. "They're a little on the cold side."

"It's a rave, man, you don't really come here to get laid."

"You don't talk to girls when you go out?"

"Not really, you just get into the energy."

I have to admit, it didn't make a damn bit of sense to me.

After my hesitant moves failed to reach any of the teenagers on the dance floor, I went outside where it was damp and the streetlights made the road glitter like tinsel. I was at the foot of London Bridge, the one they used to make me sing about back in elementary school, the one that was forever falling down. The fog was heavy and I couldn't see it, but I was quite sure that it was still falling down, just like we were all falling down all the time, our dead skin dropping from our bodies, our brain cells evaporating without warning.

The sun was vaguely coming up and I walked a bit in the gray morning, hoping not just to see something, but to *feel* something beautiful, something worth crossing the ocean for, but all I could think about was how everything dies—your teeth, your heroes, your will, smiles, moments, honor—even your own grandmother who cooked you pancakes on Sundays, even she dies and they pump her full of chemicals and rip out her organs and lock her in a box and throw six feet of earth on top of her so she won't start to stink and upset the mourners.

As the Ecstasy rained down on my head like globs of warm ice cream, I walked through London's Gothic landscape and thought to myself that history was nothing more than a series of events manufactured by soon-to-be corpses to disrupt the inescapable boredom of life. The idea, I guess, was to leave a name behind, a grunt, a sound to which people would attach your face and deeds from here to Armageddon. The Pistols did that and good for them. The rest of us, we go down like that tree in the forest that nobody hears and, brother, in a hundred-thousand years you tell me if we made a sound.

The next morning me and Richard met his friends in a pub before seeing the Pistols. I downed a prenoon Guinness and listened to the talk about England's victory over Spain the previous day in the Euro Cup semifinals. Listening to all the football talk I laughed at the irony that it was the Pistols that ended my interest in sports, back when I was first growing hair on my pubes. At the time I was playing for both the school baseball team and my local little league, but I was already losing interest. When you "won" you didn't win anything. Why was I sweating so much?

Around that time I heard the Pistols in my local record store. The guy at the register, a coked-up Andy Gibb type, said, "Let's hear a little 'God Save the Queen'," and put them on as a joke. It was no joke to me, though, it was more like I'd heard the crackling leaves of the Burning Bush. My favorite band was the Who, and the Pistols sounded like the Who would've if a bear trap had just closed on their nuts. *Never Mind the Bollocks* was the most frightening thing I'd ever heard. Once you let a thing like that into your heart, tossing baseballs around while coaches yell at you loses its mystique.

I listened to the sports talk with the ears of a foreign traveler. The Brits love their football. They see it as something they invented, a game that, no matter where it is played, is still something quintessentially British. They saw punk the same way—as their creation. When I heard them say that, I had to interrupt and defend the honor of CBGB's. There was no way the Brits would have come up with punk themselves. They're just not that violent of a people.

"Punk is American," I told them. "Skiffle is English."

"Look at the Ramones! They look like a bunch of hippies!"

"I'm talking about the *music* . . . "

"It doesn't matter! It's not punk! Sid Vicious was a punk, mate! The Damned! X-ray Spex!"

Whatever.

We got to Finsbury Park just as the Buzzcocks were playing "Ever Fallen in Love?" If fifteen years before, I had found that mythical genie's lamp, rubbed it, and was granted three wishes, a Buzzcocks reunion would have been number two, right after the Syd Barrett world tour. When the moment finally arrived, I figured my time was better spent on the beer line. Looking around I noticed it was mostly geezers well over twenty years old who turned up for this historic event. I figured all those crusty squatter punks would be throwing bottles outside the gates, but I guess your average sixteen-year-old anarchist had bigger problems to solve.

I wandered back to the blanket Richard's friends had laid out, and choked on a couple of hash and tobacco joints. The crowd started singing what I guessed were football chants. Brits enjoy a good sing-along. Pubs, trains, bathrooms—suddenly everybody starts chanting like life is just one big Sham 69 album.

Two straight-looking dudes who I'd never seen before walked out on the stage and the crowd went ballistic. One of them was footballer Stuart "Psycho" Pearce, whose penalty kick had clinched the game for England the day before. Apparently a thing like that gets you canonized in Britain. The sports heroes introduced the band.

The curtain opened, revealing a canopy of old Sex Pistols newspaper clippings from the days when they were the biggest threat to English middle-class morality since the buzzbomb. Johnny, Glen, and Steve ripped through the canopy, picked up their instruments, and opened a twenty-year-old wound with the gruesome first chords of "Bodies." They milked that pause before the verse, as if wondering whether the intro alone was enough to collect their paychecks, and then:

> *She was a girl from Birmingham!*
> *She just had an abortion!*

I was at least 150 feet from the stage, but before I knew it I was pulled into a punk *jihad.* Beers and spit started flying, arms and legs started flailing. As I was being bludgeoned, I was bootlegging the show on my crappy little mono interview recorder, and that tape makes the *Filthy Lucre Live* disc recorded at the same concert sound like *Tubular Bells.* All you hear is the furious crowd, screaming the lyrics to every song. This was Johnny's hometown and the Pistols were the prodigal punks. There were a few shouts throughout the show about Johnny's weight and apparent poverty (actually, he had plenty of money via his heiress wife), but there wasn't any of the "chaos" I'd crossed the Atlantic to see.

Once I was able to stand and watch the band, I started to notice some very un-Pistol-type details, most of which centered around Johnny's wardrobe. He looked like Arsenio Hall on a bad hair day. He wore a checkered sports coat buttoned up to his neck, like something he'd picked up at Rod Stewart's last garage sale. His usual crowd-baiting remarks were replaced with appeals for rock 'n' roll affection. "You want some more? Then don't be so fucking shy! . . . We're not that fucking bad after all, are we?"

They went through the greatest hits, playing all the songs I used to kick holes in my bedroom wall to, but when it ended I was relieved. As I hunted through the crowd for Richard and his friends, I could feel this hole swimming through my body. I wasn't sure what it was, this little bit of emptiness cruising through my veins. It was as if something inside me had been removed and my system was adjusting to the loss.

When I met up with the group, they asked me if I liked the show.

"Well, you know, it was fun . . . " I said. There was an uncomfortable pause as I tried to think of something more to tell them.

"Of course he fucking liked it," Richard said. "They were fucking great!"

I appreciated his interruption; it was a question I wasn't sure how to answer.

Germany started hating me as soon as I stepped off the plane. After retrieving my bag at the luggage carousel, I walked up to the information desk and asked for directions to my hotel in Hamburg. When the dominatrix in the Lufthansa uniform heard me speak English, this look came over her face like I'd just asked her for a blow job. She was about forty and attractive, save for the lines of disgust that had etched their way indelibly into her skin. She gave me directions, wincing when I asked her to point them out on my map. I guess she figured Americans should know their way around Germany, since we spent so much time there fifty years before.

I checked into a cheap hotel near the Central Station. My room was small with a sink, and there was a bathroom in the hallway. Everything was immaculate—the floor, the windows, the sheets, but the room had a strange smell. I couldn't figure where it was coming from, this odor of booze and sweat and death like Fatty Arbuckle was hiding in the closet.

Since I'd never been to the Fatherland, I asked around the office before I left if anybody had a contact there. Peter Gorman gave me the phone number of Hans-Georg Behr, a prominent marijuana activist, who I promptly called after I checked in. On the phone he was pleasant and invited me to drop by his house for dinner.

As the cab swung around the quaint streets of Hamburg, I wondered how the Pistols were going to approach this upcoming gig and the potential skinhead element. Would they play "Belsen Was a Gas," their offensive piss-take on Nazis, suicide, and death in general? Would they be at all menacing, or would they take the money and run like they did in London?

Georg was not in when I arrived. A young junky answered the door, drunk and slurring his already poor English, "Yezzzz doooooo commmme innnn yezzzzzz . . . "

Covering most of his body were needle marks like he'd just spent a week partying with the Allman Brothers. I sat at a small kitchen table and watched while a middle-aged hippie prepared a mushroom dish for dinner. The junky kept looking at me and laughing, saying things I couldn't understand to the hippie who seemed slightly amused by his drunken idiocy. Sometimes he talked to me in German and I sat there with what I imagine must have been a pretty dumb look on my face.

Georg came home, introduced himself to me, and then started screaming at the junky, chastising him, and finally asking him to leave.

"Please forgive me," Georg said. "But he was told never to drink in this house and now . . . " he paused, thinking of the phrase, "He has embarrassed me. But come—"

Georg was in his fifties, with a dark mustache and beard—the European artist type. I knew he was an accomplished actor, psychiatrist, and the author of many books including *Talking About Hemp*, considered by some to be the definitive text on the subject.

"I will show you something," he said and left the room. He returned wearing a fisherman's tackle vest and carrying a box of antique cannabis pipes. He collected them, he explained. Some he showed me were made from meticulously etched silver and came in their own carrying cases.

"You see these?" he said, pointing to the pockets on his vest.

"When you go fishing, you can store your pipes in the pockets," I commented.

"Excuse me, my American friend who I've known only ten minutes now," he spat back at me. Okay, so he's easily offended. The smile returned to his face, and indeed that was the punchline as he started pulling even more paraphernalia from his pockets—antique pipes and cigarette holders.

Guests were showing up for dinner and we all sat in the library, smoking herb from Georg's pipes. A few times, when they were stumbling for the right word in English, the guests asked me "You don't speak *any* German?" to which I shrugged my shoulders and changed the subject. We talked about the different pot scenes in Germany and America. I asked if there were any hash bars in Hamburg, now that Germany had decriminalized marijuana.

"There are places, but they are secret," Georg explained.

"Do you think you could show me one?" I asked. *High Times* was spending so much money on this trip, I figured I'd get another story for them.

"If we took you to them, then they wouldn't be a secret, would they?"

I'd heard beforehand about Georg's obsession with the idea that American marijuana writer Jack Herer had stolen part of *Talking About Hemp* in his own book *The Emperor Wears No Clothes.* I was going to mention it and see what his reaction was, but he began his rant without any prompting.

"Jack *Herrrrer,*" he sneered, spitting the name out like he was clearing his throat. "He could not write a book such as me. He is nobody. I wish . . . I wish I had the *liberty* to live off of my book, the way Jack *Herrrrer* lives off my book."

"Jack's a nice guy," I offered.

"Nice? How can you be nice? When you do such a thing? Ahhh—" he wearily dismissed the issue. Dinner was ready. "Come," he said. "You will enjoy an authentic German meal."

We sat around a small, impeccably set table, and Georg handed me the champagne to inspect before he opened it. I nodded my approval.

"You see this tablecloth? It is two hundred years old. One hundred percent hemp." Again I nodded approval, wondering if I was going to be quizzed on this material at the end of the evening. As we sipped our champagne, Georg took out another pipe, this one a silver "kif" pipe about a foot long with a slim stem made by one of Kathmandu's special goldsmiths. The pipe went around and as I started puffing, Georg interrupted me, "Please," he said placing my hand further down the stem. "Like this."

I did as I was told.

Georg asked me for permission to speak German to his friends, as he hadn't seen them in a while.

"Sure," I said. As long as they kept the champagne coming, I didn't care if they lighted their farts.

As they spoke, the mushrooms were served. I sat and listened to the strange tongue, amazed I'd actually managed to con a trip all the way to Germany. It was a new record for me. Suddenly, Georg started yelling at the hippie for overcooking the mushrooms.

"I'm sorry the mushrooms are dry. Take your spoon like this," he said, dipping his in the champagne and sprinkling it over the mushrooms. I commented that the fungi tasted fine to me and he picked up my spoon and put it in my hand. "Please," he insisted, and I sprinkled some champagne over them according to his instructions.

A course of cold cuts was brought out, turkey and smoked deer. I served myself and started eating. I noticed Georg looking at me as if I'd insulted him. I was pretty sure I hadn't—I don't do that sort of thing while I'm being fed because I don't want people spitting in my food when I'm not looking. He stopped eating, put down his silverware, and let out a sigh like I'd just made a pass at his wife.

"Hold them like this," he said, taking the knife and fork out of my hands and placing my fingers in their correct positions on the silverware. I started laughing. I figured he was taking the piss out of me. I kept trying to hold the fork his way but I couldn't satisfy him. "Like this!" he demanded.

"I've been eating now for quite some time," I said. "I've never went hungry once." I was the only one who thought this was funny. Everyone else at the table stared at me like I was Quasimodo yelling in their face about women and bells.

The hippie brought out the main course, a pot of chicken legs in a thick, red paprika sauce. He gave us each a bed of spaetzle and everybody started serving themselves again. When it was my turn to ladle out my dinner, I kept looking at Georg, waiting for his reproach. Timidly I picked up the spoon, holding it like I thought he wanted me to, and attempted to serve myself. Before I could get my portion to my plate, he jumped in to correct my fingering and I watched as a chicken leg bounced off the side of the bowl and onto his treasured tablecloth.

"This tablecloth is two hundred years old!" he growled.

"You were making me nervous . . . " I said, panicked.

"Irreplaceable—" I could see he was hurt and I apologized, though I

still didn't think it was my fault. "It is ruined," he said, adjusting his composure. "But . . . don't concern yourself . . . it is destroyed, but let's not let it ruin dinner . . . "

The rest of the meal came off without incident. For my benefit, English was spoken, but the conversations all started out with sentences like, "Americans are very . . . " or "The thing I don't like about America is . . . " as if I were Uncle Sam's personal felatist with the ability to get their complaints heard at an executive level. Mostly I just agreed with them and that was even more confusing. They couldn't imagine a person who wouldn't rise up to the defense of his country.

As coffee was being served Georg showed me pictures from a recent trip to Vienna he took with his lover. Mixed in with the bunch was a picture of his mother.

"My mother . . . she was a Nazi from 1933 to the seventies," he said and laughed at his own joke. He showed me the picture—an old woman smiling at the camera wearing potleaf sunglasses. "My mother is dying," he confessed. "She has cancer and I have been treating her with marijuana." He seemed like he was in a better mood now, and I suggested we put her on the cover of *High Times*. The guests laughed louder than I thought the joke deserved, and Georg angrily put the photos back in their envelopes.

"*High Times*! Bah! You should see what they write about me!"

Not only did he hate Jack Herer, he told me he'd canceled his *High Times* subscription long ago. Sometime in the eighties, we'd done an article on him he didn't like. He dug it up and shoved it at me.

"Look at that! Can you imagine such an article!"

I skimmed it, only to find that it was a very flattering piece. It described at length his work counseling drug addicts, his book *The Power Drug* about the links between international heroin and arms traffickers and narcotics agents, his investigations into local corruption in Hamburg, his travels in the Orient and India. . . . Anyway, I abandoned my idea for an interview.

"Let's go to the pub," he said. I was drunk like I'd just been to a bar mitzvah. I liked Georg. Not knowing me from a serial killer he invited me to his home for a huge feast and somehow I'd offended him at every opportunity. It's not often you get a chance to do a thing like that.

I walked back to the library and grabbed my coat and books. Georg came back, and I thanked him and apologized again for the two-hundred-year-old tablecloth.

"What are you doing with your things?" he asked, watching me grab my pack.

"What? I'm taking them back to the hotel."

"Well . . . " he smiled. "Surely you are spending the night?"

As he said this I thought to myself, I either misinterpreted his invitation or I was in the company of someone who had the biggest balls of anybody I'd ever met. I told him no, I was going back to my hotel after the bar, and he seemed to understand.

By the time we reached the pub, it was closed. I thanked Georg and company again for the delicious dinner and the etiquette lessons. The next time I'm feeling uncouth, I told him, I'd give him a call.

"Scheiss" means shit in German, and "pissen" means piss. There are places you can go on the Reeperbahn where, for a mark a minute, you can sit in a little booth and watch naked people pass these things back and forth like they were playing a game of fooz-ball. I watched one movie that starred this huge, hairy man who looked like Chewbacca. He had an attitude like he'd been working at Venus Records all his life and he tossed his scat with glee. Watching it, I wondered if we didn't all want to see what we looked like to each other in hell, and the Germans were just being honest about it.

"Scheiss!"

"Pissen!"

"Nein! Nein!"

It's the type of thing you want to forget fast. I left the peep show and walked around in circles until I couldn't stand myself anymore and decided to get drunk.

I ducked into a nondescript bar with a view of the whorehouses. The bartender was an Irishman, and when I told him I was writing a story on the Sex Pistols for *High Times* magazine, he started giving me free drinks. He was a big fan, he told me, and I laid a couple copies on him. Before long I was getting smashed with the bartender and a couple of Germans. I asked the Germans about the Pistols concert and they didn't know what I was talking about. It was becoming obvious to me that I was probably the only idiot on planet earth who thought the Sex Pistols reunion was anything other than slightly amusing.

I met an African musician from Senegal, a tall guy with the physique of a boxer, named Simon. We started talking about the Bad Brains, who we were both big fans of, and Jamaica.

"I haff a friend, Michael, you must meet," he said. "He is Jamaican. He will show you the real Hamburg."

"Are there any hash bars here in Hamburg?" I asked him. I thought maybe Simon would take me where Hans-Georg Behr wouldn't.

"Ask Michael!" Simon said. "He'll take you where they haff the goot herb!"

It turned out Michael had lived for a while in Trench Town, and knew Massive Dread and Chinna and some of the other people I'd met there. He took me to another bar that spun dub music, and people smoked herb in the open.

"Is this what you were looking for?" Simon asked.

"Yeah!" I said. It was not a hash bar per se, but at that point I was looking for anyplace with a mellow vibe.

I was still wondering how I could get a story out of this trip to Hamburg. I felt guilty for wasting so much *High Times* money, wandering around Europe depressed. I'd already crapped out with Hans-Georg Behr, the only hash bars were in my mind—what about the live sex shows? I figured I could write a story about watching strangers have sex. I asked Michael if he knew any particularly gruesome ones.

"Yeah, mon! I've got a friend who works at the door of one place, he'll let you see the show for free!"

Simon was tired and ready to split home.

"Some day you come to Senegal and I'll really show you a time!" he said and walked on into the night.

When we reached the sex club, Michael's friend Charles greeted us both with respect. Outside the theater, the passageway was crowded with tourists. Charles was another African, from Somalia. He worked at several different clubs on the Reeperbahn and assured me this was the roller coaster of sin I was looking for.

Charles started haggling with the manager, a fat old kraut in suspenders who, fifty years before, was probably on the receiving end of many a wedgie back at the Hitler Youth barracks. He wore rings on his fingers like Liberace, and when Charles showed him my *High Times* business card he looked at me and said "Heeez *dronk!*" and refused to let me in.

"I didn't come halfway around the world to be chastised by this third-rate pimp!" I told Charles.

"Don't worry! I'll talk to him!" he said and then rounded up a few of the local prostitutes who assured the bugger-meister that I was indeed a wholesome pervert, a sex fiend of the highest caliber. Finally he let me in. I had to pay, of course, but I was told I should be grateful. Michael didn't have the money so he split home to his girlfriend.

"Doon't worry, mon," Charles said. "I'll take care of you."

Inside the club was a small stage with a catwalk that extended into the audience. About twenty people, mostly couples, had come to see the ten o'clock show. I sat back at the bar. For all I knew, Chewbacca was going to come out and do his Harlem Globetrotters act, and this not being Ocean-world, I didn't want to sit in the "Splash Zone."

An emaciated woman came out and pranced around for a few minutes

like she was God's gift to crack. A second girl walked around on her hands
with her two legs wrapped around her neck. Another talented young lady
placed a cigarette in her pussy, squatted in front of an elderly German couple, and asked the lady for a light. Eager to please, the woman complied.
The actress then proceeded to blow smoke rings out of her pussy, and the
audience applauded like it was Trigger onstage, and he'd just counted to
three.

Then came the main act: the genuine swapping of bodily fluids, LIVE
SEX. (Dead sex was part of a different package, I guess.) Some introduc-
tory music was played and then the announcer shouted in broken English,
"Ladies and gentlemen! Mr. Bombastic!"

Mr. Bombastic was none other than Charles the ticket-taker. From all
appearances he was moonlighting right under the bugger-meister's nose.
As the audience welcomed him with warm applause, he walked to the
center of the stage, and revealed a member about the size of a gooseneck
lamp. His partner was introduced, a slightly overweight brunette, and the
crowd applauded politely. A quick blow job, and then they did that thing
we all like to do.

After a few groans and grinds, I realized that sex doesn't transfer well
to the stage. The dialogue is limited, as are the set, costumes, and plot. It
has more action than your average O'Neill play, but the cast of *Cats* sweats
more.

I'd evaded the bartender's eyesight long enough, and now he demanded I buy an overpriced beer. Bored and wondering what any of this
had to do with the Sex Pistols, I took out my journal and figured I'd try and
justify the expense of this ridiculous downtime with a few brilliant words.
The girl who blew the smoke rings sat down at the bar and looked at me.

"Vaat are you writink? Vat she doez?" the cigarette lady asked me as
she watched me scribble. "Who do you tink you arrrre?" Apparently it's
okay in Germany to blow smoke out of your pussy in public places, but not
okay to write down your thoughts. What would Hans-Georg Behr have
done in this situation?

When it looked like the girl on stage was about to fall asleep, Mr.
Bombastic put his lamp away and the curtains came down. I sat for a moment and finished my very expensive beer. On my way out I saw Mr. Bombastic, back punching tickets at the door.

"You're leaving?" he asked. "There's a second show!"

"I'm pretty beat," I said. "I've gotta see the Sex Pistols tomorrow . . . "

"You enjoyed it, I hope?"

"The finest I've ever seen!"

"All right, mon, you take care."

I said good-bye and then walked back to my hotel room with the funny smell.

It was raining the next day. The last time I talked to Tresa Redburn, the Pistols' publicist, she told me there'd be tickets waiting for me at the gate. I took a cab to the sports arena and started writing down questions I'd ask Johnny Rotten if by chance I got an interview. I couldn't think of anything that I didn't already know the answer to, so I started writing down things like "If there was such a thing as reincarnation, what form would Sid come back as?" and "Why are you doing this to me?"

As we approached the stadium, I noticed that the parking lot was empty. No cars, no punks, not even a homeless anarchist. Over by one of the gates there was one lone groundsperson hanging posters. I told my driver to wait and walked dejectedly towards the man, knowing that when I reached him, I would find out that I'd fucked up yet again.

"They're not playing?" I asked him.

"Next month. Next month they reschedule."

I slumped back to the cab, which took me back to my hotel room. Maybe it was just the German in me responding to my surroundings, but after I failed in my mission to see the Pistols, I had an overwhelming desire to chew on a cyanide pill. I couldn't stomach my room anymore so I decided to walk around in the rain until I caught cold and died.

I walked the streets of Hamburg, past the bizarre architectural mix of medieval churches and modern, glass boxes. Europe has always been a place of unspoken promises for me. Just the word "Europe" conjures up Lewis Carroll and Wagner and Marlene Dietrich—Gothic fairy tales and femme fatales. There's a certain eroticism to the gray skies and the cobblestone streets. As I walked, I dreamed about meeting a rich blond princess who would carry me off to her palace in the Black Forest where I'd spend the rest of my days pissing in the Rhine and drinking wine in front of blazing fireplaces.

I called my ex-girlfriend from a public phone near the harbor. Because of the time difference she was still asleep. I hung on the receiver, listening to her fall in and out of consciousness wondering, as I guess you always do in that situation, whether she was alone. I had no right, but I still found some way to justify feeling cheated. After I hung up I walked down to the harbor and stared into the water, wondering if the fish weren't staring back at me and calling me an asshole.

Then I had an idea as to how I could feel better about myself. I decided to get drunk again. I went to a faceless pub down the block from my hotel, memorable only for its fine view of the street.

After a while I struck up a strained conversation with an overweight

German woman with a Dorothy Hamill haircut. She could barely speak English, and I didn't want to drag out any of the phrases I'd learned on the Reeperbahn. We exchanged funny looks for an hour or two, until we both got apocalyptically drunk. Through a bizarre mix of sign language, sound effects, and *weissbier*, we managed to both agree that it would be a good idea to go back to my hotel and fuck. The language of love, someone once called it.

As I pumped away (using a few new moves I'd copped from Mr. Bombastic), her face stared up at me like a broken mirror. There was a brief moment of clarity and I realized when you sleep with somebody you actually become them and they become you. Polaroid posterity. I looked down at myself—a fat German woman who probably wouldn't have sounded too smart if I did speak English—and wondered why my parents spent all that money to send me to college.

After we abandoned the gropefest, we both sat on the bed in our respective comas, the blinding light from the bare lightbulb above shining down on our idiocy. She kept babbling to herself, repeating the same two-syllable phrase which, if I had to guess, was probably German for "cuckoo."

I turned the light off and laid my head on the pillow, finally realizing that the funny smell I was so curious about was nothing more than the sweat and tobacco of a hundred other morons who had laid in that bed before me. I tried to sleep but she started snoring like a hound. I laid there in bed, free-associating poetic lines to the rhythm of her grumbling.

I felt like there was too much going on, even though I knew there was nothing, nothing happening at all. I was stuck in a hotel room with nothing to do except think about why the hell the Sex Pistols decided to get back together again.

I had to piss, but I didn't want to put my clothes back on to walk out into the hall to the bathroom, so I opened the window and pissed on as much of Germany as I could. In an instant I heard the fluttering of wings as a bird two stories below scrambled to flee the unexpected downpour.

"Life is like that sometimes," I yelled out to it, but it was already gone.

The sun came up. I watched an old gardener tend to a patch of tomatoes in the yard behind the hotel until it didn't seem like an inhuman act to ask my *fräulein* to leave. It started to rain and the gardener kept working. As she opened the door to go, a breeze entered the room, and I meditated upon the wet smell of the German morning and the sounds of people driving efficiently to work.

Walking into New York's Roseland on August 8, I was expecting a bloodbath. The day before, NASA announced that they'd found a meteorite that gave evidence that primitive life existed on Mars 3.6 billion years ago. I couldn't decide which was the bigger miracle—that, or the fact that the Sex Pistols were going to play in New York City for the first time ever. Johnny had been slagging New York for twenty years, basically since the Pistols' inception. If the Pistols came out and walked on water they wouldn't have gotten much more than a smattering of applause. New York audiences only move their arms at a show when they're wiping drugs from their nose.

Again the band opened with "Bodies." This time Johnny wore an orange-and-yellow plastic suit. If he'd've had a blinking light on his shoulder and a "Men at Work" sign on his chest, he probably could have pulled in a few extra bucks working for the city as a human pylon. Johnny's hair stood straight up, half yellow and half red, like a court jester's hat. Crowd reaction was mixed, with half the audience getting into it and the other half either standing still or contributing to the fountain of spit that rained down on top of Johnny's head. This is good, I thought, he's gonna get pissed off, we're gonna see some rock-hero fireworks tonight. Having only, their legend to go by, I'd always heard the Pistols played better when they're angry.

But they didn't get angry. Johnny picked out one guy who was throwing coins and said, "If you're going to throw money, bills only, please," a line he'd been using for twenty years. As a younger, cooler man, Johnny used to stalk the stage with a maniacal stare, clinging to the mikestand like some living abortion who never quite learned how to walk straight. Now in his forties, he danced like he'd been taking lessons from Lou Reed.

"You're paying for it! Get your money's worth!" he said, as if the very fact that he was taking the crowd's money vindicated his ambivalence. The crowd gobbed more, threw their jackets at the band, and Johnny did the "Hustle." I wanted to see him cut into the crowd, to pull out a flamethrower and take out the first few rows of spitters, but no, this was a new Johnny Rotten, one who turned the other cheek—not the one on his face, either. During "New York" he turned around and pointed to his ass and then continued his Mr. Roboto dance. What seemed like harmless punk nostalgia in London became a seemingly intentional trashing of his former glory. I guess it was pretty funny, but I didn't go there to laugh. Like a kid failing his classes to get his parents' attention, Johnny seemed to be dancing on the grave of his legend to prove to us how little it really mattered.

When the show ended, music industry types nudged each other in and out of position near the backstage entrance. Whoever was in charge of the backstage access had given out several different colored passes. The green ones were good and the yellow ones were invalid, a placebo. I didn't have a pass of any sort and after much hassle I managed to procure a yellow one, which I brought up to the guard and was then informed of the joke.

At the door I saw Bob Gruen, the photographer who took most of those famous shots of Led Zeppelin and John Lennon you see hanging on dorm room walls across America. He said a few words on my behalf to the skeptical guard.

"The guy's drunk!" the guard said pointing to me. "He needs to go to A.A., not backstage."

"So what if he's drunk," Bob argued. "It's the Pistols, for Chrissakes!"

I had a déjà vu, only now it wasn't the local sex workers who were arguing in my defense, but Bob. Without knowing it I'd been bumped up with the big guys.

They relented and I was given admission to the backstage where I proceeded to get even more obliterated on whiskey. One after the other, I drank shots like I was hanging out in the local trailer park. I didn't want to see them up close. I wanted to keep that hazy seventh-grade memory intact. What was I going to say to them? You guys were my idols but you suck now? What right did I have to criticize the Pistols?

After a long wait Glen and Paul entered the room. Suddenly the same people who were slagging them off moments before were patting them on the back and saying, "Good show."

Now I've been in bands, unsuccessful bands but bands nonetheless, and nothing put me off more than those people who you know didn't see the show or didn't like the show and still came up to you for their own slimy reasons and patted you on the back. "Good show" always sounded like "Fuck you" to me but I guess it's part of the culture.

"Hey, man, there's your interview!" the *High Times* people told me. Glen and Paul were making the rounds.

"I can't," I said.

"What do you mean? You're blowing it. Get in there."

They were each surrounded by four or five people. To grab their attention I would have had to get right in their faces, something even drunk, I didn't want to do.

Finally somebody brought me directly to Glen and said, "Glen, this is Chris from *High Times*."

"Oh, *High Times*!" he said. "I remember you guys." He held out his hand to me, which I shook. There was a moment there where I could have asked him anything I wanted, anything in the world.

"I've always been a big fan," I said and let him get back to his autographs. There was a collected gasp from the *High Times* crew. It was not unlike the *whoosh* that five thousand dollars in expense money makes as it is being flushed down the toilet. Fuck it, I said, I can barely walk, and stomped outside to the city street.

It was raining again, and as I watched a caravan of yellow cabs piss down Broadway I wondered why I was taking this all so seriously. We've been going the wrong way down a one-way street for so long we might as well take a match to our heroes and warm ourselves at the blaze. Twenty years ago the Pistols earned the right to basically do whatever the fuck they want on this earth. Regardless of the Filthy Lucre tour, I figured I'd still play *Never Mind the Bollocks* as loud as I ever did.

I walked up Seventh Avenue, trying to put the whole thing into perspective. Pot activists, rock stars, German princesses, scat tossers—it was a very strange world I had created for myself, a movie I was sick of living in. I felt like I'd forgotten how to breathe. In the face of that, the Pistols reunion was a nonissue.

I remembered Holly, my blond stripper friend in Oregon. I'd just gotten another letter from her telling me that I needed to visit her and meditate upon the ocean and the redwoods and the sky and leave all this urban confusion behind. The city was the devil's playground, she argued, and right then and there I could only agree.

11

The Teflon Shaman

I told *High Times* if I didn't leave the city within a few weeks those sweet South American women who clean the offices at night were going to be picking pieces of my skull off of my "Stoned Ag'in" poster and saying "Eet's so sad . . . he haff so much to live for . . . "

"You just got a break!" they said. "Drank your way across Europe and didn't even get a story!"

"That wasn't a break," I argued. "That was a midlife crisis."

The main idea at that point in my life was to keep moving. The minute I stopped, as soon as I turned the key to my apartment door and dropped my luggage, I started to rot. The Pistols proved I could rot on the road, too, but at least the scenery was better.

I pitched them a story on Moses, the righteous grower I'd met at the Rainbow Gathering. He had a crop that was ready for harvest somewhere in Portland, and I told them if they bought me a plane ticket I'd write them the first marijuana cultivation story to ever win a Pulitzer.

Of course my underlying motivation was to see Holly. She'd just sent me a bunch of pictures someone had taken of her at work. From what I could see, Oregon looked like a beautiful place.

Teflon Shaman: Outlaw life. (*High Times* archives)

High Times bought my Moses pitch, and a few weeks later, I was sitting at a bar in JFK en route to Oregon thinking I had the best job in the world. The place was your average airport establishment, with a view of the gift shops and the runways. I sat down and ordered a Jack and Coke, and after a few minutes I started talking to this salesman who looked to be about fifty. He had a briefcase and wore a wrinkled suit. He told me about his life, how lonely it was on the road. He gave me the whole show—took the photos of his kids out of the plastic windows in his wallet to give me a better view. Rubber balls were his thing. He sold them to distributors up and down the East Coast. We traded business cards and bonded over a few shots of booze the way company men do.

He started giving me his pitch—I wasn't looking to buy any rubber balls, he knew that, he just wanted to do his dance. He had these balls that you could spin a certain way, so that when they hit the floor they bounced diagonally back into your hand. He started showing me, but the trick didn't work, so there he was drunk, scrambling around on the terrazzo after his wayward balls. It was beautiful, like a scene from a movie, and in a way I felt like I'd made it. It looked like a fun way to spend your life, drinking with other people's money, and it gave me hope for the future.

It seemed like a symbol, too, his balls for sale, but I didn't want to kill too many brain cells thinking about that one.

After a seven-hour plane ride with a stopover in Denver, I landed in Portland, and Holly greeted me at the airport by blowing a cloud of glitter in my face and then giving me a loud hug.

"We'll drop your stuff off at my house and then we *have* to go to the hot springs! Oh, you have to see this, Chris. The first time I saw this place I couldn't believe it was real. *The sun is shining!!!!!*"

She grabbed my hand and led me out of the airport in a wide-eyed hurry. Along the way she starting telling me how much fun we were going to have and how happy she was that we finally met. She had a house in the suburbs outside of Portland where we dropped my luggage. After I called Moses and made plans to see him and his victory garden the next day, Holly took me out to her backyard to meet her dog. I tossed a ball to the pooch a couple of times and then she loaded me back into her four-by-four en route to her nudist paradise.

"I was coming back from the coast the other day . . . " she said, swerving down a twisted mountain road with huge walls of trees lining both sides of the highway. "Chris, if only I could describe in words the strength and beauty of this wonderful coast. *Agggh!* I wish you could *feel it* running through my fingers . . . "

Holly sang along with the Beatles and kept telling me how much I was going to love the coast. "I brought a camera and I'm gonna take a picture of it for you to hang on your wall back in your office!" She talked loud, like an FM deejay. As we drove further, I started debating with myself whether traveling three thousand miles for a blind date was a smart thing to do.

As we drove, she told me about her life, how she had been a Deadhead for a while, and that she swore off drugs after she took the rap for a thousand hits of her boyfriend's acid and spent a year in the joint. Now she was a spiritual missionary, she explained. Her grandmother was the only family she was in touch with and, being a daughter of the world herself, she knew how important the kindness of strangers could be.

"Oh! I almost forgot to tell you!" she said. "I was coming home a couple weeks ago and as I crossed the bridge I saw a person sitting on the side of the road. I usually don't pick up hitchhikers but I still feel I owe a few rides back for the many I've received. His name was George and he was eighteen. He just graduated high school. Let me tell you Chris, I was *ecstatic*! I decided then, I was this kid's destiny for the next couple days. I took him to the hot springs and now I'm taking you."

Destiny is a word I always like to hear, because inherent in its definition is the fact that I don't have to work to get it. Everything was going as I had hoped, and I was already trying to decide what tape I'd play during the seduction. A little Zeppelin to start, I figured. I'd save the Black Sabbath until after I'd proved myself.

We parked at the hot springs and Holly made the mistake of saying hello to a scrawny, bug-eyed old man who looked like his world has never been the same since Mama Cass died. He followed us from the parking lot, into the woods, and up to the springs where I started to realize this creep was just waiting for us to take our clothes off. I told the guy to leave and he acted like I'd insulted him, telling me I'd just caused a serious deficit in my karma bank.

When we got to the springs we stripped down and waded out into the warm water the earth had sent to the surface for our delight. There were about fifteen people of various ages swimming around in five different pools. It was the first time I'd ever partied naked with a bunch of hippies and I didn't know the etiquette. Were boners rude? I wasn't sure. Holly looked at me a few times to see if the hot springs were doing anything to melt the ice in my veins, and I tried to look relaxed.

When it got dark we put our clothes back on and wandered from campsite to campsite. People sat around campfires jamming on acoustics and smoking joints. Several of them grew pot themselves and told me of massive gardens out in the woods that they had to hike overnight to reach. I started to think that coming to Oregon was not too desperate of an act after all. Back in New York I would've been on my tenth beer and here, I was instead hanging out with this life-lusting woman who'd only met me once before in her life and decided to be my destiny for the next few days. As we said goodnight to everyone I started shifting into my Isaac Hayes mode, stepping up to the center of the stage and ready to sing the words that women want to hear. In a situation like this, it's easy to get all sorts of rock star delusions about yourself.

But here's a lesson to all you would-be dope journalists out there—if you want the women, learn how to play guitar. When we got back to the four-by-four I soon learned that my strange brand of funky love was not in demand that night. In fact, it was downright frowned upon. After staying up half the night comparing the pros and cons of this Northwest misadventure, I finally thought fuck it, there were a lot of miles between me and the office and even that guy with his balls for sale seemed a million miles away.

I forgot what Moses' real name was. He was from Queens and he'd been growing pot up and down the West Coast since the sixties. After Holly went to work at Wiggles the next day, I called him up.

"Moses! Whas up, baby!"

"Hey, brother Chris, c'mon over!"

Moses had a modest house in a suburb near Portland—the kind of town where you don't expect to find multiple felons. He greeted me at the door and asked me to remove my shoes before I entered. He looked like a holy man with his long dreadlocks and ecologically sound hemp pajamas. His place was like a New Age museum, decorated with colorful crystals, each of which had some kind of cosmic significance. Moses believed in crystal healing, and told me that certain rocks had medicinal powers when administered by a spiritually enlightened hand. His, he explained, was such a hand.

Not only did Moses grow the strongest pot I've ever had, he smoked more pot than anybody I've ever met. He led me into a room, the centerpiece of which was a little altar topped with karmically blessed rocks, pipes, and twigs. He introduced me to a few of his stoner guests and sat cross-legged on a hand-stitched pillow, where he proceeded to load pipe after pipe with trichomes, the crystallized THC that can be shaken off properly cured herb. He handed me a long smoldering pipe as heavy as half a brick.

"Hand-carved from sacred stone," he explained. My memory is spotty, I don't remember what was carved on the pipe. Some hippie thing. All I know is within ten minutes I'd forgotten how to form speech. I kept laughing to myself thinking: What am I doing here, coming all this way just to hang out with people who smoked pot? Was this journalism, or just a cheap excuse to get wasted?

As I looked around the room at the long-hairs, I realized I was back in Rainbow territory and shouldn't get so far out that I couldn't defend myself if I had to. After "Fear of a Groovy Planet" I had become the sworn enemy of many a disgruntled long-hair in the letters page. They even started slagging me off in the Hemp 100, *High Times'* monthly open forum. I knew I hit a nerve when they started attacking me there. It meant the spuds were out to get me, too.

"This is . . . " I said, raking through my vocabulary for the right words, "good stuff . . . "

"What I've noticed about indoor growing," Moses lectured, "is that the human being that's relating to the plants becomes the artificial sunshine, besides the lights. It's very important, the spirit of the grower. You can have the perfect food, the perfect lights, the perfect ventilation, moisture, but if you don't have the right spirit it's not going to do the beautiful sacred thing it's supposed to.

"It's like this Hash Plant number one—" He took out a new jar for me to see. "This is grown by someone who lets greed sweep them away and even though it's primo bud, the fact that that person lets greed sweep them away takes away from the quality of the high."

The four or five stoners waiting to buy his righteous bud all grunted in agreement, and Moses sat back and puffed his pipe with a big, self-satisfied smile.

I sat there on the floor, studying the social order of the room. These were Moses' business hours. I watched the familiar exchanges of money, drugs, promises, and favors, that age-old custom as much a part of the American social landscape as Friday night poker.

The dealer/client relationship falls somewhere between business and social life. Buying drugs is more fun than going to the dentist, but there is always that feeling that you are visiting a specialist and paying him for his services. Most of the dealers I've known in my life like to talk. This is unfortunate because nothing they say ever seems to be relevant or even coherent. They know they have you where they want you, and like it or not you're going to listen to *and agree with* whatever crap comes out of their mouths until they hand you their product.

"Now I have to ask you this, Moses," said one disgruntled customer. "I know you're a righteous man, and we're all *brothers*, but I just want to know why this stuff is four hundred fifty dollars an ounce when last month it was only four hundred dollars."

"It's like *August*, man. I had everything to do just to get ahold of this herb. My stuff doesn't come in until November. You try and find this cheaper somewhere else. I'm telling you, like . . . it ain't gonna happen—"

"Man, I'm just sayin' we're *brothers.* I'd hate to think you were taking advantage of me because of the drought—"

"I'm not making *anything* on this. I'm making *less* than when it was four hundred dollars . . . "

"That's all right, man. I just had to, like . . . ask."

"Peace, brother."

"Peace."

Holly came by after her shift at Wiggles, and when she saw all the crystals she started telling me that Moses had a very expensive aura.

"This crystal right here," she whispered to me, pointing to one of the rocks on the altar, "goes for two thousand dollars . . . "

"Oh, I didn't pay that," Moses said, overhearing. He didn't want a *High Times* editor thinking he was a sucker. "I traded a few ounces of herb for it. Not a bad deal, hunh? Hey, check this out . . . "

Moses pulled out a little wad of folded wax paper from a hemp satchel. Wrapped inside it were small flakes of sheeted crystal.

"Toad," he said.

"Bufo?" I asked.

"Yeah. I've never done it. I've done DMT—*organic* DMT, but never toad. It'll be a trip, hunh?"

I was stoned and found myself shaking my head affirmatively, but all I could think was if Moses wanted me to smoke the sweat of a poisonous South American toad with him, he'd better start rubbing his rocks together, because barring a direct order from some kind of deity, I was keeping my body amphibian-free for the week. There was only so much I was going to do for a free vacation. I'd ask him some questions about growing dope and that was about it.

For the next hour or two I sat there, until Moses started baiting his girlfriend, saying things that pissed her off. She cursed at him and stormed out of the room. He laughed in such a way that invited me to share his amusement, then Holly and I finally split.

"He does have this . . . energy . . . you can't deny it," she said as we walked out.

"If we could get cars to run on bullshit," I said, "we might be able to put that kind of energy to work."

The next day I was hoping to get my interview with Moses done early so I could split to the coast with Holly and give my Isaac Hayes act another try. Moses showed up with a couple of his business partners—two kids about my age, both with the red-glazed look that a day of constant marijuana smoking will give you. Jeff was a mellow, dreadlocked Deadhead who talked about the medicinal uses of various herbs to me. The other kid,

Jason, was more of a wild-eyed street urchin who looked as if he was trying his best to see me through the fog.

"Hey, man, guess what?" Moses asked me.

"You tell me."

"It's my birthday. Fifty years today, man."

I congratulated him and asked him when we were going to do the interview.

"All things in time," he said. He apparently had something else to
show me and we drove off in his Winnebago to a local park.

As Jeff navigated the Winnebago through the Portland streets, Moses
told me about all the things he was doing to save people, the good works
he performed with his healing crystals and herbs.

"I help many different sick people, not for money but for medicine. It's
worth any risk you can take. I save lives. I always call it the sacred herb."

Moses always talked like he was practicing to be famous. He wouldn't
have been the first ego case to go mainstream. I could picture him with his
dreadlocks and his sacred herb, laughing with Regis on daytime TV and
frightening armchair grandmas across the nation with his Hippie Christ
Superstar act.

We parked, and Moses led us out into the woods. After comparison-
shopping several different vibes, he decided on a semisecluded field fifty
feet from the parking lot. He instructed Jason to lay out a hemp blanket for
us to sit on and unwrapped his treasured glassine envelope. When I saw
the familiar crystals, I tried to think of an excuse to refuse when my turn
came.

"Who wants to go first?" Moses asked. He didn't want to be the ce-
lestial guinea pig. "How about the *High Times* editor?"

I told him I was on the cosmic rag right now and not ready for inter-
course with the gods. He seemed a little hurt until he realized that that
meant more for him.

"Hell, I'll do it," Jason said and Moses packed him a bowl.

He presented the pipe to Jason like Obi-Wan handing Luke his first
light saber. Jason's eyes gleamed with the look of a boy going off to war and
hoping to come back a man. When the flame hit the bowl, the sweat crack-
led like burning hair. When he finished sucking back his smoke, Jason's
mouth split into a wide Dr. Seuss–sized grin.

"Do you feel it?" I asked him. "Are you becoming the toad?"

His face contorted wordlessly. I imagined all the little thoughts that
life had given him, all those cataloged beliefs and images and dates and
phone numbers suddenly tossed into a lawn mower and spread across the
front of his skull like a Jackson Pollock abortion. I had to imagine that

somewhere on this earth Jason's dad was wondering what his son was doing with his life since he quit college. Jason exhaled and gave us all a funny look that I interpreted as meaning his trip was a success. He didn't say very much for the rest of the afternoon.

Jeff went next, but he didn't get off.

"That's all right," Moses said, taking the pipe. "You gotta drive."

Then it was Moses' turn.

Moses sat cross-legged and meditated for a while, R.S.V.P.ing his invitation to God's barbecue. Both Jeff and Jason looked at me, as if to say, "Check out Moses, he's doin' his thing . . . " He was mumbling prayers and blessings, thanking all the gods for everything and basically spreading his chips across the divine table. Pieces of his private conversation were sometimes coherent, things like "the great goddess Kali . . . " and "may we thank the Great Spirit . . . "

When Moses finished being heavy, he loaded one of his stone pipes up with the toad crystals, praised Jah, and put his Bic to the bowl. His head shot back like he'd managed to morph himself into the Zapruder film. A shiver worked its way from his neck to his shoulders to his fingers, where whatever energy was running amok inside him was suddenly called back into possession by its master. No way Moses was going to let expensive vibe like that leave his body. He exhaled the smoke and exploded with benedictions:

"I CAN FEEL THE GREAT CHRIST CONSCIOUSNESS FROM THE FORESTS TO THE MOUNTAINS REACHING OUT FROM AFRICAN DESERTS TO THE CRYSTAL WATERS OF THE SEA OF JAPAN. THE BROTHERHOOD OF MAN IS PULSING IN MY HEART—"

Jeff and Jason stared at him like they were witnessing the hippest event this side of the Tibetan Freedom Concert.

"THE GREAT CHRIST CONSCIOUSNESS FLOWS OUT OF MY HEART TO THE WORLD, OH, IF ONLY . . . IF ONLY SOMEONE WERE WRITING THESE WORDS DOWN . . . IF ONLY THERE WAS A TAPE RECORDER THAT COULD SEND THESE WORDS OUT TO THE WORLD . . . "

I was ready to go. I wanted to get back and see Holly, Christ consciousness or no Christ consciousness. As Moses continued on about Jesus and tape recorders, I started thinking to myself that I really didn't want to interview the guy. Why encourage him? After his body gave one last prolonged quake, Moses collapsed back onto his blanket.

"Is everybody about ready to leave?" I asked, but Jeff and Jason were still fixated on Moses and waiting to see what he'd do next. When he finally came to, the boys helped him back into his cross-legged holy man position.

"Did you get it?" he asked.

"Get what?"

"What did I say?"

"I dunno . . . something about Jesus . . . "

"Oh man . . . " he seemed a little disturbed. "I mean . . . someone should have . . . What I mean is, a lot of people could have learned from me if . . . I wish somebody had taped the damn thing . . . "

Back at his house Moses' girlfriend was throwing him a party. The yard was filled with friends and clients, and when Moses showed up they all started singing "Happy Birthday." He walked through the admiring crowd, hugging and kissing his constituents.

After the pizza was delivered and a few hundred joints were passed among the faithful, people started coming up to me and asking me what it was like to smoke toad with Moses. There was one dreadlocked young lady who followed me around, hounding me for details.

"What was it like?"

"I told you, I didn't smoke it."

"Not you, Moses. Did he say anything?"

"Something about the Christ consciousness . . . " She stared at me, expecting me to elaborate.

"Yeah . . . but what did he *say*?"

"Well . . . I don't really remember."

A look of angst spread across her face as if I'd just told her Bob Weir was a narc. What did he say? Who gives a shit? I asked Jason if he wanted to come with me to Wiggles. He said he was low on cash but I assured him I'd buy a few rounds and we split.

We wandered into Wiggles and as "Highway to Hell" echoed through the club's sound system, Holly waved at me from the stage. She was swinging around on a long metal bar like some sort of erotic gymnast. Jason suddenly retrieved his senses enough to say, "Whooa . . . she's with you?"

I gave him an ambiguous smile. I was a *High Times* editor and he was a burnout. I didn't want to spoil his toasted dreams with the pathetic realities of my own life.

We watched her shimmy around on stage for an hour. By this point I was just looking forward to seeing the surf. I'd come to Oregon to meditate after all, and the ocean will always give you a bit of perspective on whatever predicament you're in. It warns you if you keep running straight, you're gonna drown.

I wondered if maybe one of Moses' gods really did exist, and this whole twisted vacation was planned this way for my own good. Since I wasn't tumbling around at night, locked in an erotic interpretation of the Normandy invasion, I'd managed to get some rest. After the toad incident, I wasn't too interested in softening my skull with drugs. Hanging out with Holly was the most fun I'd had in months, and her unrestrained optimism kept me smiling in spite of my lecherous intentions. Even Moses was a laugh when he wasn't picking on his girlfriend. All things considered, this was the best trip *High Times* had sent me on since Jamaica.

After Holly finished her act, the three of us walked outside to the parking lot. Waiting for Holly was another desperate sort: a trailer-park speed freak who obviously thought that she'd been sending him coded messages from the stage. She talked for a few minutes with the harmless stiff while I hung around with Jason by the four-by-four.

"Dude," he said. "You are like . . . " He paused for a moment. He was still having difficulties with his speech. "*Dude!* You got the best job in the world."

"Uh . . . you think so?"

"Yeah, man. You get to go places and do drugs . . . hang out with strippers."

"I was doing that before I started working at *High Times.*"

"Cool, dude," he smiled. "Outta sight."

Holly sent her stalker back to his meth lab and asked Jason if he needed a ride home.

"Sure . . . what are you guys doing?"

"We're going to the coast," I said. "I got one more night before my plane leaves. I wanna see the Pacific."

"You ain't gonna visit Moses' garden tomorrow?" Jason asked. "I thought you made plans?"

"I'm going West, young man. Send the shaman my love."

"What are you gonna write the article on?" he asked. I think he was even in awe of me for fucking the whole thing up. It gave him a bit of hope, I guess.

"Oh, you know . . . " I said as Holly pressed a button on her key chain, causing the car alarm to chirp. "These things have a habit of writing themselves."

12

Gringo Like Me: Spring Break in Cancún

I decided to expand my program a bit. I now had a reputation around *High Times* for vacationing at the magazine's expense, and to a certain extent the other employees were depending on me to outdo myself with each successive assignment. If I could keep doing what I did and not get fired, it meant job security for the rest of them. They'd always be able to say, "Well, shit, you think I'm bad, what about Simunek?"

When I got the idea to check the pulse of our nation's future while swilling beers at Spring Break, I insisted that the only way to do the story right was to bring a friend. I wanted to go on one of those package tours, and it just wouldn't have worked if I went alone. What was I going to do, get drunk at a wet T-shirt night by myself? They asked me if I wanted to bring a photographer, and I said fuck the photographer, I want to bring Mort Todd. Comic artist and all-around expert in things ridiculous, I needed Mort to help me navigate the collegiate waters.

Bungee jumping into the future with the next generation. (Mort Todd)

I'd been hanging out with Mort a lot since he'd quit his job at Marvel. He would come by the office and together we'd often enjoy a liquid lunch in one of the various bars around Park Avenue. I knew he could draw, and I also knew he could drink like a Teamster. In my eyes he was more than qualified. For weeks the phrase "I can't believe you and Mort are going to Spring Break" resounded around the office like a mantra, and I felt proud that I'd set a new record for the flimsiest pretense that ever got a pair of drunks two plane tickets to Mexico.

At the editorial meeting I argued that, with the onset of the millennium, other magazines were going to be drawing up their lists of faces to look for in the twenty-first century, so why shouldn't *High Times* take a realistic look at the future and write about the spuds? If you want an accurate portrait of the next generation, then you have to look at the majority. Namely, the ones who will be canceling your health insurance or refusing you a bank loan. If there's one thing the sixties should have taught us, it's that while the spokespeople of a generation are busy looking good on camera, history is being made by the ants.

Spring Break was like the ant Wailing Wall. It was where they all journeyed for one last stab at freedom before they became the grease that lubed the great American machine as it plowed over other people's lives. It seemed like a good idea, at least until the plane landed and the two of us boarded the School Spirit Inc. tour bus en route to our hotel.

As the white sun blazed through the bus window, creating a greenhouse effect so hot I thought my teeth were going to melt, I could see Cancún approaching on the horizon like a bear trap. A host of corporate logos hung from the buildings—Hard Rock Café, Burger King, All-Star Café. The whole place looked like it was designed by a game-show host. A clear blue sky hung over a turquoise ocean so pure I half expected to see Flipper cutting through the waves with a frozen margarita in his fin.

"Do you want to use the intercom?" I heard the driver say to Fred, our twenty-something School Spirit Inc. representative. Fred wore an XXL T-shirt that said "Just Do It" over a large Nike slash.

"No, man," Fred said with enthusiasm, "I prefer to just belt it out. Here . . . " Fred handed his clipboard to another rep, jumped up on one of the seats and screamed, "Welcome to Spring Break '97!"

There were a couple of grunts from the faithful, but for the most part the ants were tired. The plane had come five hours late and had no air-conditioning. Those who were able to keep their dinners down spent most of the time shivering from food poisoning. They were the lucky ones; their fevers kept them cool.

"Didn't it say the foam party and the bullfight were free?" Mort asked as he sorted through the various pamphlets that came with our tickets.

"Here it says they're forty bucks a head. We can't miss the foam party, or what the hell are we doing here?"

"Look, people," continued Fred. "We all want you to party hearty in Cancún, but there's a couple of things I gotta say. Last year we had an unfortunate accident, so the local people told us to tell you—the balcony-jumping has got to stop. You don't want to visit a Mexican jail. I've done it twice and, man, you don't want to do it."

"What are you guys doing here?" asked a coed from the seat behind me. She wasn't fat, but she had that look like she'd been struggling with her weight all her life.

"We're here to learn about your culture," I said. "The only way to destroy a beast is to know its habits."

"What I mean is . . . " she tried to smile, "Why are you here? You're . . . *old.*"

Her friends laughed and suddenly I was back on campus at SUNY Albany, surrounded by fifteen thousand jerks. I looked at Mort but he shrugged it off. "Amateurs," he said and went back to his literature.

Fred finished with his speech and decided to use the advanced social status afforded to him by his School Spirit name tag to make time with the girls behind us. With him was another rep, a goateed California surfer with thick black hair, named Barney.

When we reached the center of town, the bus made a right into the parking lot of the Hyatt Regency—a hotel as loud and as vulgar as the clientele it served. I was exhausted and shaken. I needed to get to my room and rest if I was going to make the foam party that night. The kids filed out tired but ready, the Nike slash dominating their clothing like a Gen-X swastika.

"I'm back," said one zealous spud in a "Weedies" shirt as a local youth grabbed his luggage and donkeyed it through the glass doors. "I can't believe it, I'm really back."

Mort and I paid the forty dollars to get into the foam party and then snaked our way through the sweaty, soap-covered bodies inside the Oasis. The low, mechanical thud of drum 'n' bass thundered through the club like the heartbeat of a robot god. Through the darkness and the fake smoke, I could make out shapes undulating on the dance floor. Red and blue laser lights sliced through the fog and as I got closer I could see a cannon shooting mounds of soap bubbles over the dancers.

Straddling the cannon with a cordless mike in his hand was a muscle-bound Marky Mark wannabe in a pair of Speedos and a New York Yankees hat. A bunch of women stood behind him like white slaves on auction. With all those soap bubbles around and the gold earring dangling from his left lobe, I thought for a moment they'd hired Mr. Clean to be our master of ceremonies.

"Anybody here from New Yawk?" he queried the crowd. Shouts and screams erupted in support of the Empire State.

"Yeah? Well, New Yawk can kiss my ass!" he said and whipped down his G-string, flashing his ridged ass at the crowd. The cannon shot a new load over the ecstatic dancers and I could see that Mort and I had our work cut out for us. To get any kind of story out of this trip, we'd have to find the heart of this beast. Something told me I'd have an easier time looking for Jimmy Hoffa, but that wasn't an option.

I stepped to the bar and ordered a couple of Coronas. The dance floor was like an episode of "Wild Kingdom," with the males standing around like packs of hyenas plotting the best way to mate with the females. Most opted for a kamikaze approach. They came up from behind and, without wasting time on conversation, grabbed an anonymous ass and waited for a reply. The women responded either by shrinking off towards their friends or throwing their hands in the air in a fit of Macarena-style ecstasy.

Mort kept pointing at a mousy little coed with a scarred face. It almost appeared as if she had spent the night before trying to bite her way through razor ribbon. She and her crew stood at the edge of the dance floor sipping pink slush from tall, hourglass-shaped steins or "yard" glasses.

Now a while ago, about a few thousand beers back, Mort had confided in me his affinity for scarred beauty—wounds, casts, stitches, etc. Apparently he'd read too many horror and gore comics during puberty, and cartoon violence had mixed itself into his burgeoning sexuality, creating fetishes that few, if any, shared.

"Judging by the color of the blood, it's a fresh injury," he observed.

"You can learn a lot about a society by studying its casualties," I said. "I think it's time we made a move."

We twisted up a joint and invited the girls to a dark corner for a smoke. Our weed must have made us attractive because they followed us enthusiastically. Cindy, Marcia, and Jan. They were all from the University of Georgia. Cindy, the wounded one, was an army brat, the last in a line of eight siblings. Just two months before Spring Break her parents committed her to a mental institution because she'd swallowed a whole bottle of aspirin after her boyfriend decided he wanted to take his Volkswagen bus on the road with the HORDE tour and subsequently moved himself out of her life.

"I was in love with him, and all he cared about was pot and Widespread Panic," she said as she accepted the joint from Mort's lecherous hand.

She came to Spring Break for a rest. She didn't count on falling in the pool and turning her face into something out of a Wes Craven movie. "The whole night started off wrong," she explained. "We missed the 'all-you-can-eat' Domino's Pizza buffet at Fat Tuesday's and then somebody puked on me on the dance floor." She wound up getting trashed on frozen hurricanes, going skinny-dipping at the hotel, and smashing her face on the steps of the pool.

"It doesn't look too bad," Cindy asked. "Don't you think?"

"I think the stitches complement your eyes," Mort commented.

She smiled like the stitches were just a minor setback and as soon as she got home her dad was going to pay Superman to fly around the world and turn time back to before the accident.

"Who wants to see some tits?" Mr. Clean shouted, bringing one of his women to the front of the stage. Just a few feet from our table the foam writhed and pulsed like a bacterial stew, accepting and spewing out life. From time to time the undergrads chanted, "Everybody get laid, get laid, get fucked."

"Youwannadance?" a thug said, sliding up next to Cindy.

"I wanna dance with him," she said and pointed to Mr. Clean as he lifted the T-shirt of a young woman whose father I'm sure had no idea what he was paying for. Cindy turned her back to her suitor, but he stuck his drunken head over her shoulders and said, "C'mon . . . I wanna fuck you." He really said it just like that and then Cindy pointed to Marcia and announced, "We're gay," and he slumped back towards the foam.

"I'd hate to think that this is all there is," Marcia said as she stared sardonically out at the crowd. Petite and blond, she was wearing a pair of Levi's overalls with dancing Grateful Dead bears across the front. Where Cindy came off as a little mixed-up but sweet, Marcia wanted the world to know that she was downright crazy. It was Marcia who instigated the skinny-dipping episode. She too had just ended a long relationship, and Spring Break was meant as a bit of revenge on her boyfriend. I felt sorry for the guy because she seemed like she really knew how to twist a knife. She was studying to be a grade-school teacher.

The song switched to "Brown-Eyed Girl" and Cindy jumped up. "We've *got* to dance to this one," she said and grabbed Marcia, leaving Jan with me and Mort. Jan was the only one of the pack that looked like she was having a bad time, so I assumed she was the only one with a brain. With her black dress and Misfits T-shirt, she looked like a hesitant Goth fan.

"What's your major?" Mort asked her.

"Spanish."

"Really? We're film students," Mort was quick to lie. We felt it was essential to remain undercover, lest we compromise our mission. "I go to SVA and he's at NYU."

We pressed her for details about her life and she told us reluctantly that she had no goals, no direction—I liked her.

When Cindy and Marcia returned, we made a tentative date for the Chichén Itzá tour the next day, and grabbed a cab back to the hotel.

We had a small room in the Hyatt Regency, overlooking the pool. From the easy chairs on our balcony we could see a huge crane sticking out of the center of town like a gallows. Every twenty minutes we'd watch a new bungee-jumper get lifted to the top and then pushed off into collegiate glory. Mort was watching a James Bond marathon on HBO, and as I poured drinks, he called out the names of the actors, screenwriters, and score arrangers.

"Those poolside bars are good 'cause you don't have to keep getting up to go the bathroom," Mort said as I handed him a glass of straight Mexican vodka.

"Do you think this godforsaken place has a heart?" I asked Mort.

"The heart is ambitious," he said. "You might be better off looking for a toe or a spleen."

In 1968, a Mexican tourism development agency had a computer calculate the best possible place to build a new resort town à la Acapulco. It decided on an undeveloped part of the Yucatán peninsula known as Quintana Roo. In an audacious act of political corruption, then-President Don Luis Echeverria Alvarez made a fortune helping his pals buy land in Cancún cheap and then sell it to international developers for a ludicrous markup. The first resort opened in 1974, and thanks to a few economic depressions and recessions which plunged many Mexicans into abject poverty, Cancún has remained an affordable vacation spot for international tourists. The dollar may not go far in Europe, but in Mexico it is treated with reverence.

Cancún might look like a cheap annex of Miami Beach, but there is history buried somewhere beneath those luxury hotels. Before President Echeverria and the tourists, before Cortés and his syphilis, there were others who came to this land in search of plunder and booty. They didn't wear baseball hats and their parents didn't pay their way, but their motivations were all the same.

The next morning as our bus rolled off towards Chichén Itzá, the once-great Mayan city now in ruins, Cindy said Mort and I both reminded her of her older brother who hadn't worked in years and was now in rehab and on Prozac. I was surprised the girls made it on time. Six A.M. was a mighty harsh wake-up call after a night of frozen margaritas. Standing at the front of the bus smoking a Cohiba Robusto, Fred ushered the Spring Breakers to their seats.

"Listen up, dudes," he said, taking the cigar from his mouth. "I thought you guys might want to know a little about the place we're visiting and the people who used to live there. During the classical period, roughly 250–900 A.D., the Maya were one of the most advanced peoples on earth, developing the only true written language in the Americas before the European colonists arrived, and making advances in mathematics and astronomy that the rest of the world didn't discover until the twentieth century. The Toltecs conquered the Itzá Maya, installing their own gods, and had their master architects rebuild Chichén Itzá in their image. The Toltecs brought the practice of human sacrifice to the Itzá as well."

"Do you believe in God?" Marcia whispered to me, handing me a Bloody Mary. She'd brought all the fixin's from home—Clamato, horse-radish, Worcestershire, celery salt. Marcia had class where the other Spring Breakers only had money.

"I like to think there's someone to blame," I said.

"I blame my parents," Jan said, sipping her drink.

"As well you should," I laughed, and we toasted.

"Can I come and watch your stitches get taken out?" Mort asked Cindy as he stirred his wake-up drink. It was good to see him in such top form this early.

I sat next to a kid named Ray, or "Ray-Ray" as his friends called him. I recognized him as being the spud in the "Weedies" shirt from the bus the day before. Ray-Ray had brought a whole arsenal of weed, coke, acid, and Prozac with him to Cancún. He insisted on calling me "Chrissy-Ray" and Mort "Morty-Ray" and kept saying, "Show me the money," to everything I said.

"You kinda remind me of Kramer," Ray-Ray told me as he washed a Valium down with a Dos Equis. "You know, from 'Seinfeld'? It's a show about nothin', ya gotta love it."

Fred, meanwhile, paced the aisle, flashing his Pepsi smile to any female who looked his way. He was like a slacker hybrid of Robert Chambers and JFK.

"Fred is it," I told Mort excitedly. "Fred is the heart. He's clean-cut, historically aware, politically informed—"

"The heart? You think? Looks more like the uvula," Mort cracked.

Marcia snagged Fred's attention with a smile and then offered him a Bloody Mary, which he declined, though he did sit with us for most of the trip. He told me he was taking a year off from the University of Florida. He was studying business and was now having second thoughts about his major.

"I'm worried about the environment," he explained. "I want to make a difference."

By the time we got to the ruins, the whole bus was pretty twisted. Our Indian tour guide was beside himself with boredom as he rattled on about the achievements of the Maya to a bunch of white people who couldn't have cared less.

It occurred to me that we were simply carrying on an ancient tradition in the Yucatán—the systematic rape of the natives. Each people who conquered this region brought with them their own religions, customs, and gods. There we all were covered in our Budweiser logos and pictures of Mickey Mouse, waiting to party in the remains of other people's misfortunes, before heading back to Daddy Rocks for the wet T-shirt night.

The guide led us to a huge ball court—545 feet long—where some believed games were played between neighboring city-states as a substitute for war. Oddly enough, the winner had the honor of being sacrificed to the gods.

I was trying to listen to the tour guide, but Ray-Ray kept yelling, "Show me the money" to the guy. What money? What the fuck was he talking about? When we approached the great Pyramid of Kukulcán, the plumed serpent the Mayans believed bestowed them with their advanced knowledge, Ray-Ray started saying, "I'm cuckoo for Kukulcán" over and over again until the guide asked him to stop.

"You're embarrassing me in front of the gods," I growled, but really I didn't give a shit. I had no more respect for Kukulcán than I did for any other god that sat up in the sky and watched us burn. On the other hand, I had no time for people who couldn't hold their booze.

On the way back to Cancún I had a fantastic déjà vu. I somehow got separated from Mort and the girls, and by the time I got to the bus, the only seat left was next to Ray-Ray. I watched him play quarters with Fred and the two of them had a soul-searching talk about the relative merits of Meatloaf and Bruce Springsteen. I was bored, I was fucked up, I was hanging out with people I didn't like. I finally felt like I was back in college.

The week was passing by in a blur of lousy beer and dull conversation. I decided it was time to up the ante. I was ready to eat the acid on the ride over—I thought it might have been a good test of our courage, to sweat it out there on the plane with our newfound peers, their faces exploding into geometrical shapes—but Mort thought it was best to wait for the bullfight.

The plan was to cram as much activity into our last night in Cancún as possible. We'd chew the blotter, check out the bullfight, have one last dip in the ocean, catch Fat Tuesday's St. Paddy's Day chugathon, and then sleep on the airplane home.

At first I was wary about giving LSD to the girls. I had a vision of Cindy screaming into the mirror and pulling her stitches out with a coat hanger, but she ate it and I couldn't even tell she was high. In the cab to the bullfight she blabbed on about the Mayans and UFOs and God and the millennium, attaching a lysergic significance to it all.

"You can't tell me that, in all that space, we are alone," she said, convinced. "And even if there's not actually aliens, then there are spirits. Contact is going to change *everything*."

The building was downtown, a short ride from the hotel strip. It was just like it looks in the cartoons—a large, sunny coliseum with a mariachi band playing "La Cucaracha" in the bleachers over the bullpen. Jan and I sat down on a stretch of concrete and ordered beers from a vendor. Mort sat in front of us with Cindy. (Marcia, so hung over she couldn't get out of bed, had to miss this one.)

I could feel the acid coming on. The clouds swirled above me like happy ghosts. I kept grinding my teeth and staring intently at an old Mexican woman sitting next to me in a white dress. She held a yellow umbrella between herself and the sun and watched the show with a smile. A group of traditional Mexican dancers came out and spun around with bottles on their heads.

"They're gonna kill the bull, right?" Jan asked.

"I don't know," I said. My stomach felt like plastic. "I hope not."

Fred saw us from across the arena and gave us the thumbs up.

The band kicked into an unfamiliar Latin favorite and a skinny bull with scars on his back entered the ring. I was expecting the bull to rush out the way they do in the cartoons, but he just trotted out and stared at the crowd as if wondering why the hell there were so many people there in his living room. With all the cuts on his back, the bull looked more like a sparring partner than a contender. My guess was he'd had a whole lot of matches prior to this date where he'd come out and gone through the motions for the simple reason that he knew he was going to eat dinner as soon as they were through.

The bull made a few passes and then looked up at the matador as if to say, Is that enough? A swipe of the sword told him it wasn't, and he made a few more well-trained runs, blood now running down his side.

"I got into *such* a fight with Marcia last night," Cindy said as her eyes lazily followed the bull around the court. The matador had his cape out and the bull took a few more halfhearted leaps at it. "It's like . . . all she can think about is herself, you know?"

"Oh God, she gets so drunk," Jan said. "It's like she's not even there. You can't talk to her—remember New Year's Eve?"

"I almost stabbed her on New Year's," said Cindy. "I swear I had the knife right in my hand. We were going to this party and she just wouldn't leave the dorm. She was screaming at her boyfriend because she didn't like the shirt he was wearing. Then, she started screaming at *me*—"

Without warning, the matador stuck a sword into the bull's back. It went in smooth like it was a hunk of warm butter. Blood started spurting out in rhythm with the beat of its own doomed heart. Cindy glanced down for a moment, then continued.

"Anyway, last night she was sooooo drunk. She was naked when we came home and she said she didn't remember taking her clothes off. That's what she said at first, but then she remembered most of it and started telling me. She said Fred and Barney had helped her home. We saw the three of them necking on the dance floor at Señor Frogs. I tried to get her to cool out and that's when she started acting crazy and I thought we were going to fight. I was like, fine, bitch, what*ever*. They played Truth or Dare and they dared her to take her shirt off."

I was on acid. I wanted her to shut up. I watched as the matador poked the bull until it dripped like a blood piñata. There was a drunk in front of us wearing one of those baseball hats with straws that you can screw beers into, and a shirt that said "Corona Beach Club—We're just better than you." He waved his fists and screamed incoherently.

"Kill the human!" I shouted in encouragement, but my voice was drowned out by the lustful screams of the other Spring Breakers. It would have been hard enough to watch this spectacle sober, but with a head full of acid it was like they were carving up Lassie. The matador again stuck his sword in, this time deep, delivering the fatal blow, and the stadium vibrated with applause. After the bull fell over, the matador cut its ear off and the band kicked into a tune I recognized as "It's a Small World After All." We all started laughing.

As they dragged the bull off the killing field, people started filing towards the exit. Mort mimicked, "Abe-abe-abe—That's all, folks!" as I tried to navigate my way through the acid to my feet. The wind kicked up, lifting dust and sand and Styrofoam cups into the air.

We met Fred outside the bullring and he said we should go around the back and get our pictures taken with the matador. We walked around the side and there was a crowd of people gathered around a Ford pickup truck.

"Check it out!" Fred said and quickened his pace. We followed.

The bull was hung on hooks above the Ford. The arteries were emptying out from the holes in his back, covering his head in blood which formed a pool in the bed of the truck. The bull was too big for the Ford, and a bunch of Mexicans in dirty Marlboro hats were trying to find a solution. The five of us joined a crowd of about thirty tourists and Spring Breakers gathered around the truck staring at the corpse. There was another crowd near the entrance of the stadium waiting to mug it up with the matador.

"This is a little gross," Cindy said as a man climbed into the truck and started sawing off the bull's legs. "I'm gonna go get my picture taken."

Cindy skipped off toward the bloody matador and I stayed with Jan, Fred, and Mort, watching the carnage. Looking around at the crowd of kids unable to hide their smiles, I realized I understood a little bit more about the Toltecs than I wanted to. The man sawed for a good two minutes before the last piece of shin cracked like a chicken bone and the bull toppled neatly into the truck.

"Looks like bull burgers tonight," Fred said with a naïve laugh. "I think they're gonna cut its balls off."

We split a cab back to the hotel—Mort, Fred, Cindy, Jan, and me. We were crammed in pretty tight as the driver steered wildly back to the hotel, bouncing us back and forth off the doors of the cab. It was about six o'clock and a strong wind was bending the palm trees.

"What did you think?" Cindy asked, handing me a pipe full of Mexican brown. She looked so young I couldn't believe that she was graduating college.

"The Mayans were right," I said. "We should kill all the winners."

"Maybe send them for a cordless bungee-jump," Mort cracked and Fred laughed.

"What did you think?" I asked Jan.

"What do you mean?"

"Did you like the bullfight?"

"Uh-huh."

"Why?"

"Well, on TV it's only ketchup."

Cindy agreed and started talking about a tattoo she wanted to get.

I had a plane to catch in a few hours, and after the bullfight, all I wanted to do was float around in the ocean for a while, enjoy the rest of the acid, and forget about the future of my people. These kids were bungee-jumping into the millennium, mistaking their head spins for visions. We're doomed, I figured; no reason to dwell on that fact. Back at the room, Mort and I packed our bags and then ate a few Vitamin C tablets in an effort to wake up whatever LSD was still in our system.

As we walked down to the beach, Mort and I spotted about fifteen different iguanas sitting on the rocks, some small enough to hold in your hand and others as big as standard poodles. They stared blankly out at the sea in reptilian contemplation.

"What are you waiting for?" Mort asked them. "If it hasn't happened in 25,000 years, it ain't gonna. Why don't you guys grow yourself a thumb or something?"

We walked over to the surf and I dived in. I was still tripping and I floated on my back. Above me hung the blue wonder of the sky with its clouds drifting past like smoke left over from the Big Bang. I could hear Mort splashing around, enjoying himself as the horizon turned from blue to orange, announcing the arrival of another Caribbean night. I started jumping around, diving beneath the waves, and body surfing.

"Can't get this in New York," Mort yelled.

"Sure can't," I told him.

"Watch out for the sharks," he said.

"If they got me now, I could at least say I won."

Mort started to sing.

"The record shows, I took the blows—and except for those few months at the A&P in '82—I did it myyy wayyyyy . . . "

I laughed and then I heard a scream. Then I heard somebody calling my name. "Chris!" I distinctly heard it but, hey, there are a lot of Chrises in this world. I heard it again, and when I looked over I saw Mort frantically waving me to shore.

I went over. He was lying in the sand, moaning in agony. His hand trembled as he held out his foot to me.

"What do you think?" he asked in a panicked voice.

It looked like something out of *Alien.* There were several swollen puncture marks placed symmetrically around his foot. He must've stepped on a sea urchin the size of a Heisman Trophy. He was writhing in pain and I started saying things like, "Don't worry, you're gonna be all right," but really I thought he was going to die. Whatever stung him was poisonous enough to survive on this planet unchanged since the beginning of time. What the hell was I supposed to do?

He made it to his feet and together we started hobbling towards the front desk of the hotel. The guy there looked like he sympathized with our situation, but the doctor had left hours ago. He asked if he should call an ambulance.

"No," Mort groaned.

"What do you mean?" I asked him. "These things can kill you, or didn't you see *The Blue Lagoon?*"

"We gotta . . . we gotta . . . the chugathon . . . I can make it—" He screamed as the urchin's primordial poisons absorbed deeper into his body. Again, this was an instance where the acid wasn't helping things any. "We gotta . . . we gotta . . . a . . . a . . . story to do . . . AHHHHHHHH—" I was impressed by his valor. He looked like Captain Kirk waving the *Enterprise* on while he died with the Gorns. Still, I saw through his act.

"You just want to see Cindy again, don't you?" I finally figured it out. This was all about her. "You don't give a shit about the story, you just want to see damaged flesh." His eyes rolled back into his head. He wasn't listening.

Almost on cue, the girls walked out of the elevator. They ran up to us.

"Smile," Marcia said and snapped a picture. Mort growled and they stepped back a bit.

"What happened?" Cindy asked.

"S-s-sea u-urchin . . . " Mort said. She looked down at the moonscape on his foot, and then back at him. No words were uttered, but I could hear what they were saying. For a moment it was as if they were speaking to each other out of their wounds. *What becomes of our relationship now that we're both scarred?* The question lingered, then Cindy said, "We're going to the chugathon." With that, they turned and walked towards the exit. They didn't want anything to do with us now that we were cripples. Couldn't they see we were cripples all along?

"We're leaving," I said, and heard a chorus of "Good-byes" from the backs of their heads.

"Hey, what do you want me to say about your generation?" I yelled out.

"Just say it sucks," Jan said, and they all laughed.

I got Mort back up to the room and threw a blanket on him. *The Man Who Saw Tomorrow*, the Nostradamus story with Orson Welles, was on HBO. It was an old film, and according to Welles the world was going to end in 1987. Here it was 10 years later and from what I could see we weren't going anywhere.

"L-look, th-th-they're using f-f-footage fr-from *Earthquake* for the a-a-apocalypse scene . . . " he said before unleashing a vicious howl. I walked out to the balcony to get a break from his screams.

A few knuckleheads two floors below us were indulging in the forbidden art of balcony-jumping. As I looked down, one of them was standing on the rail, holding on to the wall for balance. He stared up at me and drunkenly screamed, "FFFFFFFFUUUUCK YOUUUUU!" I had to wonder what his motivation was.

Ray-Ray was standing next to him saying, "C'mon, man, don't yell at him, just do it."

"FFFFFUUUUUCK YOUUUUU!" he screamed again like a crackhead. He was three floors up, readying himself for a death-defying feat, the

only virtue of which was its meaninglessness. He was evil, dark—like
somehow Satan managed to squeeze just enough pus up from the bowels
of hell to penetrate the terra firma in the form of a fat kid with a baseball
hat.

"Just do it," Ray-Ray said. And he did.

Our cab to the airport came sooner than the "fuck you" guy's ambulance.
Mort's foot was too big to fit a shoe on, so I just wrapped it in a towel and
laid him down in the back seat. A crowd had formed around the "fuck you"
guy, who lay prostrate on the concrete in front of the hotel.

"I didn't know legs could bend like that," our driver remarked.

"They can't," I said, and we shared a laugh as we drove off into the
night.

By this time, Mort's shrill screams had given way to a low, dull moan.
I was convinced he wasn't going to die, so I turned my mind back to the
story.

What story?

The word "story" implies that something happened. That wasn't the
case here. Just as "Seinfeld" was a show about nothing, this was a generation about nothing—the bastard child of my own denuded generation,
which was about next to nothing. As our cab drove through Cancún and I
got my final look at the corporate strip, I just hoped that when the little
bastards grew up, they'd stay the hell away from my life. I doubted that
they would, but I had to dream.

Our car drove out of the city and into the mossy grasslands, over sand
that had been soaked and resoaked with native blood over the past few
thousand years. I wondered what the ghosts of the Maya were saying to
each other as they watched from their ethereal portholes as we turned
their homeland into a vacation paradise. My guess was they were doing the
same thing I would in their situation—kicking back with their peace
pipes, putting their feet up on their cosmic coffee table, and saying, "Enjoy
it while it lasts, gringo, 'cuz you can't take it with you."

13

Rastafari Now: Haile Selassie's Earthday and the Knights of the Nyabinghi

By this point in my journalistic career, I had an agent, a publisher, two lawyers, and an accountant. I didn't have any money, but these people were perfectly happy to handle my dust. I also had a few drug dealers who I spoke to regularly, and a serious drinking problem. There was no way around it—in four short years I had become a narco-yuppie.

I was getting sick of drugs. I didn't stop doing them, I was just tired of talking about them. I only ever saw drugs the way everybody, from my guidance counselors to my parents to the people who sent me hate mail at *High Times* said I shouldn't—as a crutch, as a way to get from one end of the evening to the other without falling asleep from boredom. Anytime I tried to use them for something else—writing, fucking, thinking, driving—they failed me eight times out of ten, and I figured that was a batting average I could maintain without assistance from anything.

When I got back from Spring Break I started thinking about all the things I'd written about and realized that, for the most part, I had been visiting places and attending events that only confirmed my worst fears as true. After a while I started laughing when people's eyes got wide and they told me, "Man, you got the greatest job in the world!" I'd look at them and think, What are you talking about? I'm a gravedigger.

They all saw glamour in my life. What was so glamorous? Hanging out backstage at rock concerts? It made me want to tear the veins out of my arms with my teeth. Name-droppers and industry jerks ready to eat each other over guest lists and drink tickets, and performers who would never remember your name or your face and who probably dreaded having to talk to you at all. I liked the cheap/horny/Mrs. Robinson/divorcée chic of airport bars and Holiday Inns, but outside of that I was running around trying to get people to talk to me about dope. Who wanted to talk to strangers about anything, much less what drugs they did?

I never felt as if I did anything that any other idiot couldn't do himself. It wasn't like I spent my afternoons lying on a beach in Nice snorting heroin with the Stones. I wasn't out there fucking supermodels. I hardly got laid at all. Where was the glamour in that?

At the same time I was reevaluating my career, I was listening to a lot of reggae. It was the only music that pacified me anymore. Since my first visit to Jamaica a year and a half before, all I had to do was hear an old Don Drummond song and suddenly I was back on that green hill in Nine Miles looking out at the farms and the clouds. It was the first music that had saved my life since the Black Flag days, and after a while I not only wanted but *needed* to get back to Jamaica.

I'd kept in regular contact with Brian Jahn, and for months he'd come to my office and we'd try and find some angle that would get us back to the island. A story came through to the *High Times* Buzz section about a Rasta demonstration in Kingston on the 100th anniversary of Ethiopia's victory over Rome in the Battle of Adwa. Organized by the Rastafari Centralization Organization (RCO), celebrity participants included Mutabaruka, Yami Bolo, and Bunny Wailer. It was the largest demonstration for the legalization of herb in Jamaican history, and that provided the hook we needed to pitch a story that took us back. We didn't just want to write about pot, but about the whole Rasta culture. We wanted to immerse ourselves as deep as possible in the Rasta way of life.

At the next editorial meeting, Brian and I proposed an extensive article that would cover the current state of the Rasta movement and its efforts to legalize herb, a visit to a Rasta sacred ceremony known as the Nyabinghi, and, as the clincher, an interview with the reclusive Bunny Wailer on . . . well, whatever Bunny wanted to talk about. I also promised to get a picture of Bunny suitable for the cover of *High Times*, an iconic image that would make the kids at the newsstand want to pay for the issue twice. By this time I'd learned the game—promise money and you start making all kinds of new friends around the office. The editors were surprised, if not impressed, by our detailed pitch and we planned to build a special issue of *High Times* around the mysterious Rastafari brotherhood.

After landing in Jamaica, the first bit of business Brian and I went to take care of, once we dropped our bags off at Chinna's house, was scoring. We needed a few pounds to photograph for the centerfold and then to pass around to the brethren at Chinna's. Not that we needed to bribe anybody around Chinna's, but it was always fun to see the smile on a Rasta's face when you put a shopping bag full of herb on the table.

Our connection was Tex, a half-Jamaican, half-Chinese gangster who hung out in an alley between a bank and a Kentucky Fried Chicken in New Kingston, the city's commercial district. Along with his small crew of street kids and ragamuffins, Tex sold ganja and "protection" to whatever local tourists were brave enough to wander outside the barbed-wire security of their four-star hotels. You want to see a lush, green Jamaican herb field?

Talk to Tex. You want to party in the ghetto with Uzi-toting gangsters? Tex was your guide. You want to change money? Wipe your enemies off the face of the earth? Tex made things happen.

As our cab approached the Kentucky Fried Chicken, we could see Tex and his crew hiding from the yellow glow of the street lamp beneath a small tree. It was late, but they were still hanging out. When Tex saw us climbing out of the cab, he let out a chesty laugh that was at once sincere and calculated. His laugh was like a status report, a moment-by-moment evaluation of the scene. When Tex didn't laugh, people got scared.

"You're back, Brian! Ha haaaa!" His laugh pinched off into a squeal, and we knocked fists with the crew in respect. We told Tex what we wanted, and he said it would take a day, but he was pretty sure he could help us. For now, he said we could sample some of his "private stock."

"Rottweiler!" Tex called out to a youth no older than twelve, wearing only a pair of sweat pants with an ice pick stuck in the waistline. Rottweiler handed over a bag of herb and Tex told us to help ourselves. "Today Rottweiler beat up Leroy Smart!" Tex said. "Ha ha! Five men looking for him!"

"Why are you picking on Leroy Smart?" I asked him.

"He vex me up," Rottweiler said, and then asked me for change.

"Why you here now?" Tex asked us. "What you working on?"

We told him about the Rastafari Centralization Organization and their efforts to legalize the herb.

"The people who cut down the ganja are devils! Devils!" he sneered and then spat at the ground. "If you dance, you are a dancer. If you pick up the garbage, you are a garbage man. If you do the devil's work, you are the devil." Arch criminal that he was, Tex had a way of convincing you that his was the voice of righteousness in a world of thieves.

As I puffed my spliff and stared out at the empty street, I felt that strange hybrid of relaxation and paranoia that I remembered from the last time I was in Kingston. The place never left me totally at ease. When I mentioned to the crew that I was trying to get in touch with Bunny Wailer, I was suddenly surrounded by six kids who told me they'd find him for me, and that I should make a "contract" right there for them to be my driver and personal bodyguard until I left the island, and perhaps even beyond that.

"I am true ragamuffin!" said Razor, a kid of fifteen with two dozen machete-chop scars covering him. "I find you Bunny Wailer," he promised, hoisting his ice pick in the air.

"I don't want his head on a stick, I just wanna talk to the guy."

Razor smiled as if to say, What's the difference?

Brian and I hung out for another hour and a half, smoking joints, de-clining offers and illicit favors from the crew, and listening to Tex's stories about being shot and stabbed. He told us how someone once macheted his hand off, rolling up his sleeve so we could see where they sewed it back on crooked. All that violence to finally gain control over an alley littered with crushed soda cans and broken glass. Tex's story was a microcosm of Jamaica's own—the bloody struggle for the control of debris.

Despite our protests, Razor insisted on driving us home that evening. I was no expert in Jamaican etiquette, but I knew that, by allowing him to do this, we were agreeing to let him sucker us for the rest of the trip. That was the "contract."

So I wasn't surprised when I woke up the next morning and found Razor waiting for us in Chinna's driveway.

"Brian . . . we're partners," he said. "We made a deal. I look out for you. I take you anywhere you want—you want women, cocaine, anything. Nobody mess with you if you have me . . . "

Brian had more patience in these situations than I did, so I let him deal with it. After much negotiating, he gave Razor two hundred Jamaican (about six dollars U.S.), which he begrudgingly accepted and drove away.

The morning began with the usual phone calls that led nowhere and accomplished nothing. Bunny Wailer was a long shot and we knew it. Back in New York, Brian and I kind of led on that we were old friends with Bunny, that all we had to do was call him once we got to the island, and he'd tell us anything we needed to know about herb, Bob Marley, or Rasta-fari, and then toss us the keys to his Lexus to use for the rest of the week.

Reality was a bit different. Bunny was a virtual recluse. In the Wail-ers, Bob Marley was the superstar, Peter Tosh was the radical, and Bunny was the enigma, a reputation he still upheld. This was a man who quit the Wailers because he didn't want to fly in planes, a man who stood up a headlining gig at Madison Square Garden. He was the last living Wailer and in Jamaica that's like being the last living Beatle. It was clear from the start—if we wanted him to talk into our tape recorders, we would have to find him first. We called around to his manager, his band members, and even a few old friends, but nobody knew where he was. We anticipated that, and instead moved on to Plan B: speak to the Rastafari Centraliza-tion Organization, the new activist arm of the Rastafari brotherhood.

Since Bunny Wailer was a strong supporter of the RCO, we thought they might be able to talk to him for us, and through them we also hoped to gain entrance into the Nyabinghi that was being held all that week in celebration of Haile Selassie's birthday on July 23. The Nyabinghi was the Rasta equivalent to Christmas, and was off-limits to journalists except by permission. Basically, we figured, if we were down with the RCO, we were down with everybody. Our only problem was we didn't know who or where they were.

Brian knew that reggae singer/poet Mutabaruka was also connected to the RCO, and that he could usually be found in a little bookstore he ran downtown. Sidney, one of Chinna's brethren and former percussion player for Jimmy Cliff and Ras Michael, offered to give us a ride downtown, and we split. As we drove through Half-Way Tree to downtown, Sidney told us he wasn't busy that week and if we wanted, he'd be our guide. Brian and I accepted immediately. A good-natured, unarmed Rasta like Sidney was better company than an ice-pick–wielding psycho like Razor.

As we cruised deeper into Kingston, past the familiar shantytowns whose wood and zinc shacks were lit unforgivingly by the volcanic afternoon sun, Sidney told us it was election time again, and the streets were less safe than usual. Since our last trip, Massive Dread had been shot and killed in Trench Town by a neighboring gang, giving the city a doomed new look for me. From "JLP Territory" to "PNP Zone" and back to "JLP Forever," the allegiance of each ghetto was spraypainted on the stone walls that surrounded each neighboring section. At one point the traffic slowed and a little kid who looked about ten walked up to the cab with his fingers shaped like a gun. "White man," he said and fired an imaginary bullet into my head. We drove on.

A young dreaded woman at the bookstore told us Muta wouldn't be back for another hour. As we browsed through the small selection of Rastafari and Black Power literature, I came across a curious pamphlet with the headline: "Secret Society to Destroy Whites Reported to Be Existing with Headquarters in Ethiopia: Nya-binghi, Its Origin." It was printed in Rasta colors with a picture of Haile Selassie on the front.

This, I later found out, was a reprint of the original racist propaganda article, written by an anti-Ethiopia Italian propagandist in 1935, that unintentionally spawned the Nyabinghi movement in Jamaica. It goes on to report that a secret conference of eighty-two African leaders convened in 1930 in Moscow to address the problem of European colonialism. There, Haile Selassie was crowned "King of the Nyabinghi," whose mission it was to defend black supremacy in Africa. It talked of attacks that had already been made against the Ku Klux Klan, claiming that leaders of that organization across America had been stricken with a mysterious, fatal disease. It also spoke of a "black avalanche" that would soon eclipse European rule if something wasn't done soon to stop the nya-men. Strength, roots, and organization—the early Rastas liked what they read way back in the thirties, and have since considered themselves the inheritors of the Nyabinghi legacy. Whether the original article was real or mythical is unimportant.

Since then "Nyabinghi" has come to mean "Death to black and white oppressors" in Jamaica.

I paid for the pamphlet, and then, since we had time to kill, we rode over to see if Tex had gotten our herb together. He hadn't, but again invited us to dip into his personal stash. Seeing Sidney, Razor demanded to know what our relationship with him was.

"We made a contract, Brian!"

"Uh . . . no, we didn't."

Razor went on like a jilted lover and before he could reach for his trusted shank, we beat it back to the bookstore where we found Muta sitting calm and sage-like behind the counter, a small triangular patch of gray hair in the dreads above his forehead giving him an aura of royalty. When we asked him about the RCO, he scratched us out a little map of downtown Kingston with directions to the organization's headquarters. We thanked him, he wished us luck, and after two days in Jamaica, we finally began the business of dope journalism.

As we followed Muta's map down a couple short blocks, the streets narrowed until we arrived at a little storefront with "Black Power" spray-painted above the door. A sign outside read: "Rastafari Nation on the Move."

Brian went inside and I watched him talk to an older Rasta until they both waved me in. Sidney told us he'd meet us back at Chinna's, and drove off.

"We've been waiting for you!" Ras DaSilva said and smiled. We knocked fists, and he told us that the RCO had been in existence for over a year, but we were the first journalists to come and speak with him in person. The headquarters was a very small room, big enough to fit seven or eight people, with signs covering the walls announcing marches and meetings. DaSilva introduced us to Ras Campbell, the organization's secretary, who asked me, "Have you ever read *The Emperor Wears No Clothes?*"

"Sure," I said.

"In it it says that the brain has certain receptors only for THC! What does that tell you?"

"That Jah must want us to smoke herb," I said.

"You know it, mon!"

DaSilva pulled out some newspaper clippings from a manila envelope, and passed me their formal resolution, addressed to Jamaica's Prime Minister P.J. Patterson:

"Be it therefore resolved that the Rastafari Community, under the leadership of H.I.M. Haile Selassie I and under the banner of the RCO, calls upon the government to make a provision within the Constitutional Reform which will ensure the rights of the Rastafari Community to their

Religious Culture and Political Activities . . . Therefore, we call upon the Government of Jamaica to legalize our Sacred Sacrament—the HERB [ganja] for spiritual/religious, recreational, industrial, medicinal, and economic purposes for the development of our nation."

When I asked what inspired them to form the organization, Ras DaSilva explained how, in 1961, a special delegation of Jamaican Rastafari met with Emperor Selassie in Ethiopia to discuss the possible repatriation of Jamaican blacks. The Emperor commanded them to "organize and centralize" the Rastafari nation before seeking repatriation. It was in compliance with this command that, thirty-four years later in 1995, the RCO was created.

Their first objective was the "total unification of the Rastafari movement, both nationally and internationally," explained Ras DaSilva. Only after that was completed could they begin working towards the ultimate goal of repatriation back to Ethiopia. "In order for I and I to get deliverance, I and I must have proper representation, and it is up to I and I to organize ourselves so we can be one voice for all."

The number two item on their agenda was the legalization of herb, and they were discussing the issue with representatives of the country's political parties—JLP, PNP, and the New Democratic movement. DaSilva also mentioned that there was talk of the economic promise that the cultivation of industrial hemp could bring, but Rastas had a real problem with the "low THC" concept.

"How are you going to take the THC out of the plant?" Ras Campbell asked me, his forehead wrinkled in confusion. "Why would you *want* to take the THC out of the plant?"

"You're asking me?"

When I asked about the possibility of interviewing the two of them, they told me to come back in a day or two, when they had more time. DaSilva also told us he'd speak to Bunny. They were old friends and he felt confident he could make something happen for us.

As we walked outside the RCO office to take some pictures of the two Rasses in front of the shop, an army Jeep filled with soldiers carrying M-16s drove by like a float in a parade celebrating human misery. Listening to the enlightened talk of the RCO, I had almost forgotten where I was. We thanked the Rasses and promised to check back in a day or two, then headed back to Chinna's.

The next few days passed by in a blur of ganja smoke and unproductive phone calls. We couldn't find Bunny, Tex couldn't find our weed—there was nothing left to do but sit around Chinna's eating mangos and watching TV. Chinna was out of town, on tour with Ziggy Marley, and had left his housekeeper Bigga in charge. Bigga grew up with Chinna in Greenwich Town, one of the ghettos in Kingston. Bigga was a large Rasta with medium-length dreads, and he spoke with a heavy patois. Brian and I both agreed it would be easier to give Bigga some money to cop us some herb, rather than show up again and again at Tex's corner with Razor giving us ice-pick stares.

Bigga left with thirty dollars American and came back two hours later with a half pound of medium-grade herb. The three of us sat out on Chinna's porch, and Bigga gave Brian and me a lesson in chalice smoking. The chalice is the Rastaman's sacred ganja water pipe, and smoking from it is an act of holy communion, a physical concourse between man and Jah. I watched Bigga chop up the herb with a knife, mixing it with an equal amount of tobacco.

"Why tobacco?" I asked.

"Ta' back up the herb," he said. He took the chalice—this one constructed from a steer's horn which had been sealed off at one end, with a clay bowl and rubber hose for smoking added to it—thanked Almighty Jah for these gifts of life, herb, and good company, and then instructed Brian to light him up. He took a deep hit and put his head down in reverence. When he exhaled, the smoke drifted up through his dreads.

"Selassie I!" he rejoiced, and then handed the chalice to Brian. Brian knocked back a medium-sized hit, sans benediction, and then handed the pipe over to me. I sucked back a few baby-sized hits and then coughed for two minutes straight.

"No more for me—I'm driving," I said, and handed it back to the now hysterically laughing Bigga.

Rasta Now: Chinna (behind smoke) licking chalice in Trench Town. (Brian Jahn)

Now that we were properly lifted, we went through our growing list of phone numbers in search of Bunny. He'd become our holy grail by this point, and I knew if I came back without an interview, the magazine would bust me down to copy editor and I'd spend the rest of my journalistic career fetching coffee for Peter Gorman.

Sidney came by and, seeing the dejected looks on our faces, offered to drive us by Bunny's house.

"Isn't that . . . rude?" I asked him.

"No, mon—jus' show 'im de magazine. Him not live far at all . . . "

I was a bit nervous about busting in on a superstar in his home, but even more aghast at the prospect of never being given an expense account again, so I agreed.

Bunny's house was only twenty minutes away from Chinna's, making me wonder what kind of journalist I was that I never thought to drive past and see if the man might just be outside mowing his lawn. Sidney drove us through an area that looked like Watts, with its single-floor ranch houses with iron gates over their windows. When we turned the corner of Bunny's block, I saw an almost militarized-looking complex surrounded by ten-foot concrete walls covered with barbed wire and protective statues of the Lion of Judah at all four corners. Considering the assassination attempt on Bob Marley and the murder of Peter Tosh, I still wondered if this was enough to keep the vampires out.

When we got there, Bunny was sitting on his porch, smoking a spliff the size of a carrot and talking with six or seven Rastas. I've never been trained in the etiquette of harassing legends in their home, so I just walked up to the gate, stuck a copy of the magazine through the bars, and shook it a little. Bunny sent one of his brethren to see who was bothering him. We handed the messenger the magazine, and waited to see if we'd be granted an interview, or if we would have to run back to the car dodging machine-gun bullets. Bunny examined the magazine cryptically, not even opening it, just looking at the picture of Bob Marley on the cover, and then sent the Rasta to let us in.

Bunny greeted us warmly, remembering Brian from an interview he did with him for his book *Reggae Island.* The brethren dispersed, and Brian and I sat alone with Bunny on his porch, each party slowly acclimating themselves to the others' presence. Bunny continued smoking his spliff until he decided it was time for him to talk. Bunny liked to talk. I don't think he liked to answer specific questions, but he was pleased to tell us what was on his mind at that particular juncture of time and space. That subject, lucky for us dope journalists, was herb.

"Before the first slave was enslaved," Bunny began slowly, hitting his spliff for added inspiration, "man used to smoke his peace pipe. Herbs is everything planted by seed. So why concentrate on one herb when there are so many other herbs? Why make one illegal? Why make one brother the sinner? We still await that liberal day where we can burn our spliff without worrying about being penalized and thrown in the dungeons.

"Herb still is what it has been through the ages. Natural seeds you put in the earth, water it, grows in the sun and wind and rain, and the power of the sustenance of life that was injected in billions of ages ago still is there. It is not something you can add to, although you could take from it, yeah. Not like man's machines who have not yet seen a pea grain come out one of those machines. We don't see all these seeds . . . what you call it? Cyber-herbs! Cyber-herb! We don't see any natural seeds coming out of those machines . . . "

Bunny stopped for a moment and let out a slow, staccato chuckle. Bunny took his time with everything he did, and laughing was no exception. "Heh-heh-heh . . . they've attempted, you know . . . Machines are made by man. Man was given choices. If you think right, and invent right, it's all about you. Everything would be all right, but if you fool around thinking wrong things and inventing wrong things you will hurt yourself, and until you stop doing that you are going to keep hurting yourself. It is going to be a continuous hurt on the earth."

"How was the Rastafari Centralization Organization formed?" I asked him. "How did you get involved with them?"

"Rastafari himself, Haile Selassie I, tell us that we should motivate ourselves as a people to centralize and organize at home and abroad. So we are like the ant and we practice ant-ology, so that the Rastaman within his revolution will develop the stages necessary to obey Rastafari's word of centralizing, organizing within the unification of the Rasses. It's a command of Jah Rastafari."

"We've been hearing a lot about the Nyabinghi," I said, "but nobody has told us exactly what it is . . . "

"The Nyabinghi is the order," he replied. "So the trumpet sounds from the Nyabinghi, because Nyabinghi is first, then reggae comes out of the Nyabinghi and it brings nations together. That is what made reggae and will ever be reggae, it comes for all nations. It brings everybody together and though sometimes the message is hard, it doesn't hurt."

Bunny smiled. That was a good enough explanation for him, obviously. I decided to shift the conversation back to marijuana.

"Why do you think people are afraid to legalize herb?"

"It is reasons," he said. "You see, most things have to have reasons. They did not have any reasons in the first place to penalize people for it, so it is hard to find a reason for them to legalize it.

"Bill Clinton claim he didn't inhale, who is there to say he didn't? These leaders I think they sit down in their offices too much. They don't go amongst the people, eat out of the pots they eat of, smoke out of their pipes, sit on the corner, talk, reason, fall asleep. You could fall asleep on the bench and wake up and the people are there with you. They need that. They are afraid of the same people that put them there. Humpty Dumpty sat on a wall . . . he became an egg, he stayed away too long, heh-heh-heh. Why can't the President go among Americans if God bless America? He need some spliff, some chalice. These guys worry too much, they don't pray as often as they worry, something is wrong.

"You have got to be careful of that monster who sucks the soul from man, who feeds from the soul of innocence and says he has power. One can't get strength from the weak. If you have a little baby you can't feed off that baby's legs, arms, whatever, until he can't stand on his own two feet . . . you can't get strong from a baby other than giving him strength so that when he is strong he will defend you with the strength you gave him. But if you think you are going to feed upon his little weakness, you better pray that he does not get strong."

A few more brethren showed up, and Bunny went into the house and reappeared on his porch with a brown shopping bag full of herb. He pulled out five different colas for us to inspect.

"Did you grow this?" I asked, holding one of the colas up to my nose for further inspection.

"The sun and the wind and the earth grow this," he laughed. His stash had that musky, almost minty smell indicative of Jamaica's finer strains, and I realized that if Bunny ever lost his gig as a founding father of reggae, he could still make a decent living as an herb farmer.

"Can we get some pictures for the magazine?" I asked him but he was busy smoking his spliff.

"Come back tomorrow, same time, we'll do it."

With that, Brian and I took our cameras and our sunburns and said good-bye. "Same time tomorrow," Bunny reminded us, and we thanked him for the herb and split.

For the rest of the night and into the next morning, Brian and I were so pleased with ourselves, the idea that Bunny might have something better to do the next day besides pose for our cameras never entered our smoke-clouded heads. The next morning Brian, Sidney, and I waited for three hours in Bunny's driveway, along with a small entourage of people who seemed to do nothing all day *but* wait for Bunny. Even his wife drove by looking for him. Once the sun had burned mine and Brian's flesh to a bright crimson, we decided to abandon Bunny and drop in on the RCO.

Sidney drove us back down the narrow downtown streets and dropped us off at the headquarters. When we arrived, Rasses DaSilva and Campbell closed down the shop. They wanted to show us their latest project, the site of a community center they were hoping to build if they could find the funding.

As we walked the three blocks to the center, I tried to find the right way to phrase the question I'd wanted to ask the two elder Rastas since I'd first walked into their headquarters several days before. It was a simple one, really. I wanted to know what it was like to see God.

Judging by their long, gray locks, I figured they would have been old enough to have been there on April 20, 1966, when Haile Selassie visited Jamaica for the first and only time in his life. Unbeknownst to His Imperial Majesty, waiting in the rain to receive him at Kingston's Palisades International Airport on that date were a hundred thousand people, ten thousand of whom were devout, ganja-burning Rastas who believed that their God had finally come to take them back to Ethiopia. Ethiopian flags flew high in the rain as Rastas chanted, drummed, and licked chalice. They predicted that the rain would stop the moment the Emperor's plane landed, and it did. Intimidated by such a strange reception, the Emperor waited an hour before leaving the plane. When he finally greeted the fanatic crowd, legend has it he wept.

As I expected, both DaSilva and Campbell had been there.

"It was like Christmas," explained DaSilva as we sat in a hollowed-out building he hoped to turn into a thriving Rasta community center. "I was working in Kingston driving a garbage truck. That morning I went to work, I tell the boss that I am not working today. Him say, 'Why?' I say, 'My God a come, so I no work.' We jump inna back of de truck and gwan down airport road. When we look His Majesty and the Governor General inna de car wave to the people, mi head swell. It was a sealing, His Majesty come to seal the people."

The Jamaican government allowed a group of about sixty Rasta leaders to attend several of the events celebrating the Emperor's visit, including receptions at King's House and the Sheraton Hotel. Aristocrats and dreadlocks socialized together for the first time in Jamaica's history. Each Rasta was given an official invite card and a gold medal from the Emperor. Campbell, then a representative of the Rastafari Brethren United Front, was one of the select few who met and touched the hand of his living God.

"I held His Majesty's hand," he recalled. "It was as if I put my finger in a socket and I could feel electrical vibrations. That is what I personally and truthfully felt at that moment. I bow down and I look in His Majesty's face and try to see his eyes like I see yours right now. I could not see the white and the black, all I could see was depth of space. It is not a matter of exaggeration, but what I personally experience, seen? And His Majesty said, and I never forget, 'Continue the work and the good work.' "

Whatever benevolence the Jamaican government had shown the Rastas during the Emperor's visit was soon to end. On July 12, less than three months later, two hundred and fifty police armed with guns, bayonets, pistols, and clubs stormed Back 'O Wall, the largest Rasta settlement in Kingston and the predecessor to Trench Town. Bulldozers plowed over the Rasta shacks, fire spread through the community, and after three days hundreds of Rastas were left homeless. Ras Campbell picked up his remaining belongings and moved into the local cemetery.

Rasses DaSilva and Campbell gave us a tour of the work-in-progress that was their latest mission. The building was two stories tall, with a half-dozen rooms on each floor, still just a foundation, without doors or windows. The RCO envisioned a place where Rastas of all ages could come and eat ital (vegan) food, smoke ganja, and educate their children.

"We want to occupy this building on a daily basis," explained Campbell. "We want to bring the community the reality that Rasta is here to do cultural work. Our program is intertwined with the program of Ethiopia and the restoration of the government of His Imperial Majesty where the herb is our ancient sacrament. We want the government to realize that the herb is what give the Rastaman the sense of meditation by which he can find the reincarnated divinity."

After the interview, we walked outside to Heroes Park, where we bought some peanuts from a woman on the street, and waited for a cab. I asked Ras DaSilva whether the organization was planning any kind of event to commemorate the Emperor's birthday, and he corrected my language and told me it was His Majesty's *earth*day, because you only can have one day of birth, and that no, there were no marches planned. However, he told us we were welcome to visit the Nyabinghi in Spanish Town anytime during the week.

"What exactly is a Nyabinghi?" I asked him.

"It is when the Rastaman ask Jah for peace and justice, a time for the brethren to dwell together in unity and love."

On Haile Selassie's earthday, the day we decided to visit the Nyabinghi, we realized that we'd smoked our way through the half pound. Sacramental smoke was an essential element of the celebration, so we sent Bigga out on another ganja quest. Bigga wasn't exactly Federal Express, and took about four hours to return with the herb. Spanish Town not being Beverly Hills, I had hoped to get in and out of the Nyabinghi while there was still some daylight left, but getting Rastas to adhere to any sort of schedule is kind of like asking the rain to stop falling. It was already dark once Bigga started loading the chalice for everyone, and I knew we'd be lucky if we made it to Spanish Town by midnight. I figured it was all part of Jah's plan, and after a few licks of the chalice, I sat back and listened to the tree frogs chirp and the insects buzz and the world seemed so kind at that moment, I was sure we were going to be all right.

"Chriiis," Bigga said in a deep, heavy voice as he handed me the pipe. "Some day I go to New York, mon. Open ital restaurant. Yeah, mon!"

"You should call it Bigga Burger."

"Yeah, mon!"

" 'We do it Jah's way!' "

"Selassie I!"

After Bigga decided that we'd all smoked ourselves to Selassie I's satisfaction, we called a cab to come take us to the event.

At night the streets of Kingston are deserted. When you pass the shantytowns during the day, you see people inside them going through the motions of their daily lives and they have a picturesque charm. In the evening the ghettos are desolate, and as I stared out the car window, I watched the outlines of their humble structures pass by like charcoal sketches on top of the dark horizon. As we smoked our spliffs en route to Spanish Town, they looked to me almost haunted, as if there was something sleeping behind the short stone walls that did not want to be woken up.

As our cab got closer to the site, we saw many Rastas on foot, bike, and moped making the same pilgrimage. Bigga yelled out to one young dread on a bike.

"Lion!"

"Yes, Ras!"

"Where the 'binghi at?"

"Up the road, Ras!"

"Selassie I!"

"Down wit' Queen Elizabitch!"

"Fire!"

We drove a little further into Spanish Town and turned down a dirt road. Our cab bumped its way through the brush until we reached a field, at the center of which was a drum circle and a huge, brilliant bonfire. At the perimeter of the parking lot, people hung out around little barbecues and shacks. I felt at ease. It looked like a summertime St. Anthony's fair, only without the Ferris wheel. Our driver asked us if three hours would be long enough, and we said sure, and agreed to meet him back in the same spot at one A.M. Bigga excitedly led us over toward the tent, meeting

friends along the way and knocking fists with exclamations of "One Love!"
and "Selassie I!"

"This is mi' bredren from *High Times*," he told them, and they
knocked fists with us in respect.

We walked over to the large tabernacle, where inside a hundred or so
Rastas—some in flowing, colorful gowns—drummed and chanted. I was
expecting a party, but I quickly saw that this was a religious ceremony that
owed more to African tribal rituals than it did to Bob Marley albums. The
Rastas swayed together in unison, smoking their chalice, and praising Jah
in almost trance-like reverie. Ethiopian flags were draped around all sides
of the tent and at the center of the drum circle was an altar upon which sat
a portrait of His Majesty and a tall herb plant. Shouts punctuated the air.

"Jah *Rastafari!*"

"Se*las*sie I!"

"Fire!"

We stood there for a long time just listening to the songs and the drums
which went on without interruption, the crowd knowing mystically when
to change the chant. Bigga walked around, joyously saluting old friends,
and Brian and I quietly smoked our spliffs.

> *By the Rivers of Babylon, there we sat down*
> *Yeah we wept, when we remembered Zion . . .*

A Rasta elder came over and welcomed us. Seeing Brian's camera
equipment, he told us not to take any pictures until he gave us permission.

"No problem," we told him, and went back to our smoking. Groups of
kids passed by staring at us and whispering to one another. Bigga had wandered off. I wasn't sure if it was my own suspicious imagination, but after
about ten minutes, the crowd seemed to distance itself from us.

> *For the wicked carried us away in captivity*
> *and required from us a song*
> *How can we sing King Alpha's song in a strange land?*

Someone shouted "Kill the white race," and I snapped to attention like
a deer hearing a gunshot.

"You hear that?" I asked Brian.

"Don't worry," he said. "It's not personal."

The drumming rose to an intense peak and then smoothed out again.
Smoke from the fire wrapped itself around the crowd, the smell of the
wood mixing with the scent of the herb. The kids came back and started
circling in a little closer to us. Brian didn't look concerned, so I tried not

to either. One kid approached, stood a foot in front of me, and stared directly into my face. I tried to ignore him, to act like he wasn't there, but I wasn't fooling anyone, least of all myself.

"Burn the pope!" one shouted.

"Slay the white dragon!" replied another.

I turned to Brian and asked him whether he was worried about this scene, but he told me to forget it, that they weren't talking about us.

A skeptical Rasta approached and asked who invited us. When we mentioned Ras DaSilva's name he seemed only slightly appeased. He wanted to know what we were doing there, and we told him we were writing an article on Jamaica's struggle to legalize the herb.

"Me don' wyan de herb legal! Den Rastaman be right back on government plantations, a slave to the ministers again!" I struggled to keep a conversation going, but my mind was more concerned with the kids that kept going away and reappearing closer and closer to me. Bigga had disappeared, and the number of "bloodclot whiteman"s were starting to outnumber the "Selassie I"s two to one.

I hear the words of the Rastaman say
Babylon your throne go down, go down ...

I wasn't concerned about the Rastas, who seemed too lost in their prayers to be worrying about Brian and me, but the packs of teenage baldheads snaking in and out of the crowd had me wondering how close we were to one A.M. I asked Brian what time it was and he said it was 11:30. The drums thundered on.

I hear the Angel with the seven seals say
Babylon your throne go down, go down ...

Finally, the Rasta I forgot I was having a conversation with told me he'd find Ras DaSilva for us, and we followed him through the crowd. We found Ras DaSilva, lost in reverie, wearing a long, draping robe. We'd caught him in a state of bliss, and he opened his arms and greeted us with a warm laugh. I got the impression he couldn't believe we had the nerve to show up, but he was happy we did. His demeanor put me somewhat at ease.

"You might meet some judgment tonight," he warned in a friendly way.

"I think we've had a few trials already," I said, and he laughed again.

The fire reached higher and higher in the air, and though I was standing at some distance, I could feel the heat and smoke on my face. The wild

frenzy of the flame sent shadows flying back and forth over people's faces
like bats. The drums slowed down again, and I asked one of the elders
what the fire represented.

"The fire there symbolizes the presence of divinity and also signifies
the presence of destruction if you fall contrary to tradition. It is good for
the good, and it is bad for the bad. At times you throw herb in the fire, bags
of herb to send up that incense, a glorification and a sacrament, seen? This
is spiritual, and the aroma, fragrance, and the prayer and the chant and the
spirit that you feel when you are within the herb will uplift you. You concentrate on the drums and work within the beat and you can realize that
it is really trying to settle you, and when you look at the earth and you see
the mystery in that beating of the drums, you can go out there and face
those who don't even realize that this tradition exists."

I listened to his words and watched the fire, concentrating on the
drums like he instructed. Just as I was beginning to feel comfortable, a
young, large Rasta with short locks stormed over to Brian and demanded
to know what was in his camera bag.

"You cyan't bring you Babylon inventions to de Nyabinghi! Dere are
strict rules . . . " He was livid—cursing and spitting at the ground.

"Dese bredren here come wit' invitation," DaSilva interrupted in our
defense. "Dem here to tell the people about fi' herb . . . go ahead," he said
to me. "Show him the magazine."

"I don't want to see ya' Babylon magazine! You should not be here!"
he said. His shouting had caused a few eyes to turn my way, and soon I was
the unwilling center of a growing controversy. I kept quiet, hoping somebody else would tell the young Rasta he was an asshole, but that voice was
slow in coming. "On the Emperor's birthday dey bring white man inventions to spread poison and radiation to our people!"

A few more elders joined with Ras DaSilva and tried to calm the
growing crowd of young Rastas and baldheads, but they were being overwhelmed by the louder, angrier youths. A few of the kids started yelling
"Fire burn!" directly in my face. I looked toward the huge bonfire and for
a moment I really wished I had made that contract with Razor. The loudest kid in the group was standing right next to me wearing a cape and
holding a staff. His eyes grew wider and whiter with each insult he flung
at me.

"Fire burn!" screamed the Caped Crusader, waving his staff above his
head. It was a statement I couldn't argue with.

"I cyan't relax knowing de Babylon inventions is here," said my original tormentor.

Ras DaSilva took me aside and said, "Go and leave your cameras in
the parking lot and come back." I told him there was no one to leave them

with, and also that I didn't want to wander too far from the elders, who were the only support I had at the moment.

"Fire burn!" cried out the Caped Crusader again, in case I misunderstood him the first time. I wiped his words from my face and looked over at the huge bonfire reaching twenty feet up in the air. I started thinking, Jesus, I hope they stab me first and don't throw me into the flames until I'm good and dead.

"Why do you come here?" I heard an angry, anonymous voice ask me.

"I'm uh . . . trying to legalize herb . . . " It wasn't the best response, but it was true in a way, and besides I was so frightened I was just glad words were still coming out of my mouth and not bile. Fear was something I could deal with, but pain was where I drew the line. But as I watched the bonfire turn the half tree that was sticking out of it into one glowing orange coal, I realized that that line was not for me to draw.

Brian didn't seem alarmed at all and just watched the scene from behind me with a bemused gaze.

They closed in tight on me, shouting and cursing. I could no longer understand what they were saying, but their intent cut through the dialect like a machete. I didn't have a hell of a lot of moves left. I couldn't stay there, but I knew if I left the elders, I might not live to see the parking lot. Things were not looking good for the I.

"You see that fire?" said the Caped Crusader, his eyes popping out of his head like marbles. "That's for you!"

I could take a hint. Brian and I started walking over to the parking lot, and I could almost feel the anonymous ice pick sticking between my ribs. When we reached the lot someone flashed their headlights on us, letting the whole place know we had come to party.

We stood there for about a minute before we were descended upon by yet another gang of youths. Before I even understood what they were saying I started walking back towards the fire, just to get away from them.

Finally, we saw a blissed-out Bigga. He came towards us with his arms raised in exhultation. "Respect mi' bredren! Selassie I! Jah *Rastafari!*"

I informed him that we were seconds away from being lynched, and he got real hard on the gang of youths pursuing us, telling them that their treatment of us would not please Jah one bit.

"Don't worry about the likkle youts," he told us. "The 'binghi beautiful, mon."

We hung out with Bigga until our cab arrived. I couldn't speak and just stood there thinking, my mind going over and over all the peaceful words I'd heard from all my Rasta friends that week. I felt a victim of the same racial bullshit I always thought they were dead against. Once we were on the road, the driver saw the vacant glare in my eyes and asked me what happened. I couldn't even bring myself to answer him, I was so wrung out.

"Some yout's was persecutin' him," Bigga said. "It's too bad, Chriiis, you have to see dat. The 'binghi wonderful, we go back sometime and you see."

One morning a few days after, I woke up, ate a bowl of porridge on Chinna's porch, and caught Bigga outside licking chalice and praising the Almighty. I sat down next to him, shoveled his heavenly breakfast into my mouth, and waited for a turn at the steer horn.

"Selassie I lick up the fire on that likkle yout' who was persecutin' you," he told me. "Selassie burn up de yout!"

"What?"

"The yout who want to trow you in de fire, he jump in de fire himself and burn up!"

My first thought was that this was just Rasta superstition and Bigga, seeing how quiet and reserved I'd gotten since the Nyabinghi, was just trying to provide me with some type of closure to the event that would ease my mind. I told him I didn't believe him, but he insisted it was the truth.

Ashanti Roy, founding member of one of my all-time favorite reggae bands, the Congos, visited with some of his brethren and confirmed Bigga's story. He was there when it happened. He said the Caped Crusader climbed on top of the bonfire, sat down, and yelled a few "Jah Rastafari"s as he burned to death. I still told them it was bullshit, only now I wondered which one of us I was trying to convince.

I spent the afternoon and most of the night licking chalice on the porch with Chinna's brethren. The porch had become my sanctuary. I didn't want to go to the beach, I didn't want to visit the country, I just wanted to smoke the chalice until my head exploded. After the sun went down, the brethren took their last sacramental smokes and wandered off into their own herb dreams. Brian dumped the water from the pipe out onto the concrete and walked away, too, leaving me there in my meditation.

I looked down at the mark the water had made on the concrete. It was like a Rorschach test, a blot of shapeless patterns. I sat and stared at it until the patterns started moving and shifting around like plasma. I looked away thinking I was too fucking stoned to deal with this, and when I looked back I saw the Lion of Judah marching defiantly with a crown on top of its head. I'm not saying that I *thought* I saw it, or that I saw something that *looked* like it. I saw the Lion as if I were looking down at a drawing in an illustrated Bible. Fuck me, I thought. What's next?

The patterns shifted, multiplying and dividing like ectoplasm until they reformed in the shape of the Lion roaring head-on. I could see its

mane, nose, and teeth, and its eyes looked up at me like I'd just kicked it
in the nuts. As I stared at it, I could hear Bigga talking and praying to himself in the backyard. His deep baritone climbed through the air to my
ears.

"Behold how good and how pleasant it is for brethren and sistren to
dwell together in unity and love . . . "

He laughed and the watermark shifted again, the patterns sliding
around like liquid mercury, until the shape of a face appeared, twisted in
pain like it was on fire. I saw the eyes, the teeth, the nostrils—like someone was drowning down there in that puddle and wanted me to save him.
"Fuck this," I said and got up. I walked away and came back and it was
still there. I went and washed my face, drank a glass of water, and when I
returned it was still there, staring at me and screaming for revenge.

I thought back to that quote from Revelations, the part where the
angel falls before the Lord who holds the scroll with seven seals containing His will and testament. The angels search heaven and earth looking for
one worthy enough to open the seals, and decide upon the Lion of the
tribe of Judah. But when the Lion is called forth, they find he's not a lion
at all, but a lamb. The Lamb of God opens the seals, and the wicked are
punished, the good are delivered, and the world comes to an end.

So now I was waiting for my vision to complete itself. I was waiting for
the Lamb to appear, but it didn't. All I could see was the twisted face, staring up like an accuser, until the water evaporated.

Great, I thought, I risk being immolated to write an article that most
people are going to flip right past on their way to Bud of the Month, and
what's my reward? I'm fucking cursed. My hair is probably going to fall out
and my kids are going to be born deformed. Fuck *High Times*, I thought,
fuck life, fuck everything. I drank a few Red Stripes and went to bed.

The day before I left, I drove around Kingston with Brian and Sidney in
one last futile attempt to find Bunny. We went to his house and to the various hotels and parking lots he was known to frequent, but his Lexus was
not to be found. Finally we went back to Chinna's, where Bigga had
promised to cook us a bunch of his favorite ital stew so we'd leave Jamaica
with the right taste in our mouths.

As I waited for Bigga's culinary present, I sat out on the porch again
and opened the *Sunday Gleaner*. One article in particular got my attention:

BURNT TO DEATH AT RASTA CELEBRATION

A man identified only as "Mickey," about 24 years old, of
Pusey Hill, Manchester, was burnt to death early yesterday

morning during a Rastafarian celebration at the Irish Pen community in Spanish Town.

Reports from the Spanish Town police say that "Mickey"
jumped into a bonfire which was lit during the celebrations
and burnt to death. The body was removed for post-mortem
examinations.

Karma has a funny way of kicking you in the ass like that. I guess
someone was going into that fire and, short two dope journalists, Mickey
figured he'd do it himself. A Rasta whose name I didn't get, one of Ashanti
Roy's brethren, saw me pondering the article.

"These youths are still ignorant and they embarrass us," he said. "But
that is why we are here. To teach. The Lord says, 'Suffer little children and
come unto me, for theirs is the kingdom of heaven.' "

Somehow, when he said that, I understood what these Rastas were
trying to tell me all along. It wasn't about hanging around all day smoking
herb and playing guitar and rapping about Jah, it was about trying to save
the world. The Rastas weren't trying to kill me back there at the Nyabinghi,
it was the poor schmucks they were trying to help. And maybe, just maybe,
by letting me hang out with them and lick the chalice and eat good food
and have intelligent conversations about the future of the planet, the Rastas were even attempting to salvage *me*. At a time when I was wondering
about all these dope travels I took throughout the world, and what the
point of them was, I felt like I at least had some kind of a story, even if it
was of no use to anyone but me.

As Bigga called me to dinner, and lobbed a steaming plate of vegetables in front of me, I felt like my curse had been lifted. It no longer seemed
like a curse, but a vision—like those images had shifted one last time, and
the whole experience had come full circle.

The Lion in that Rasta bongwater was no longer an attacker, but a symbol of strength, the ferocious part of life that came naturally and instinctively and needed to be tamed. The Lion was that angry soldier inside us
that needed to be smacked back into line from time to time.

Mickey was not an accuser, but a messenger. The twisted face I saw
was a person-to-person call from one idiot to another. He had reached out
from beyond the grave to tell me to stop being a fool, to tell me you can't
beat death, you can't even tie it, and that's why you made it last on your
list of places to visit. It was pretty nice of the little psychopath to die for
my sins like that, and if I ever get to where he is, I'll have to buy him a
drink.

As I ate Bigga's stew and talked with him some more about that restaurant he wanted to open up in New York, I remembered the no-show of the

Lamb and wondered why the thing would have left me there in my confusion instead of running to my rescue.

But then, what did I ever do to deserve it? No one was going to give a freak like me a break, I knew that. The Lamb was smart and knew to run away from beasts. I ate my ackee and didn't worry much more about it. I figured I'd catch glimpses of that holy mutton in my life, and I knew it would all come in time. In the meantime I'd go back to New York and keep looking for the fucker, turning over the rocks, digging for whatever gold was left in the ruins of the twentieth century.

14

Epilogue: Welcome to America, Bend Over Please

But hold on, it's not over.

I have to tell you the story of Vlad the Inhaler, of what happened when I went to visit him along the route of a *High Times* promotional tour I was sent on. Imagine that. In a few years I went from being a liability in the eyes of my fellow employees to autographing bongs and rolling papers in head shops up and down the Pacific Coast. I was a cannabis success story, a dope-smoking Horatio Alger.

I could tell you all about how we reconciled during our trip to Jimi Hendrix's grave (it's hard to hold grudges under the watchful gaze of the Master) and how, encouraged by the spirit of the moment, I convinced Vlad to accompany me and a couple hits of acid up to Vancouver Island to spend the weekend in a state of lysergic omniscience, but I'd rather start at the crucial decision we made that got me thinking about just how fucked up things have gotten here in the Land of the Free, and how people I have never met have basically botched up the twentieth century, and how even fools like Vlad and I can find some way to live with it.

It was always a slap in the face seeing Vlad again after an extended absence. He always had some new plan to conquer the world

One hundred pounds of "Mexi" en route to the Land of the Free. (Malcolm MacKinnon)

without ever having to get out of bed. I wanted to hear about it the way I want to hear about earthquakes and disasters on the news.

"I'm telling you, man, you gotta get on the Internet," he kept saying to me. For whiz-kid spuds like Vlad, the net was opium.

"When it can serve me a beer, I'll get on the net," I said. "In the meantime I'd rather hang out at Beefsteak Charlie's."

We were standing on board a mammoth ferry en route to Victoria Island, Canada, where I was to hit the next stop of my publicity tour. I distinctly remember asking Vlad if we should hide the drugs. I'd never been to Canada before and I wasn't yet familiar with its borders. The rental was down in the belly of the boat—if there was any concealing to be done, this was the time.

"This is *Canada*," he said. "They just wave you through. I do it all the time."

I was relying on Vlad for guidance—neither the first mistake I've made in my life nor the last.

I get nervous at borders, I can't help it. I've seen those episodes of "Miami Vice" where cool, collected, sharp-dressed individuals carrying bags full of cocaine hand their passports to customs agents like they were picking up the check in a swank restaurant. Not me. If I have so much as a roach on me I start to sweat and I worry about how I'd make it in a federal prison for a few years being bounced back and forth from the Bloods to the Crips in a never-ending game of dickie volleyball.

High Times journalists don't win too many Pulitzers, but if they had an award for most times sodomized in the line of duty, I bet we could compete with the world press. I've been poked and prodded so many times by border guards across the world that I think I have grounds for a few palimony suits. The car was loaded with *High Times* products—magazines, T-shirts, hats—all with huge pictures of pot on them. I knew if a guard looked too closely at the back seat, he'd think he stumbled onto the *French Connection.* In hindsight my mistakes were obvious, but after a week of breathing Pacific air and smoking Northwest herb, it seemed like God was on my side.

We were talking about John Travolta's new success as an action hero and the sad fact that we were destined to see this actor whose work we both used to respect dodge explosions until we were both safely resting in our graves.

"The explosion has done to movies what MTV did to rock 'n' roll," Vlad said. "It's like a conspiracy where every movie ever made was a *Smoky and the Bandit* ripoff. They all gotta have that huge fireball towards the end, whether it's a drama, romantic comedy, whatever. I mean, I've never seen a fireball in my life. Where's the reality?"

"Hulk Hogan's got a new movie out," I said. "He's gone the action hero route."

"That just proves my point," Vlad said. "Think about it. Ever since 'Wrestlemania' that guy has had the world at his fingertips. That's where we're at today. For two decades a guy like Hulk Hogan's been calling the shots."

"It almost gives you hope."

It was windy on the deck of the ferry and the hair kept whipping into my eyes. Vlad's pubic-like perm stood defiantly rigid as he looked out into the water and talked about Pink Floyd, World War II—all the usual topics of conversation. He talked about the acid, too, about how long it had been since he had done it and how he was looking forward to doing it again. It was getting late in the afternoon and the clouds were getting ready to do their thing. The waves crashed against the side of the ship, the beat of the tide telling the moment how fast it should occur. Good sights, good company, good acid waiting for me down in the car—I was so happy with my life I felt like I was on thorazine.

When the boat pulled into the harbor Vlad and I went down to the car and waited to be admitted into Canada. I had the acid stuck in the pages of a Bible which was buried in the trunk under a pile of other books, magazines, and assorted clothes I'd bought at thrift shops along the way. We sat in the car listening to Mott the Hoople and feeling no different from any of the other tourists waiting for some clean, honest fun with our brothers to the north.

"Do birds have dicks?" Vlad asked me.

"How many years did you go to college?"

"Eight, but that's not the point. I've been thinking about this for a week. I've never seen a bird dick. I mean, I figure there must be something there."

"I'm not even going to answer that," I said. The truth was, I just didn't know. "They gotta have dicks, how else are they going to reproduce?"

"For all I know they spray pollen out of their heads."

The cars started moving out of the boat. I turned the key in the ignition and started crawling towards the exit. "They really got moose in Canada?" I asked as I inched out into daylight.

"Yeah, big fuckers like horses with horns . . . "

"What's the plural of 'moose,' " I asked him. " 'Meese'?"

" 'Mooses,' I think. 'Meese' is the plural of 'mouse.' "

I pulled out of the boat and into the parking lot, where I saw customs officials going from car to car.

"What do I do here?" I asked Vlad as a customs officer with a clipboard started waving me to the side.

"Just follow him. He's gonna ask you a few questions."

I pulled over and was approached by a mousy little man wearing thick glasses.

"Hello, gentlemen," he said.

"Whus up?" I asked.

"Are you here for business or vacation?"

"Vacation."

"How long are you planning to stay in Canada?"

"Just a few days," I said.

"How much money do you have with you?"

"Only about five dollars," I told him. "We both have credit cards, though."

"Yes, okay, and what are you planning to do during your visit?"

This is where I fucked up. I was always taught to be straight with cops. Like I said, I get nervous around these people and I didn't want to start fabricating a story I couldn't remember if he started questioning me.

"I'm doing a promotional appearance for *High Times* magazine."

"So you're here on business."

"In a way, yeah."

"And what type of magazine is *High Times*?"

"It's an alternative culture magazine." I figured that one worked on my parents, maybe I'd have the same luck with the guard.

"Would you pull into lot number six?"

"Sure."

I drove over to the side of the parking lot where I saw some agents poking through a Hispanic man's Chevy.

"This doesn't seem right," I told Vlad.

"Just be cool," he said.

" 'Be cool'? Who are you, Shaft?"

The customs agent asked Vlad and me to get out of the car, and another agent with a handlebar mustache approached me with a very happy dog.

"Down, boy!" I said to the dog as he leaped up on me like a groupie. We had killed a joint right before we boarded the ferry, and I still had that high-quality sinsemilla smell all over me like there was a skunk running around in my pants. "Friendly dog you got here, officer, what's his name?"

As I patted Rin Tin Tin on the head, I noticed the first agent examining the *High Times* promo stuff. Rin Tin Tin was getting excited, making quick, jerky movements like a dog makes when it's walking down the street and happens across a particularly pungent puddle of urine.

"What type of magazine is *High Times*?" he asked, holding up a calendar with a huge bud on the cover.

"We do some reporting on the drug war."

"I see." When he started flipping through every single page of every single book, I figured we might have a problem. I had a vintage copy of *Naked Lunch* I bought in Oregon, a book with a lot of pictures of the Rolling Stones in it, a couple of *High Times* cultivation books, and that Bible. This isn't happening, was my first thought. It was like that pleasant shock of recognition when you realize you're having a nightmare and you smile because you know you're going to wake up. I kind of knew what the man was going to say next.

"We've found six hits of acid," the guard said, holding the square-inch Ziplock baggie between his fingers. There might as well have been a sticker on it reading: "Hello, my name is Drugs."

"Acid?" Vlad said, taking some initiative. "Jeezus, officer, let's catch the guys who did this . . . "

"Slow down, son. Are there any other narcotics in the car?"

"Narcotics?" I asked with a laugh. "They're over there with the cassettes . . . " The nefarious little man started rifling through the pile of clothes and accumulated debris in the back seat. He started pulling pieces of my laundry out and holding them up to his nose. He was using the search as an excuse to fulfill some strange fetish, I assumed.

"I'll get it for you," Vlad said.

Vlad was leading the guard to what remained of our stash and I still refused to believe it was happening. Finally the guard lined us both against the wall and started patting us down. Then I knew it wasn't a dream, because the man was slapping me and I wasn't waking up.

As I was being groped by the Don Knotts lookalike, I thought back to my days as a teacher and wondered what the kids would think of me now— Mr. S getting busted. I saw a few of them go down myself, even gave a recommendation about one to his parole officer after he was busted selling crack to his classmates. He was the smartest kid in class, wrote me long, imaginative fictional essays about what an outsider he was and how school made him want to puke. If I did one thing right the whole time I was a teacher, it was giving that kid an *A*. People like us, we got to stick together.

What right did this creep with the badge have to take my acid? Why did he care what I did with my life? I don't remember seeing any instruction manual when the Holy Buggerer handed me my soul and kicked me out of the womb. The way I saw it, the soul was a gift to us to use as we pleased. Some people, like this asshole border guard, let go of theirs a long time ago, but I've always tried to hold on to mine. If nothing else I figured I could throw it over my head when it rained.

"Wait here," the guard said and walked away.

"Where you guys from?" the other guard said. Cops always love to make small talk when they're arresting you.

"Nowhere," I told him and he started petting his stupid dog.

I looked at Vlad with disgust.

"I thought you said they just waved you in."

"They used to," he shrugged. "You want to run?"

"You're going to look awful pretty in them prison blues," I told him. "I might even wait my turn and have a stab at you myself."

"You're so *condescending*," he said, finally getting pissed off. "It's like hanging out with my mom."

"If you were hanging out with your mom I wouldn't be paying for the beer."

"Don't patronize me!" he shouted. The little guard came back.

"It's going to be a two-hundred-dollar fine," he said. There was an uncomfortable silence as Vlad and me tried to process this information in our heads.

"Can we pay by credit card?" Vlad asked meekly.

"Sure, you go right in that door there to your left."

We paid the drug teller and were then informed we couldn't enter Canada anyway because I had a six-year-old drunk driving conviction. We were given our receipt and then put back on the boat.

"I think I like this new kind of drive-through justice," Vlad said as we got back into the car. "It's very nineties."

"It's very expensive," I said.

They led us back to the Shove Boat and we had a long, quiet float back to the U.S. As I watched the Land of the Free get closer and closer to me, I wondered whether I shouldn't just do Vlad a favor and throw him overboard. There was no way he'd make it in a free-market economy. He was the kind of lazy schmuck that prospered under a Communist regime, drinking vodka all day and shipping his peers off to the gulag.

I called Steve Hager from the cell phone *High Times* had given me and informed him of my predicament.

"Don't worry about it," he said. "There's nothing you can do, just catch a plane back to New York as soon as possible. Let's not make this disaster cost any more than it has to."

When we got back to the United States we had to get permission from customs to reenter the country of our birth. We parked and walked past a silver Camaro that was being searched by a cop, a bloodhound, and a soldier in Desert Storm fatigues. They had the hood up and the gas tank open, and the dog was going wild, his little pink hard-on pointing like a divining rod to somebody else's bad luck.

When we entered the little office, a policeman took our paperwork and told us to have a seat.

"By what right?" Vlad asked. The financial aspect of this misadventure was starting to awaken his chip. He never let it go without a fight. "I have to sweep the hostel every day for two weeks to make two hundred bucks. I *hate* Canada."

"You ever think maybe it's not Canada? Maybe it's just you?" I hated Canada, too (although I'd never been there), but there was no way I was going to agree with him about anything at that point. I wanted to dump him off at the youth hostel as fast as possible. He was bad luck.

"And then this shit about drunk driving," he continued. "This is Canada we're talking about, drunk driving is like the national pastime up there. That reminds me, I gotta send my mom your half of the money as soon as we get back. She's been taking care of my AmEx bills."

"What half? It was *your* acid, for Chrissakes. I haven't paid you for it."

He looked like he was ready to bite me. I almost wish he did so the policeman would have an excuse to shoot him.

"Hey—hey dude—" whispered a sweaty guy sitting next to me. I hadn't noticed him, I was so pissed at Vlad. He looked like your garden-variety greaser with a mustache and one of those eighties-style Heavy Metal haircuts—long in the back but short and puffy on top.

"Hey," he said. "Are they lookin' at my car?"

"Uh . . . I don't know. Which one's yours?"

"The silver Camaro."

"Yeah, they're looking at your car."

"How many guys?"

I had to stifle a laugh. I didn't know how to tell him so I just said it straight, "There's a cop, a bloodhound, and a guy in Desert Storm fatigues."

Blood drained from the guy's face so fast I thought he was going to wilt. He was a man destined for a cavity search if ever I saw one. One of the customs agents asked us to accompany him to our car and I left the greaser slumped over on the bench, wondering what the future had in store for him.

America searched our car again, reaching between the seat cushions to see if they couldn't find a little change for Uncle Sam, and then reluctantly let us through.

"This country is a police state," Vlad said, sucking on a can of flat Coca-Cola. "I'm ready to defect to Cuba. If you do drugs in this country you cease to have any human rights. They can manhandle you, imprison you, take your car, your home, your children . . . drug users are America's last niggers. You look at that show 'Cops.' Man, they sic dogs on our kind and it's considered family entertainment."

We drove south in silence for a half hour, winding around the perimeter of the Olympic Peninsula. The sun was starting to set and the sky had acquired a turquoise tint.

We entered a little town, the name of which I didn't get, and the neon-lit "vacancy" signs hanging over the hotel parking lots gave me an idea. Driving over all these bumpy mountain roads was bound to dig the chip deeper into Vlad's shoulder, and I figured I'd show the poor schlub some mercy.

"Look, I don't feel like driving all the way back to Seattle," I said. "Let's just get one of those little motor-inn rooms where you can drink beer in bed and keep an eye on your car at the same time. I like those places, they remind me of being on vacation with my parents."

"I'm broke," Vlad said.

"I figured. I'll take care of it." I was acting brave, I knew the magazine had me covered, and Vlad's happiness always came cheap.

The sky at this point was starting to turn colors like a Maxfield Parrish painting. I'd noticed something happening up there when we got off the boat, but it wasn't until we drove up next to a small lake that the sky opened enough for me to see the kaleidoscope. The trees around the perimeter obscured the actual sunset, but there were streaks of turquoise directly above us, and then closer to the horizon there was a band of green. Vlad noticed it, too, and told me to pull over.

"Man, you see that?" he asked. "It's fucking green. The sky is fucking green."

"There's your fireball for you," I said. "Too bad Stallone's not around to kick you in the dick."

I pulled into a parking lot filled with campers and Winnebagos. We both got out of the car and walked to the edge of the lake.

"I never knew the sky could turn green," Vlad said, staring with moronic excitement. "Far fucking out."

Scattered around the trees I could see a few families sitting down with Bud suitcases after another successful barbecue. There was one bunch who looked like renegade *Deliverance* freaks ready to take the concept of "family fun" one step further in the Winnebago. They were cackling like hounds and throwing their empties in the lake at the kids floating around in inner tubes.

"Daddy!"

"Huh-huh-huh." The parents laughed like they were watching the family dog try to fuck a squirrel.

"Check it out," Vlad said, pointing to them.

"Yeah . . . " I said. "It's like a Skynyrd concert."

We stood there for a while watching the emerald overture above. I fig-

ured I'd try one last time to talk Vlad into having some fun before I left. I
used the bait-and-switch approach. I'd loosened him up with the roadside
motel concept, he was all excited about the sky, so I figured I'd take it a
babystep further.

"Let's just go south down the coast as far as we can until my plane
leaves. We'll drive the whole border incident out of our system."

"Impossible," he said, spitting in the lake. "You don't go on after a
thing like that. If we don't pack it in we'll live to regret it, I guarantee . . . "

"You remember *King Kong vs. Godzilla*, right? What did Kong do after
he went down?"

"What? Chew on power lines?"

"Exactly. You can get more acid, right?"

"You know, I got a lot of things to do back at the hostel," he said without looking at me.

"What things to do, you're unemployed."

"Hey, man," he suddenly snapped, spitting his words out like a vicious
raccoon. "My life ain't a bed of roses like yours is, all right? You work for
High Times, Mikey just played Madison Square Garden . . . Sometimes I
have pangs, you know?"

"I'm just talking about a little road trip."

"I'm sick of panging from one end of life to the other. I'm lost in pang
wonderland here . . . "

"I pang like a postal worker but I pull through. You got to ride it like
Travolta on that mechanical bull . . . " I couldn't believe it was me saying
all this positive-thinking bullshit. I didn't want a pissed-on blanket for
company over the next twelve hours, that's all.

I'd lost him. He didn't even answer, just stared up at the green sky.

It was right around that moment when a huge bird shit on Vlad's head.
It must have been an eagle or something; it let loose on Vlad like a B-52.

"Fuck!" he squealed. *"Fuck! Fuck! Fuck!"*

I couldn't handle it anymore. The guy was such a magnet for stupid,
random cruelty that I started laughing like a retard.

"I'll tell you this," I chuckled. "Birds definitely have some kind of
ass."

"Fuck *birds*," he croaked. "Flying pieces of *shit*. Fuck *Canada*. Fuck
everything."

"Canada's one thing," I said. "But don't take your anger out on the bird
population."

"Have you ever seen me shit on a bird?" he asked as he started pulling
sloppy pieces of white gunk from his head. "To my knowledge it's never
happened."

"You're overreacting," I said as he dug around in the Dunkin' Donuts bags in the back seat looking for napkins. "It's good luck."

"Fuck good luck. What have I ever done to birds or Canadians to make them treat me like this?"

"I'm telling you, it's good luck. That and doggie-do."

He started wiping furiously, spreading the mess out. When he was done, he had the punkest version of spiked hair I've ever witnessed on this earth.

"Is it out?"

"Yeah, you can't even see it." He'd figure it out later, I thought. I didn't want to spoil the moment.

The green was gone and the night settled over us like a pillow. Vlad calmed down and the two of us watched the yokels across the lake throw more cans at their kids.

"I knew we were going to get busted with that acid," Vlad said.

"I know," I told him. His knack for self-destruction shouldn't have been a surprise to me.

"On the other hand, I never knew the sky could be green."

"You lost me."

"I'm saying that maybe it *is* good luck. The bird shitting on me, the bust at the border—maybe it was some guiding force that wanted to bring me here and show me that miracles can happen, and that the sky can turn green."

"Yeah, man, maybe you're right."

You can't help wanting to believe in something any more than you can help wanting to eat a good meal every once in a while. Some people are kosher, some say hey, if it ain't blessed then don't stick it in my mouth, but when you get desperate like Vlad and me, you find yourself in a *Lord of the Flies* situation—feasting on things that you know are wrong to eat, but too fucking hungry to give a shit about the next guy's problems. I laughed at Vlad, I laughed at the guy with the silver Camaro—the same way I laughed when that bull got stuck in Cancún or when Mickey set himself on fire in Jamaica because that's what he thought God wanted him to do. It was a laugh of solidarity—I knew what shit luck was like from the inside. A snot-faced junky begging change for a fix—I can understand him the way I could never understand the kids I went to college with—

Keep the delusions, buddy, just gimme my dinner.

It was nearly dark and I gave up trying to trick Vlad into the road trip. We'd paid a big debt to the karma bank that day, and I felt like we could now relax. The green sky was like God's apology.

Even the hillbillies across the lake seemed to be doing the right thing that night. The way they laughed as they threw the empty cans at the kids, you'd have thought they'd just invented child abuse. The children floated along on their rubber donuts, just happy their parents were paying attention to them.

We piled into the back car, and as I pulled onto the road, I looked over at Vlad, at the dumb wonderment he had on his face because he didn't know the first thing about light refraction. He gave me hope, let me know that sometimes pissing in the wind was its own reward, and that even idiots like us can stumble their way into paradise. After the motel I'd drive Vlad back to the youth hostel and he'd be happy with himself for a week, and then I'd drive myself back to the airport where I hoped to grab a few martinis and talk to a divorcée or two before heading back to New York. It's my mantra—if you can't live your life like a rock star, at least try and live it like a roadie.

What else? It ain't over 'til the fat lady sings?

Don't take any wooden nickel bags?

Fuck it.